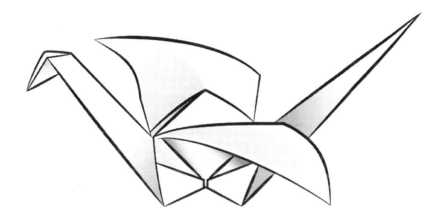

Everyone Can Learn Origami

By: Peter Saydak

Everyone Can Learn Origami, first edition copyright © 2017 Peter Saydak. All rights reserved. No part of this publication may be reproduced without prior permission of the publisher and author.

ISBN-13: 978-1978356894
ISBN-10: 1978356897

Published by Origami.me (www.origami.me)
Design, Layout, Diagrams, Photography, Cover Design and Text by Peter Saydak
Front Cover Artwork by Brenda Saydak

About Origami.me

Our goal is to teach people how to make origami, help them improve their skills and promote artists and others in the international origami community.

We maintain the largest database of free origami instructions on the Internet including diagrams, crease patterns and video tutorials.

Our blog features amazing work from a variety of talented origami artists, book reviews, guides, tutorials and lots more.

Visit us online at **www.origami.me**.

Front Cover Art by Brenda Saydak
View more of her art at www.BlissandKittens.com

Table of Contents

Tips and Advice 11
Symbols 12

Basic Folds and Bases 15

    1) Mountain and Valley Folds 16
    2) Kite Base 16
    3) Blintz Base 17
    4) Inside Reverse Fold 18
    5) Outside Reverse Fold 19
    6) Pleat 21
    7) Crimp 21
    8) Water Bomb Base 22
    9) Square or Preliminary Base 23
    10) Squash Fold 24
    11) Petal Fold 25
    12) A Common Petal Fold Variation 26
    13) Swivel Fold 27
    14) Bird Base 28
    15) Rabbit Ear Fold 31
    16) Fish Base 32
    17) Frog Base 33
    18) Open Sink 38
    19) Closed Sink 39

1-Star: Beginner Models 41

    Dog Face 43
    Cat Face 44
    Ladybug 46
    Christmas Tree 47
    Cup 49
    House 51
    Fox 53
    Swan 55
    Cicada 57
    Fly 59
    Pigeon 61
    Samurai Helmet 63
    Fortune Teller 65
    Turtle 67
    Parakeet 69
    Peacock 72
    Parrot 74
    Talking Fish 77
    Crown 79
    Rooster 81

2-Star: Easy Models 83

    Angelfish 85
    Butterfly 87
    Goldfish 90
    Piano 93
    Long Box 96
    Sailboat 100
    Chick 102
    Penguin 105
    Duck 107
    Pajarita (Little Bird) 110
    Pinwheel 112

    Angelfish 115
    Crab 118
    Bird 121
    Pig 125
    Lantern 129
    Yakko-San 132
    Chair 135
    Beetle 138
    Sitting Dog 141
    Sitting Elephant 143
    Talking Crow 146
    Carp 149
    Whale 152
    Seal 155
    Rabbit 160

3-Star: Intermediate Models 163

    Mandarin Duck 165
    Chicken 169
    Catamaran 172
    Fish 174
    Dolphin 178
    Flapping Bird 182
    Crane 186
    Crow 191
    Heron 196
    Horse 201
    Swallow 207
    Rabbit 212
    Table 218
    Water Bomb 223
    Tulip 227
    Bunny Balloon 230
    Goldfish Balloon 233
    Jumping Frog 236
    Butterfly 239
    Lotus Flower 242
    Masu Box 247
    Masu Box Lid 250

4-Star: Challenging Models 253

    Masu Box Divider 255
    Sitting Crane 258
    Star Box 264
    Owl 269
    Dragon 274
    Iris 280

5-Star: Difficult Models 289

    Dragonfly 291
    Phoenix 297
    Frog 301

Additional Resources 309

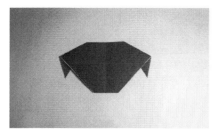
Dog Face - Page 43

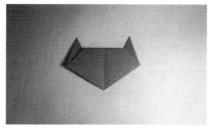
Cat Face - Page 44

Ladybug - Page 46

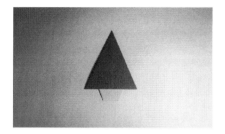
Christmas Tree - Page 47

Cup - Page 49

House - Page 51

Fox - Page 53

Swan - Page 55

Cicada - Page 57

Fly - Page 59

Pigeon - Page 61

Samurai Helmet - Page 63

Fortune Teller - Page 65

Turtle - Page 67

Parakeet - Page 69

Peacock - Page 72

Parrot - Page 74

Talking Fish - Page 77

Crown - Page 79

Rooster - Page 81

Angelfish - Page 85

Butterfly - Page 87

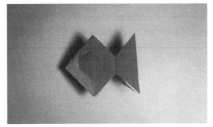
Goldfish - Page 90

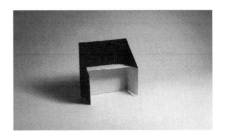
Piano - Page 93

Long Box - Page 96

Sailboat - Page 100

Chick - Page 102

Penguin - Page 105

Duck - Page 107

Pajarita (Little Bird) - Page 110

Pinwheel - Page 112

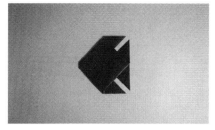
Angelfish - Page 115

Crab - Page 118

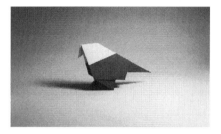
Bird - Page 121

Pig - Page 125

Lantern - Page 129

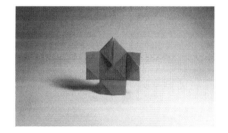
Yakko-San - Page 132

Chair - Page 135

Beetle - Page 138

Sitting Dog - Page 141

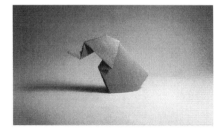
Sitting Elephant - Page 143

Talking Crow - Page 146

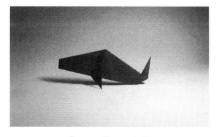
Carp - Page 149

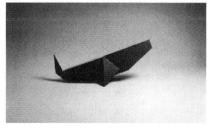
Whale - Page 152

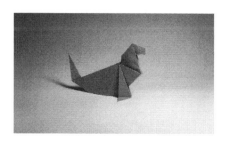
Seal - Page 155

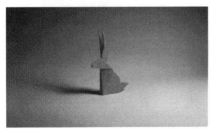
Rabbit - Page 160

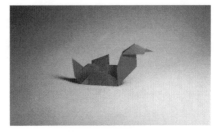
Mandarin Duck - Page 165

Chicken - Page 169

Catamaran - Page 172

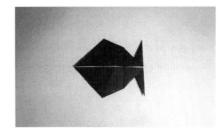
Fish - Page 174

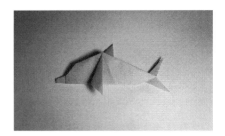
Dolphin - Page 178

Flapping Bird - Page 182

Crane - Page 186

Crow - Page 191

Heron - Page 196

Horse - Page 201

Swallow - Page 207

Rabbit - Page 212

Table - Page 218

Water Bomb - Page 223

Tulip - Page 227

Bunny Balloon - Page 230

Goldfish Balloon - Page 233

Jumping Frog - Page 236

Butterfly - Page 239

Lotus Flower - Page 242

Masu Box - Page 247

Masu Box Lid - Page 250

Masu Box Divider - Page 255

Sitting Crane - Page 258

Star Box - Page 264

Owl - Page 269

Dragon - Page 274

Iris Flower - Page 280

Dragonfly - Page 291

Phoenix - Page 297   **Frog** - Page 301

Tips and Advice

All of the models in this book can be folded from a single square-shaped sheet of paper. A couple of them require scissors to make one or two small cuts. Other than that, no other tools are required.

There are various folding tools available in craft stores and online but nothing like that is required to fold any of the models in this book.

As you fold the models in this book go slowly and make sure your folds are nice and precise. If you make an error early on it can compound and cause bigger issues later. If you do make a mistake or run into problems it's perfectly okay to start over with a new sheet of paper.

When making a fold make a soft crease first to make sure everything lines up properly. If everything is good then go ahead and crease it very well.

Look ahead to the next step or two all the time. Sometimes it can be a bit difficult to see exactly where to make a crease from one diagram. When you look ahead to the next step you can see where edges or corners line up and it makes folding easier.

Most importantly, keep practicing and have fun!

Symbols

Throughout this book you'll see the following symbols being used to indicate different folds and instructions.

Origami paper typically comes with a color or pattern on one side (usually the front) while the other side is usually plain white (the back). The color gray indicates the colored side while white is the back.

Fold: This arrow indicates the direction of a regular fold. Fold the paper in the direction of the arrow over the dotted line. This arrow is usually used for Mountain or Valley Folds.

Fold and Unfold: this arrow indicates that the paper should be folded and then unfolded leaving behind a crease.

Other Folds: this arrow indicates a more complex fold like a Squash Fold or Inside Reverse Fold where the paper is usually being squashed, or pushed inside itself.

Fold Here: this dotted line shows the line where you should make a fold.

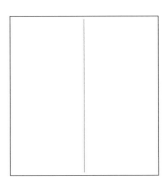

Crease Lines: these lines indicate existing creases on the paper from previous folds.

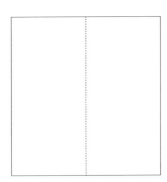

Cut Here: this dotted line indicates the path that you should cut the paper. A few models in this book require you to make one or two small cuts with scissors.

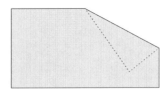

Paper Inside the Model: This dotted line shows the path of the paper inside the model after folds such as a Sink or an Inside Reverse Fold.

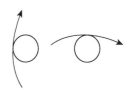

Turn Over: this symbol indicates that the paper should be turned over in the direction of the arrow so you can see the other side.

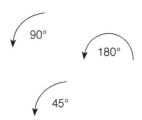

Rotate: these symbols indicate that the paper should be rotated a certain number of degrees in the direction of the arrow.

Scissors: this symbol indicates that the paper should be cut with scissors along the dotted line.

Look Here: this symbol indicates that you should view a certain part of the model, usually the underside. This section will be magnified for the next several steps.

Inflate: a few models in this book require you to blow air into a small hole to inflate the model like a balloon. This symbol indicates where to do this.

Basic Folds and Bases

Before you start folding any of the models in this book take a few minutes to learn these basic techniques and bases. Once you have a good understanding of at least techniques 1 to 16 then you should be ready to fold most of the models in this book.

1) Mountain and Valley Folds

Every fold in origami is either a Mountain Fold, a Valley Fold or a combination of the two.

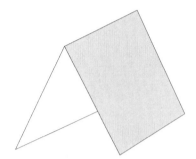

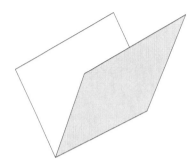

With a mountain fold the paper is folded so the crease is at the top and the paper resembles a mountain.

With a valley fold the paper is folded so the crease is at the bottom and the paper resembles an open valley.

2) Kite Base

The shape of this base resembles a kite which is where it gets its name.

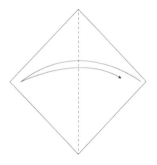

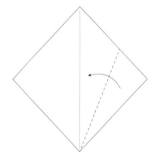

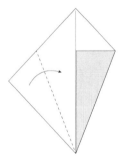

1) Start with a square of paper rotated 45 degrees. Fold it in half vertically. Crease this well and then unfold it.

2) Fold the right side of the paper to the center along the dotted line.

3) Fold the left side of the paper to the center along the dotted line.

The completed Kite Base.

3) Blintz Base

Sometimes this is referred to as a Blintz Fold. If you make these folds right at the beginning then it's a Blintz Base but you can still fold this sequence later as well. If you ever see instructions saying to make a Blintz Fold it means to fold all four corners to the center like what you do here.

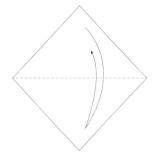
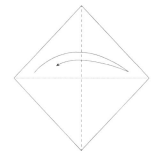
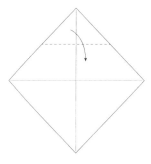

1) Start with a square of paper rotated 45 degrees. Fold it in half horizontally from one corner to the other. Crease this well and then unfold it.

2) Fold the paper in half vertically from one corner to the other. Crease this well and then unfold it.

3) Fold the top part of the paper to the center along the dotted line.

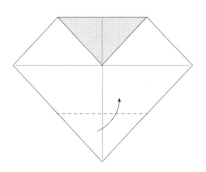
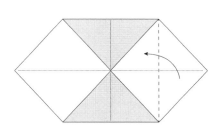
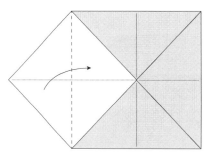

4) Fold the bottom part of the paper to the center along the dotted line.

5) Fold the right part of the paper to the center along the dotted line.

6) Fold the left part of the paper to the center along the dotted line.

Basic Folds and Bases

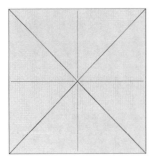

The completed Blintz Base.

Typically I find it a little bit easier to fold the opposite corners first like what you see here. Top, then bottom, right and then left.

While I feel doing it this way makes the Blintz Fold a little bit more precise there's no rule here and you can fold the corners in any order you want.

4) Inside Reverse Fold

The Inside Reverse Fold is a very common fold where the paper is folded inside itself.

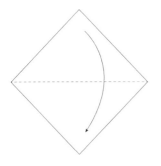

1) Start with a square piece of paper rotated 45 degrees. Fold it in half horizontally.

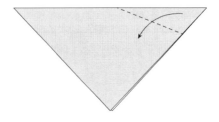

2) Fold the right side of the paper along the dotted line.

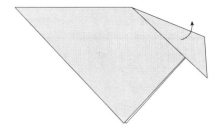

3) Crease this well and then unfold it.

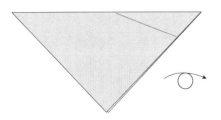

4) Turn the paper over.

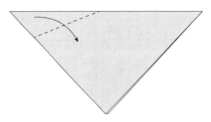

5) Fold the left side of the paper along the dotted line. This will be the opposite side of the crease you just made.

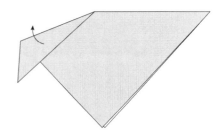

6) Crease this well and then unfold it. Now you will have folded this crease in both directions.

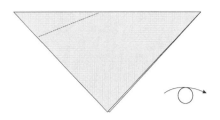 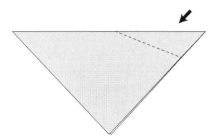 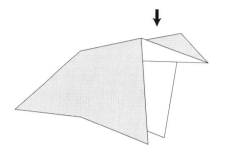

7) Turn the paper over back to the way it was before.

8) Push the paper inside itself along the existing crease.

9) Once the paper is inside following the existing crease push everything flat.

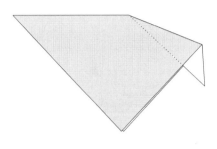

The completed Inside Reverse Fold. The dotted line show the path of the paper inside the model.

The easiest way to make an Inside Reverse Fold is to fold the paper in one direction and then the other. This gives you creases in both directions and makes it much easier to fold the paper inside itself.

It's not always possible to do this however and sometimes you just have to push the paper inside without any pre-existing creases to help.

When you get more confident with origami you may find that you can make Inside Reverse Folds without making the previous two folds in both directions. You might also find that you only really need to make one fold in one direction before making the Inside Reverse Fold as well.

If you want to be as precise as possible though it's best to fold the paper in both directions before pushing it inside.

5) Outside Reverse Fold

This is the opposite of the Inside Reverse Fold. Instead of folding the paper inside itself you fold it outside itself.

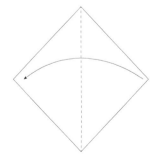  

1) Start with a square of paper rotated 45 degrees. Fold it in half vertically along the dotted line.

2) Fold the top part of the paper down along the dotted line.

3) Crease this well and then unfold it.

Basic Folds and Bases

Page **19**

4) Turn the paper over.

5) Fold the top part of the paper down along the dotted line. This will be the opposite of the crease you made earlier.

6) Crease this well and then unfold it. You have now folded this crease in both directions.

 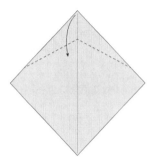 

7) Fold the paper outside itself along the crease you just created.

8) To make this fold a bit easier open up the paper and pull it back along the dotted lines. These are existing creases.

9) As you pull the paper back outside itself fold it back in half following the crease from step 1.

Just like with the Inside Reverse Fold it's easier and more precise to fold the paper in both directions before making the Outside Reverse Fold.

It's also not always possible to do this though and as you get more confident with origami you may be able to make these folds without any previous creases to help as well.

The completed Outside Reverse Fold.

6) Pleat

This is a very simple fold where you basically fold the paper one direction and then fold it back the other direction.

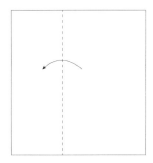  

1) Fold the paper along the dotted line to the left.

2) Fold the paper back towards the right along the dotted line.

The completed Pleat.

7) Crimp

The crimp is almost like a combination of a Pleat and an Inside Reverse Fold.

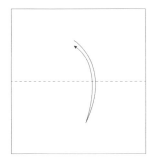 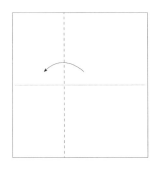 

1) Fold a square of paper in half horizontally. Crease this well and then unfold it.

2) Fold the paper vertically along the dotted line.

3) Fold the paper back along the dotted line, just like a Pleat.

Basic Folds and Bases

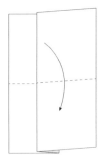

4) Fold the paper in half horizontally.

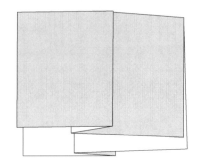

The completed Crimp.

8) Water Bomb Base

These are the first several steps to folding a traditional origami Water Bomb which is where this base gets it's name. This base is used for a number of inflatable origami models and is sometimes called a Balloon Base.

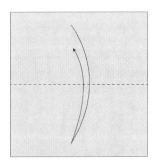

1) Start with a square of paper with the colored side up. Fold the paper in half horizontally. Crease this well and then unfold it.

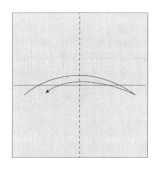

2) Fold the paper in half vertically. Crease this well and then unfold it.

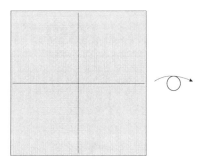

3) Turn the paper over.

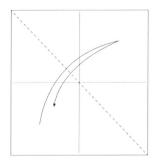

4) Fold the paper in half diagonally. Crease this well and then unfold it.

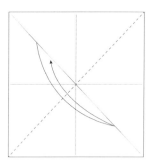

5) Fold the paper in half diagonally the other way. Crease this well and then unfold it.

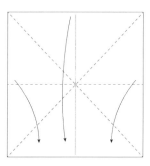

6) Following the existing creases bring the left and right sides of the paper as well as the top edge towards the bottom.

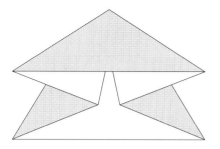

7) The paper will begin to take a shape that looks like this. Push everything flat along the existing creases.

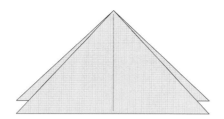

The competed Water Bomb Base.

9) Square or Preliminary Base

The Square Base (also called the Preliminary Base) is probably the most common base in origami.

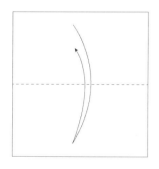

1) Begin with a square sheet of paper with the white side up. Fold it in half horizontally along the dotted line. Crease this well and then unfold it.

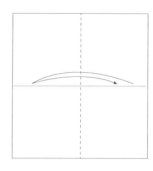

2) Fold the paper in half vertically along the dotted line. Crease this well and then unfold it.

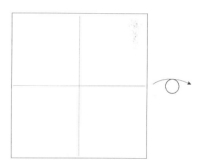

3) Turn the paper over.

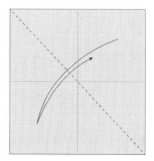

4) Fold the paper in half diagonally along the dotted line. Crease this well and then unfold it.

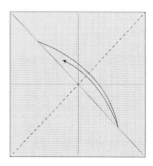

5) Fold the paper in half diagonally the other way along the dotted line. Crease this well and then unfold it.

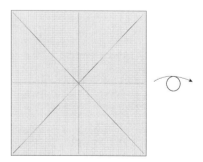

6) Turn the paper over.

Basic Folds and Bases

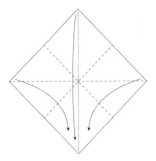

7) Using the existing creases bring the left, right and top corners to the bottom.

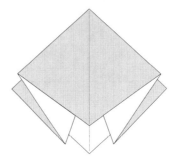

8) The paper will take on a shape that looks like this. Press everything flat along the existing creases.

The completed Square Base.

10) Squash Fold

With this fold you basically take a flap of paper and squash it flat.

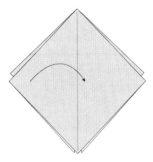

1) For this example start with a Square Base. Fold the top left flap towards the center.

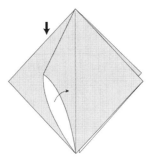

2) As you bring the flap towards the center push down on the crease along the top of the flap.

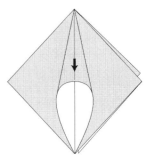

3) Continue pushing along the crease at the top. Squash everything flat. Make sure the crease is in the center and both sides are symmetrical.

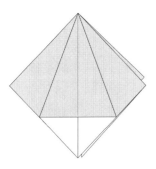

The completed Squash Fold.

11) Petal Fold

There are a few different variations of this fold. This is the basic one and it's used in the Bird Base.

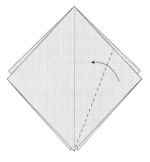

1) Start with a Square Base. Fold the right flap of paper to the center along the dotted line.

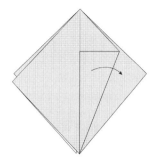

2) Crease this well and then unfold it.

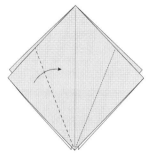

3) Fold the flap of paper on the left to the center along the dotted line.

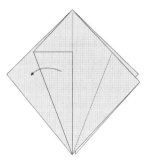

4) Crease this well and then unfold it.

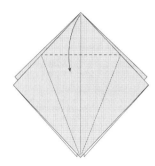

5) Fold the top of the model down along the dotted line. The ends of this dotted line will line up with the ends of the previous two creases you made.

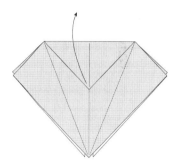

6) Crease this well and then unfold it.

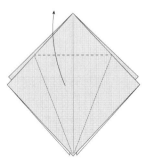

7) Lift up the top flap of paper along the horizontal crease you just made.

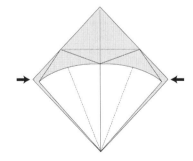

8) As you lift the paper up fold in both sides along the existing creases.

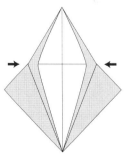

9) Push everything flat along the existing creases.

Basic Folds and Bases

Page **25**

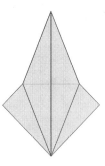

The completed Petal Fold.

12) A Common Petal Fold Variation

This is a slightly more difficult variation of the Petal Fold. You'll see this variation in the Frog Base.

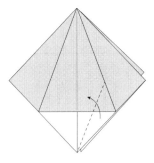

1) Start off with a Square Base with a Squash Fold on one of the four flaps. Fold the right side of the paper to the center along the dotted line.

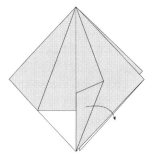

2) Crease this well and then unfold it.

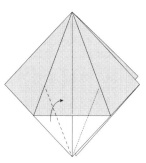

3) Fold the left side of the paper to the center along the dotted line.

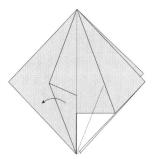

4) Crease this well and then unfold it.

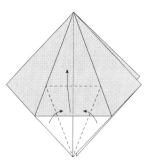

5) Lift the top flap of paper up along the horizontal dotted line. The ends of this line will touch the ends of the previous two creases you made.

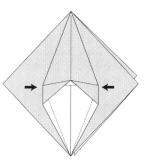

6) As you lift the paper up fold in both sides along the two creases you just made and push everything flat.

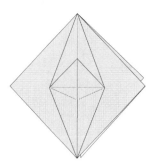

The completed Petal Fold.

This fold is a bit more difficult than the regular petal fold because you don't have an existing horizontal crease to use when folding the paper up like the one made in step 5 of the regular Petal Fold.

You can fold the paper down and make this crease between steps 4 and 5 however this will result in creases across the rest of the paper because of all the layers. These creases will most likely be visible on the final model and may not look great. This is why this step is usually omitted.

In the beginning you can use this extra crease to make this Petal Fold a bit easier but try practicing using the instructions here and skipping it.

13) Swivel Fold

The Swivel Fold is kind of like half of a Petal Fold but it's a little bit different.

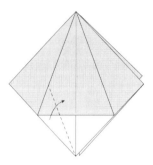

1) For this example start with a square base with one of the 4 flaps Squash Folded down. Fold the left side of the flap to the center.

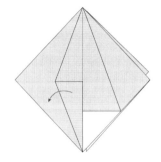

2) Crease this well and then unfold it.

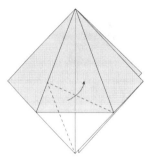

3) Fold along the top dotted line. As you fold along this line fold the paper on the left back using the crease you just made.

4) The paper will "swivel" up and to the right. Push everything flat.

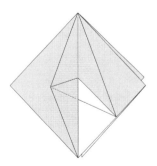

The completed Swivel Fold.

Basic Folds and Bases

14) Bird Base

This base is used to fold the traditional origami crane as well as several other birds which is where it gets its name. It begins with a Square Base and then uses two Petal Folds.

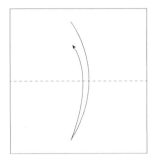

1) Fold the paper in half horizontally. Crease it well and then unfold it.

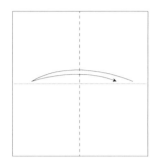

2) Fold the paper in half vertically. Crease it well and then unfold it.

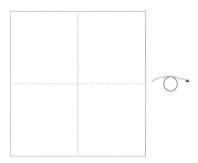

3) Turn the paper over.

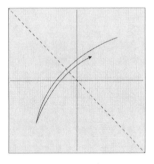

4) Fold the paper in half diagonally. Crease it well and then unfold it.

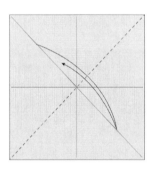

5) Fold the paper in half diagonally the other way. Crease it well and then unfold it.

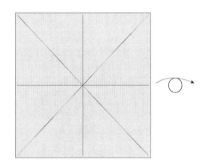

6) Turn the paper over.

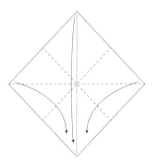

7) Fold the paper along the existing creases bringing the left, right and top corners to the bottom.

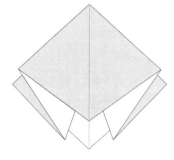

8) Continue folding the paper along the existing creases. Flatten everything well.

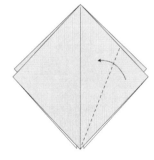

9) Fold the flap of paper on the right to the center along the dotted line.

10) Crease this well and then unfold it.

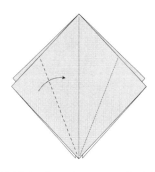

11) Fold the flap of paper on the left to the center along the dotted line.

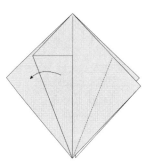

12) Crease this well and then unfold it.

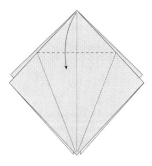

13) Fold the top of the model down along the dotted line. The ends of this dotted line will line up with the previous two creases you made.

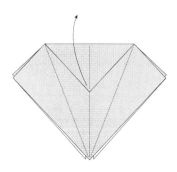

14) Crease this well and then unfold it.

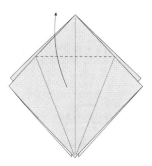

15) Lift up the top flap of paper along the horizontal crease you just made.

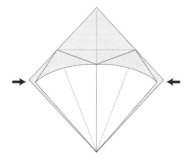

16) As you lift the paper up fold in both sides along the existing creases.

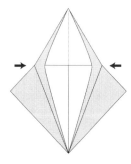

17) Push everything flat along the existing creases.

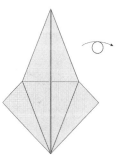

18) Turn the paper over.

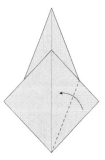

19) Fold the flap of paper on the right to the center along the dotted line.

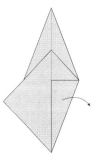

20) Crease this well and then unfold it.

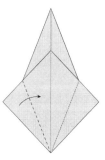

21) Fold the flap of paper on the left to the center along the dotted line.

Basic Folds and Bases

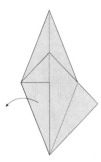

22) Crease this well and then unfold it.

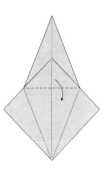

23) Fold the top of the model down along the dotted line. The ends of this dotted line will line up with the previous two creases you made.

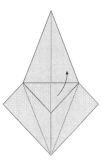

24) Crease this well and then unfold it.

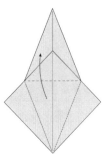

25) Lift up the top flap of paper along the horizontal crease you just made.

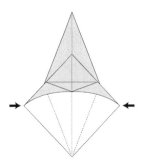

26) As you lift the paper up fold in both sides along the existing creases.

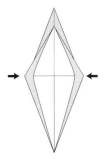

27) Push everything flat along the existing creases.

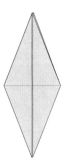

The completed Bird Base.

15) Rabbit Ear Fold

This fold kind of resembles a rabbit's ear which is where it gets its name.

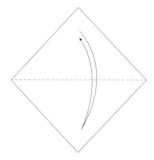

1) Start with a square of paper rotated 45 degrees. Fold the paper in half horizontally along the dotted line. Crease this well and then unfold it.

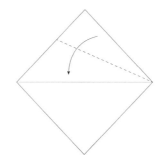

2) Fold the top right part of the paper to the center line.

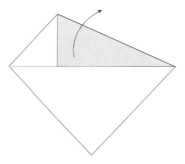

3) Crease this well and then unfold it.

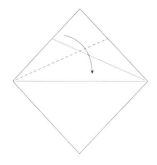

4) Fold the top left part of the paper to the center line.

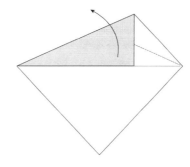

5) Crease this well and then unfold it.

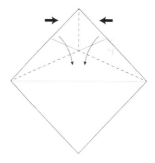

6) Fold both sides of the paper to the center using the existing creases. The paper in the middle will form a triangle-shaped flap like a rabbit's ear.

The little triangle ear-like flap from step 7 can be folded to either side depending on what the instructions ask for.

You can also try folding it to both sides which may help the whole thing stay a bit more flat.

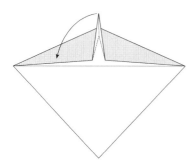

7) Fold the triangle flap to the side and flatten everything.

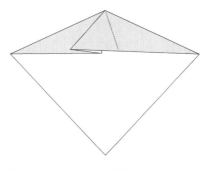

8) The completed Rabbit Ear Fold.

16) Fish Base

The Fish Base is folded using two Rabbit Ear Folds and is used to make several different traditional origami fish which is where it gets its name.

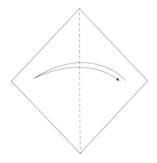

1) Start with a square of paper rotated 45 degrees. Fold it in half vertically. Crease this well and then unfold it.

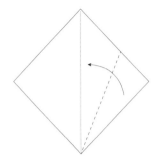

2) Fold the bottom right side of the paper to the center along the dotted line.

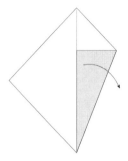

3) Crease this well and then unfold it.

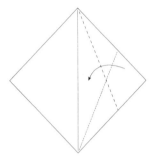

4) Fold the top right side of the paper to the center along the dotted line.

5) Crease this well and then unfold it.

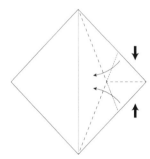

6) Using the two creases you just created make a Rabbit Ear Fold.

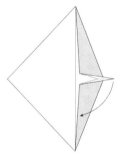

7) Fold the triangle flap of paper to the bottom.

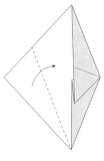

8) Fold the bottom left side of the paper to the center along the dotted line.

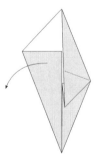

9) Crease this well and then unfold it.

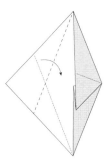

10) Fold the top left side of the paper to the center along the dotted line.

11) Crease this well and then unfold it.

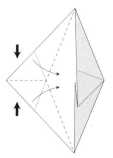

12) Using the two creases you just created make a Rabbit Ear Fold.

13) Fold the triangle flap of paper to the bottom.

The completed Fish Base.

The triangle rabbit ear flaps can be folded up or down depending on what the instructions ask for.

You can also fold them in both directions to help the whole thing stay a bit more flat.

17) Frog Base

The Frog Base is used to fold the traditional origami frog which is where it gets its name. This is the longest and most complicated base in origami and involves a Square Base, Squash Folds and Petal Fold Variations.

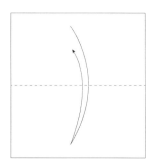

1) Begin with a square sheet of paper with the white side up. Fold it in half horizontally along the dotted line. Crease this well and then unfold it.

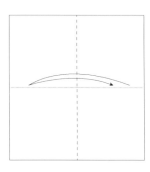

2) Fold the paper in half vertically along the dotted line. Crease this well and then unfold it.

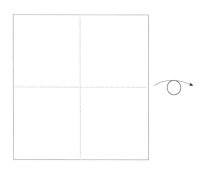

3) Turn the paper over.

Basic Folds and Bases

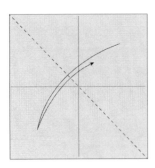

4) Fold the paper in half diagonally along the dotted line. Crease this well and then unfold it.

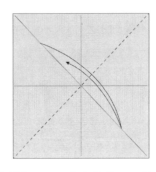

5) Fold the paper in half diagonally the other way along the dotted line. Crease this well and then unfold it.

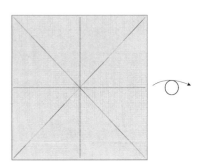

6) Turn the paper over.

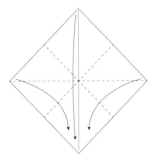

7) Using the existing creases bring the left, right and top corners to the bottom.

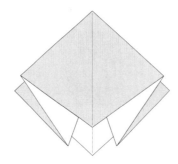

8) The paper will take on a shape that looks like this. Press everything flat along the existing creases.

9) Bring the top left flap of paper towards the center.

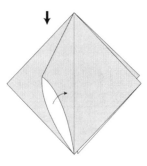

10) Squash Fold this flap down.

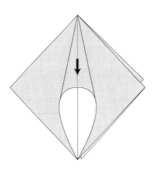

11) Make sure everything is symmetrical and push the paper flat.

12) Fold the top right flap over to the left.

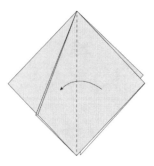

13) Bring the top right flap of paper towards the center.

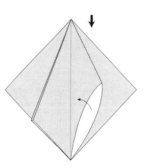

14) Squash Fold this flap down.

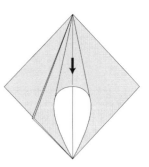

15) Make sure everything is symmetrical and push the paper flat.

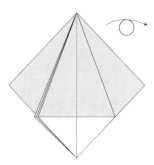

16) Turn the paper over.

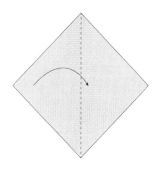

17) Bring the top left flap of paper towards the center.

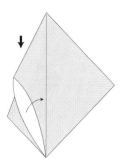

18) Squash Fold this flap down.

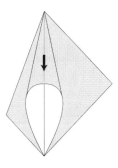

19) Make sure everything is symmetrical and push the paper flat.

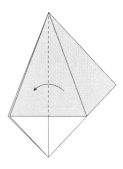

20) Fold the top right flap over to the left.

21) Bring the top left flap of paper towards the center.

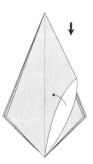

22) Squash Fold this flap down.

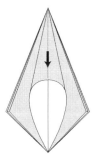

23) Make sure everything is symmetrical and push the paper flat.

24) Take a moment and make sure that you have 4 flaps of paper on both sides. If you don't, move how ever many flaps you need to the other side. The front and the back sides of the model should both look like what you see here.

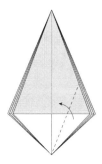

25) Fold the top right flap of paper towards the center along the dotted line.

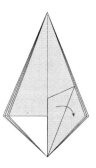

26) Crease this well and then unfold it.

Basic Folds and Bases

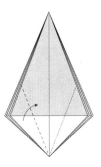

27) Fold the top left flap of paper towards the center along the dotted line.

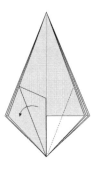

28) Crease this well and then unfold it.

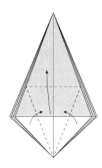

29) Make a Petal Fold using the previous two creases.

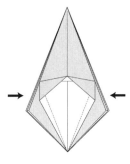

30) Finish making the Petal Fold and push everything flat.

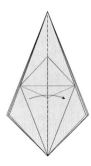

31) Fold the top left flap of paper over to the right.

32) Fold the top left flap of paper over to the right.

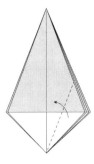

33) Fold the top right flap of paper towards the center along the dotted line.

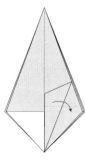

34) Crease this well and then unfold it.

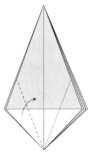

35) Fold the top left flap of paper towards the center along the dotted line.

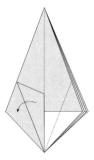

36) Crease this well and then unfold it.

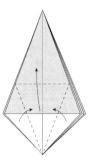

37) Make a Petal Fold using the previous two creases.

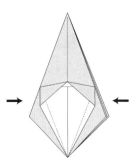

38) Finish making the Petal Fold and push everything flat.

Basic Folds and Bases

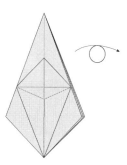

39) Turn the paper over.

40) Fold the right flap of paper towards the center along the dotted line.

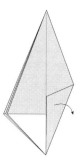

41) Crease this well and then unfold it.

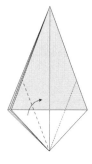

42) Fold the top left flap of paper towards the center along the dotted line.

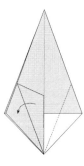

43) Crease this well and then unfold it.

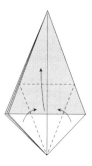

44) Make a Petal Fold using the previous two creases.

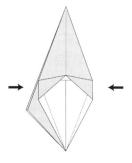

45) Finish making the Petal Fold and push everything flat.

46) Fold the top left flap of paper over to the right.

47) Fold the top left flap of paper over to the right.

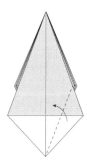

48) Fold the right side of the paper towards the center along the dotted line.

49) Crease this well and then unfold it.

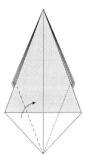

50) Fold the left side of the paper towards the center along the dotted line.

Basic Folds and Bases

51) Crease this well and then unfold it.

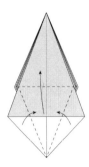

52) Make a Petal Fold using the previous two creases.

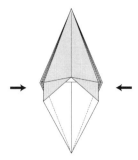

53) Finish making the Petal Fold and push everything flat.

The completed Frog Base.

Take a moment to make sure you have 4 flaps of paper on each side of the model. If you don't, move how ever many flaps you need to the other side. The front and the back sides of the model should both look like what you see here.

18) Open Sink

This is one of the more difficult folds in origami but if you make the initial creases in both directions sinking the paper inside isn't too hard since you have existing creases to work with.

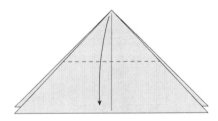

1) Begin with a Water Bomb Base. Fold the top of the paper down along the dotted line.

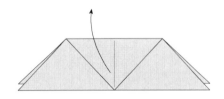

2) Crease this well and then unfold it.

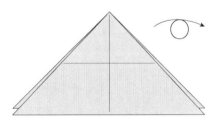

3) Turn the paper over.

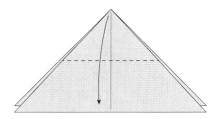
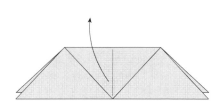
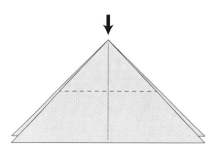

4) Fold the top of the paper down along the dotted line. This is the opposite direction of the crease on the other side.

5) Crease this well and then unfold it.

6) Push the top of the paper down using the horizontal creases.

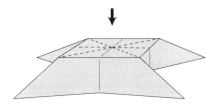
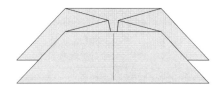

7) Open the paper up and push the paper inside following the existing creases marked by the dotted lines.

8) As the paper takes on this shape fold everything flat.

The completed Open Sink. The dotted line shows the path of the paper that has been sunk inside.

19) Closed Sink

This is probably the most difficult fold in origami. Don't worry if you have trouble with this one, none of the models in this book will require you to make this fold.

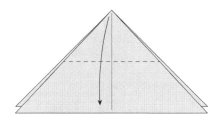
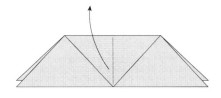
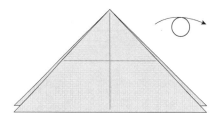

1) Begin with a Water Bomb Base. Fold the top of the paper down along the dotted line.

2) Crease this well and then unfold it.

3) Turn the paper over.

Basic Folds and Bases

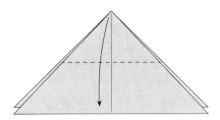

4) Fold the top of the paper down along the dotted line. This is the opposite direction of the crease on the other side.

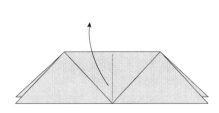

5) Crease this well and then unfold it.

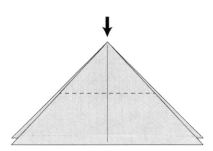

6) Push the paper down inside of the model without opening it up too much.

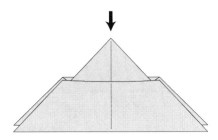

7) Continue pushing the paper down and inside.

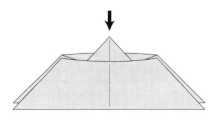

8) Continue pushing the paper down and inside.

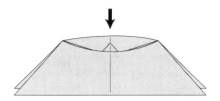

9) Finish pushing the paper all the way down, close everything back up and push everything flat.

The completed Closed Sink. The dotted line shows the path of the paper that has been sunk inside.

Basic Folds and Bases

Beginner

Dog Face

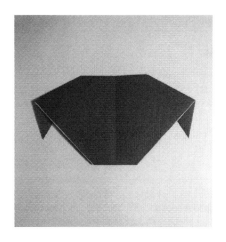

Feel free to draw some eyes on this model when you're finished to complete the face.

Techniques Used: Mountain and Valley Folds

Before You Start: Begin with a square sheet of paper rotated 45 degrees with the white side facing up.

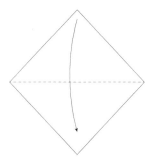

1) Fold the paper in half horizontally along the dotted line.

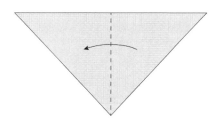

2) Fold the paper in half vertically along the dotted line.

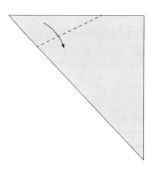

3) Fold the top flap of paper down along the dotted line.

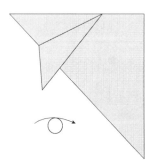

4) Turn the paper over.

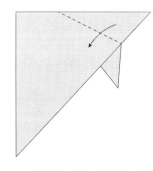

5) Fold the top flap of paper down along the dotted line.

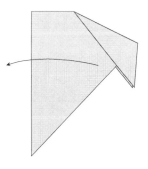

6) Open the paper unfolding the fold in the middle.

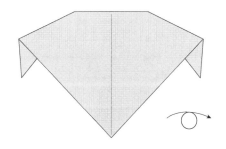

7) Turn the paper over.

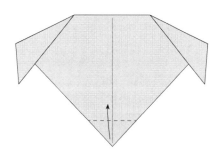

8) Fold the two layers of paper up along the dotted line

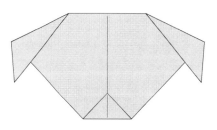

The completed Dog Face.

Cat Face

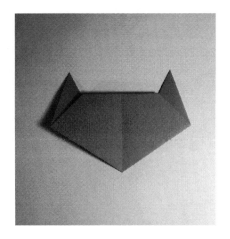

Feel free to draw some eyes, a nose and some whiskers on the finished model to complete the face.

Techniques Used: Mountain and Valley Folds

Before You Start: Begin with a square sheet of paper rotated 45 degrees with the white side facing up.

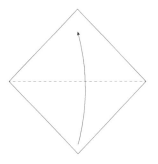

1) Fold the paper in half horizontally along the dotted line.

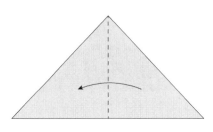

2) Fold the paper in half vertically along the dotted line.

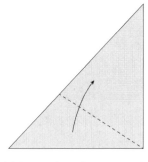

3) Fold the top flap of paper up along the dotted line.

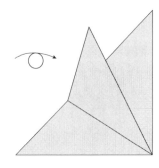

4) Turn the paper over.

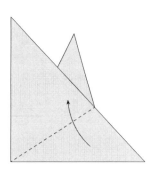

5) Fold the top flap of paper up along the dotted line.

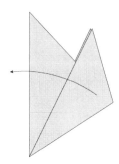

6) Open the paper unfolding the fold in the middle.

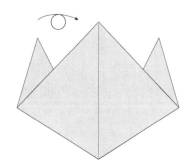

7) Turn the paper over.

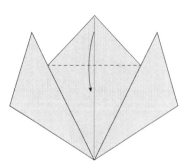

8) Fold the top two layers of paper down along the dotted line

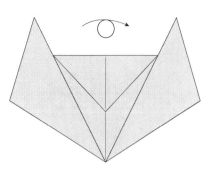

9) Turn the paper over.

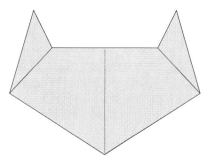

The completed Cat Face.

Ladybug

This model looks best folded with red paper and feel free to draw some black spots on the back when you're finished as well.

Techniques Used: Mountain and Valley Folds and Pleat.

Before You Start: Begin with a square sheet of paper rotated 45 degrees with the white side facing up.

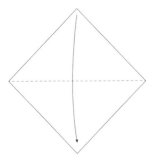

1) Fold the paper in half horizontally along the dotted line.

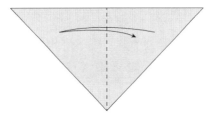

2) Fold the paper in half vertically along the dotted line then unfold it.

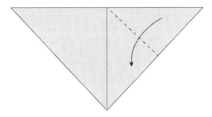

3) Fold the right side of the paper down along the dotted line.

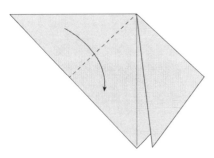

4) Fold the left side of the paper down along the dotted line.

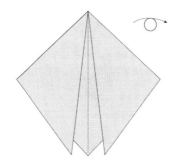

5) Turn the paper over.

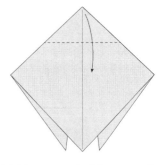

6) Fold the top part of the paper down along the dotted line.

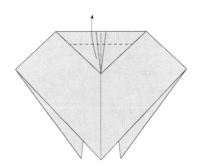

7) Fold the top flap of paper back up along the dotted line.

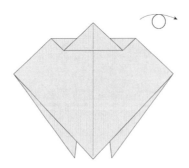

8) Turn the paper over.

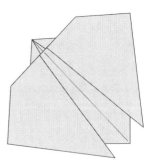

The completed Ladybug.

Christmas Tree

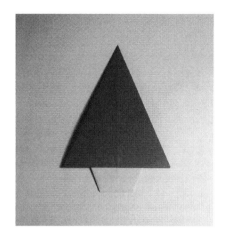

This model begins with a Kite Base. If you're already familiar with this base you can skip ahead to step 4.

Techniques Used: Mountain and Valley Folds, Kite Base

Before You Start: Begin with a square sheet of paper rotated 45 degrees with the white side facing up.

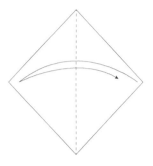

1) Fold the paper in half vertically along the dotted line. Crease this well and then unfold it.

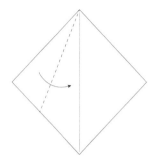

2) Fold the top left side of the paper towards the center along the dotted line.

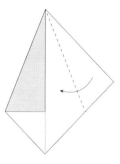

3) Fold the top right side of the paper towards the center along the dotted line.

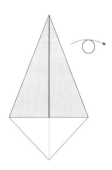

4) Turn the paper over.

5) Fold the bottom right side of the paper towards the center along the dotted line.

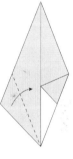

6) Fold the bottom left side of the paper towards the center along the dotted line.

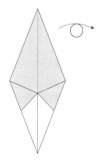

7) Turn the paper over.

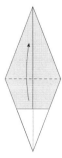

8) Fold the paper in half horizontally along the dotted line.

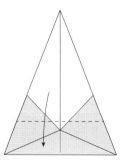

9) Fold the top flap of paper down along the dotted line.

Christmas Tree

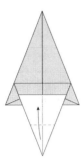

10) Fold the bottom flap of paper up along the dotted line bringing the tip of the paper to the top of the white area.

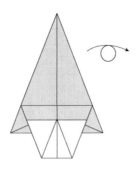

11) Turn the paper over.

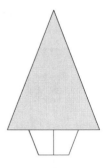

12) The completed Christmas Tree.

Cup

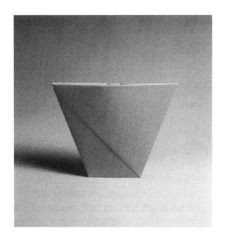

This model can actually hold water for a little while before it eventually soaks through the paper.

Techniques Used: Mountain and Valley Folds.

Before You Start: Begin with a square sheet of paper rotated 45 degrees with the white side facing up.

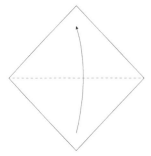

1) Fold the paper in half horizontally along the dotted line.

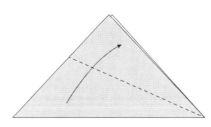

2) Fold the paper up along the dotted line bringing the bottom edge to the top right edge. Only crease a tiny bit at the left side of the fold.

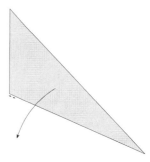

3) Crease a little bit on the left side of the fold and then unfold the paper.

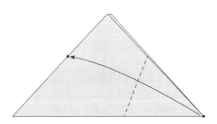

4) Fold the paper along the dotted line bringing the bottom right corner to the point at the end of the previous fold.

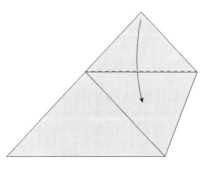

5) Fold the top layer of paper down along the dotted line.

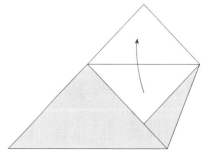

6) Crease this well and then unfold it.

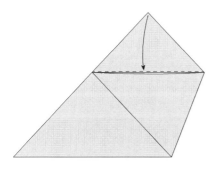

7) Fold the top layer of paper back down along the existing crease and tuck it into the pocket.

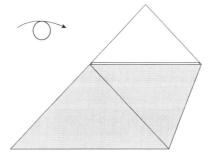

8) Turn the paper over.

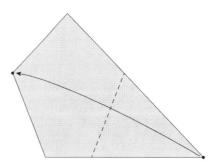

9) Fold the paper along the dotted line bringing the bottom right corner to the marked point.

Cup   Page **49**

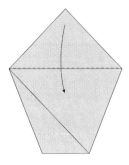

10) Fold the top layer of paper down along the dotted line.

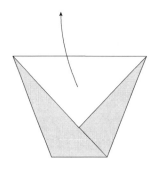

11) Crease this well and then unfold it.

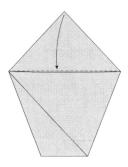

12) Fold the top layer of paper back down along the existing crease and tuck it into the pocket.

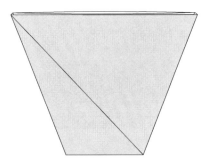

The completed Cup.

House

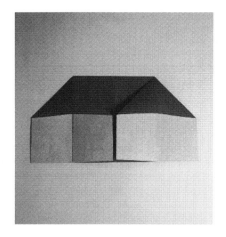

This sequence of folds is also used as the first several steps of the traditional origami piano on page 93.

Techniques Used: Mountain and Valley Folds and Swivel Fold.

Before You Start: Begin with a square sheet of paper with the white side facing up.

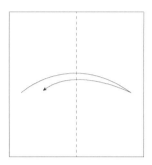

1) Fold the paper in half vertically and then unfold it.

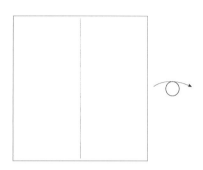

2) Turn the paper over.

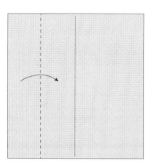

3) Fold the left side of the paper towards the center along the dotted line.

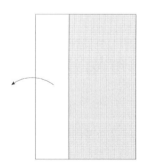

4) Crease this well and then unfold it.

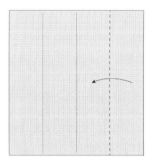

5) Fold the right side of the paper towards the center along the dotted line.

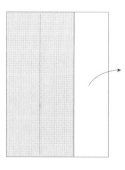

6) Crease this well and then unfold it.

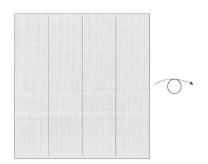

7) Turn the paper over.

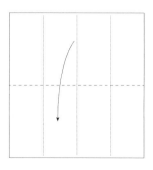

8) Fold the paper in half horizontally along the dotted line.

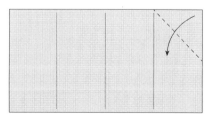

9) Fold the top right corner of paper down along the dotted line.

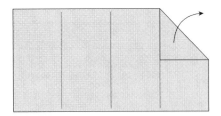

10) Crease this well and then unfold it.

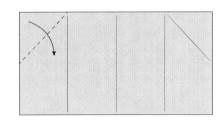

11) Fold the top left corner of paper down along the dotted line.

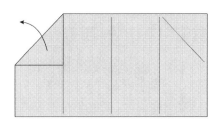

12) Crease this well and then unfold it.

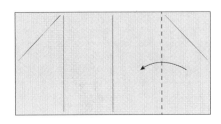

13) Fold the top layer of paper towards the center along the dotted line.

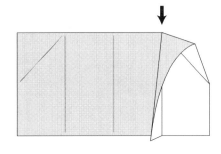

14) As the paper opens make a Swivel Fold along the existing creases and push everything flat.

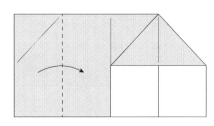

15) Fold the top layer of paper towards the center along the dotted line.

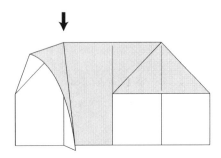

16) As the paper opens make a Swivel Fold along the existing creases and push everything flat.

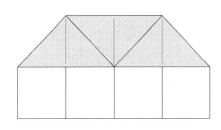

The completed House.

Fox

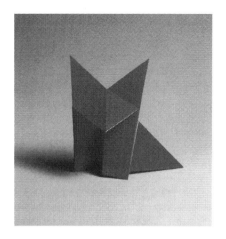

This fox is quite cute and ends up being a somewhat 3-dimensional model.

Techniques Used: Mountain and Valley Folds and Squash Fold.

Before You Start: Begin with a square sheet of paper rotated 45 degrees with the white side facing up.

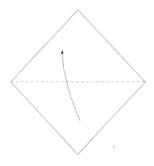

1) Fold the paper in half horizontally along the dotted line.

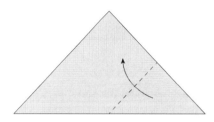

2) Fold the right side of the paper towards the center along the dotted line.

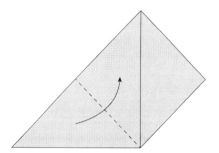

3) Fold the left side of the paper towards the center along the dotted line.

4) Turn the paper over.

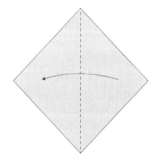

5) Fold the paper in half vertically along the dotted line.

6) Rotate the paper 45 degrees to the left.

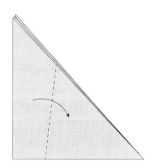

7) Fold all three layers of paper towards the right along the dotted line.

8) Unfold the top two layers of paper back towards the left.

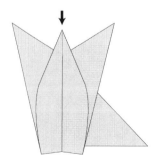

9) Squash Fold the middle layer of paper down to form the fox's head.

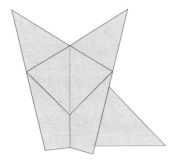 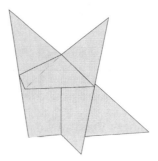

10) Push everything flat and then let the model open up a little bit naturally.

The completed Fox.

Swan

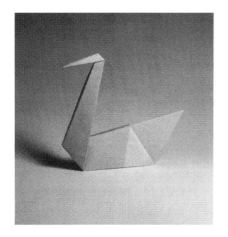

This model begins with a Kite Base. If you're already familiar with this base you can skip ahead to step 4.

Techniques Used: Mountain and Valley Folds, Kite Base, Outside Reverse Fold and Pleat.

Before You Start: Begin with a square sheet of paper rotated 45 degrees with the white side facing up.

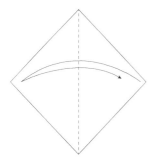

1) Fold the paper in half vertically and then unfold it.

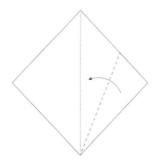

2) Fold the right side of the paper towards the center along the dotted line.

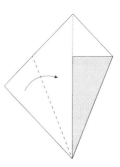

3) Fold the left side of the paper towards the center along the dotted line.

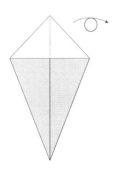

4) Turn the paper over.

5) Fold the right side of the paper towards the center along the dotted line.

6) Fold the left side of the paper towards the center along the dotted line.

7) Fold the bottom of the paper to the top along the dotted line.

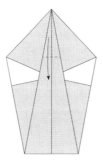

8) Fold the tip of the paper down along the dotted line.

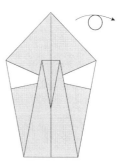

9) Turn the paper over.

Swan

10) Fold the paper in half vertically along the dotted line.

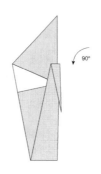

11) Rotate the paper about 90 degrees to the left.

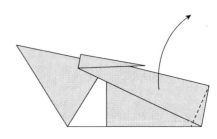

12) Pull the paper up and out in the direction of the arrow. A new crease will form along the dotted line.

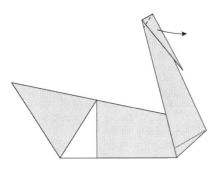

13) Pull the paper up and out in the direction of the arrow. A new crease will form along the dotted line.

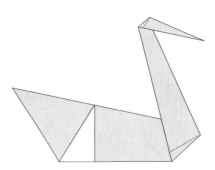

The completed Swan.

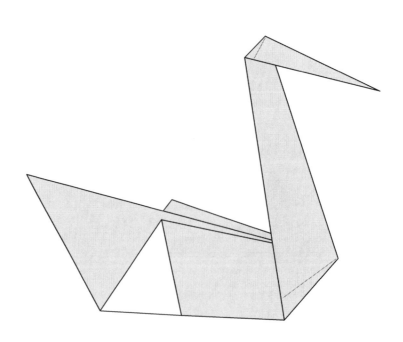

Cicada

This origami insect isn't very difficult but still looks great, especially with two sided paper.

Techniques Used: Mountain and Valley Folds.

Before You Start: Begin with a square sheet of paper rotated 45 degrees with the white side facing up.

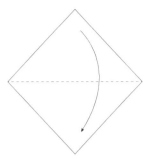

1) Fold the paper in half horizontally along the dotted line.

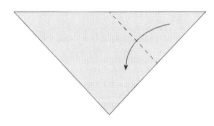

2) Fold the right side of the paper towards the center along the dotted line.

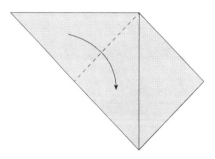

3) Fold the left side of the paper towards the center along the dotted line.

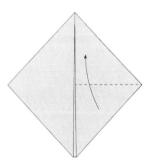

4) Fold the top right flap of paper up along the dotted line.

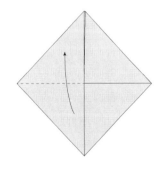

5) Fold the top left flap of paper up along the dotted line.

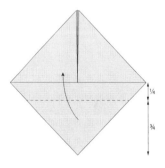

6) Fold the top layer of paper up along the dotted line. This should be roughly 1/4 of the way from the center. Don't worry if you don't get it exactly 1/4.

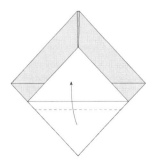

7) Fold the bottom of the paper up along the dotted line.

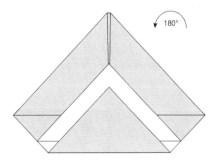

8) Rotate the paper 180 degrees.

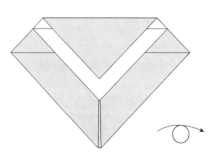

9) Turn the paper over

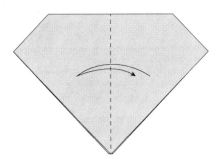
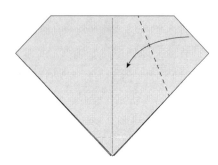
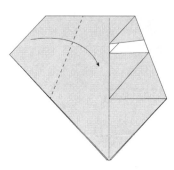

10) Fold the entire model in half vertically then unfold it.

11) Fold the right side of the model towards the center along the dotted line.

12) Fold the left side of the model towards the center along the dotted line.

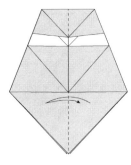
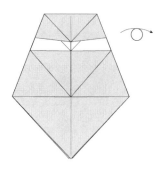
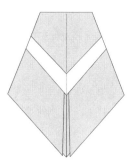

13) Fold the entire model in half vertically again. Crease this well and then unfold it.

14) Turn the paper over.

The completed Cicada.

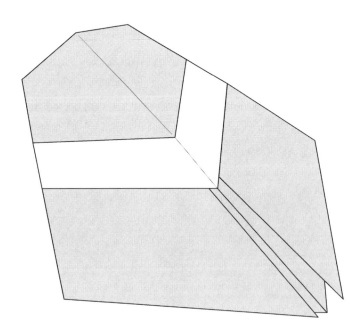

Fly

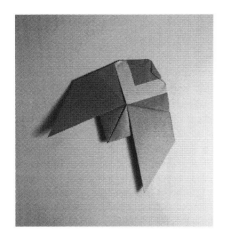

The folding sequence for this origami fly is very similar to the previous origami cicada.

Techniques Used: Mountain and Valley Folds.

Before You Start: Begin with a square sheet of paper rotated 45 degrees with the white side facing up.

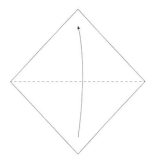

1) Fold the paper in half horizontally along the dotted line.

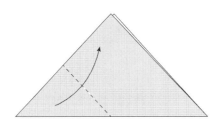

2) Fold the left side of the paper towards the center along the dotted line.

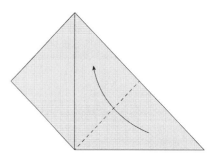

3) Fold the right side of the paper towards the center along the dotted line.

4) Fold the top right flap of paper down along the dotted line.

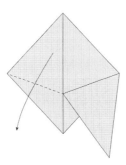

5) Fold the top left flap of paper down along the dotted line.

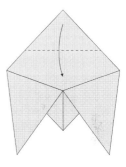

6) Fold the top layer of paper down along the dotted line.

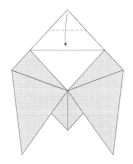

7) Fold the top layer of paper down along the dotted line.

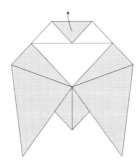

8) Unfold the previous fold.

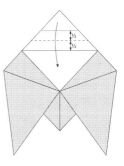

9) Fold the top layer of paper down along the dotted line. This fold should be half way between the previous fold and the point marked in the diagram.

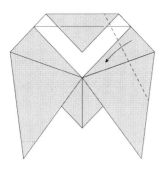

10) Fold the right side of the model along the dotted line.

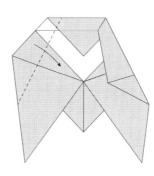

11) Fold the left side of the model along the dotted line.

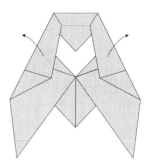

12) Crease both of these folds well and then unfold them.

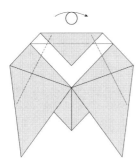

13) Turn the paper over.

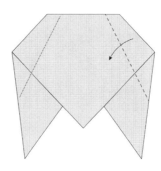

14) Fold the right side of the model along the dotted line. This is the opposite direction of the crease on the other side.

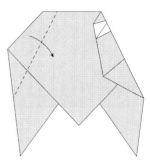

15) Fold the left side of the model along the dotted line. This is the opposite direction of the crease on the other side.

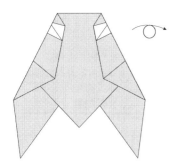

16) Turn the paper over.

17) Fold the top right corner down along the dotted line.

18) Fold the top left corner down along the dotted line.

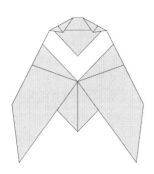

The completed Fly.

Pigeon

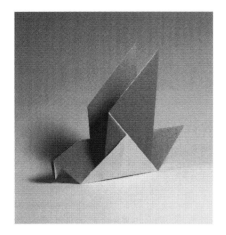

This is a really simple and great looking origami bird.

Techniques Used: Mountain and Valley Folds and Inside Reverse Fold.

Before You Start: Begin with a square sheet of paper rotated 45 degrees with the white side facing up.

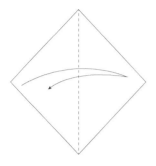

1) Fold the paper in half vertically along the dotted line and then unfold it.

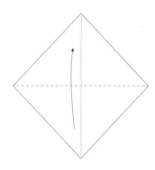

2) Fold the paper in half horizontally along the dotted line.

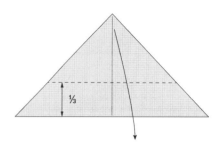

3) Fold both layers of paper down along the horizontal line. This crease should be about 1/3 of the way from the bottom of the paper to the top.

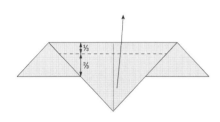

4) Fold the top layer of paper up along the dotted line. This crease should be about 1/3 of the way from the top of the paper to the marked point.

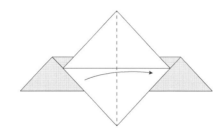

5) Fold the paper in half vertically along the dotted line.

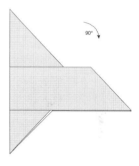

6) Rotate the paper 90 degrees to the right.

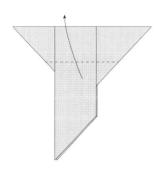

7) Fold the top flap of paper up along the dotted line.

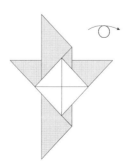

8) Turn the paper over.

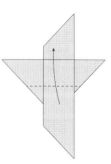

9) Fold the top flap of paper up along the dotted line.

Pigeon   Page **61**

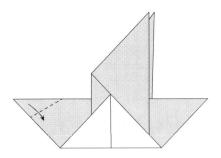

10) Fold the paper down along the dotted line.

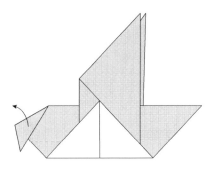

11) Crease this well and then unfold it.

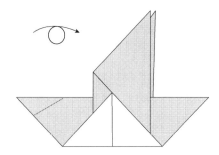

12) Turn the paper over.

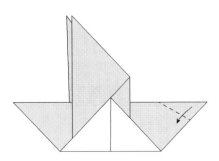

13) Fold the paper down along the dotted line. This is the opposite direction of the previous fold on the other side.

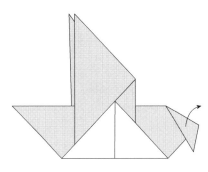

14) Crease this well and then unfold it.

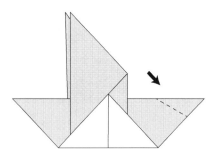

15) Make an Inside Reverse Fold along the existing creases.

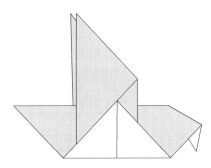

The complete pigeon.

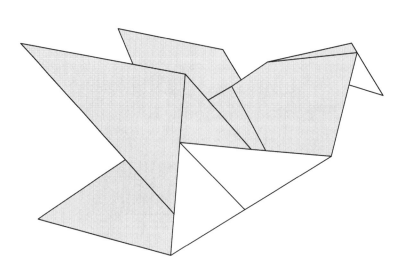

Pigeon

Samurai Helmet

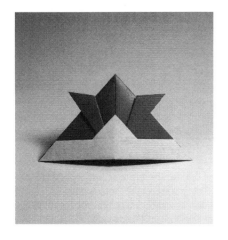

If you fold this model using a very large piece of paper such as a sheet of newspaper then you can wear it as a hat.

Techniques Used: Mountain and Valley Folds.

Before You Start: Begin with a square sheet of paper rotated 45 degrees with the white side facing up.

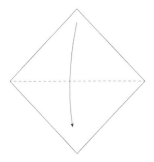

1) Fold the paper in half horizontally along the dotted line.

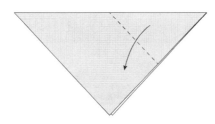

2) Fold the right side of the paper down along the dotted line.

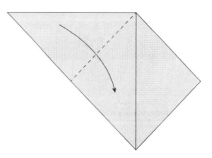

3) Fold the left side of the paper down along the dotted line.

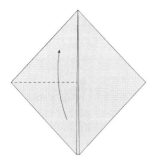

4) Fold the left flap of paper up along the dotted line.

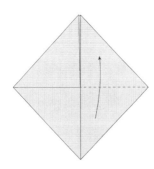

5) Fold the right flap of paper up along the dotted line.

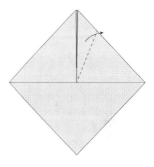

6) Fold the right flap of paper out along the dotted line.

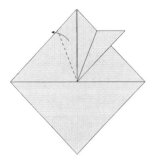

7) Fold the left flap of paper out along the dotted line.

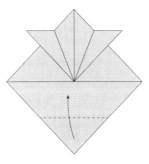

8) Fold the top layer of paper up along the dotted line.

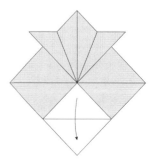

9) Crease it well and then unfold it.

Samurai Helmet

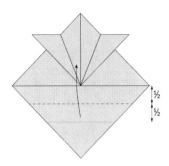

10) Fold the top layer of paper up along the dotted line. This crease should be one half of the way between the middle and the previous crease.

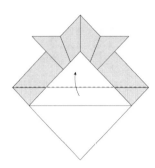

11) Fold the top flap of paper up along the dotted line.

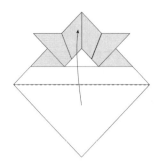

12) Fold the bottom of the paper up along the dotted line.

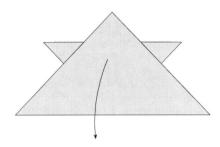

13) Crease this well and then unfold it.

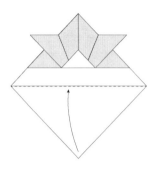

14) Fold the bottom of the paper up along the dotted line but this time tuck it inside the model.

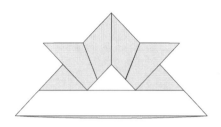

The completed Samurai Helmet.

Fortune Teller

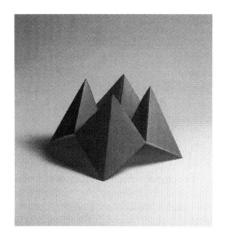

This model is also called a Cootie Catcher.

Techniques Used: Mountain and Valley Folds and Blintz Base.

Before You Start: Begin with a square sheet of paper rotated 45 degrees with the white side facing up.

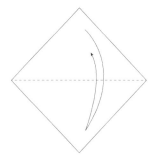

1) Fold the paper in half horizontally. Crease it well and then unfold it.

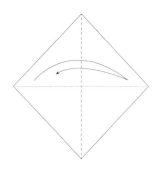

2) Fold the paper in half vertically. Crease it well and then unfold it.

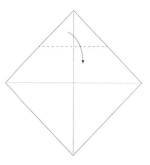

3) Fold the top corner to the center along the dotted line.

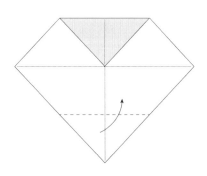

4) Fold the bottom corner to the center along the dotted line.

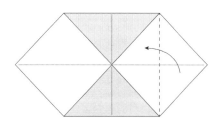

5) Fold the right corner to the center along the dotted line.

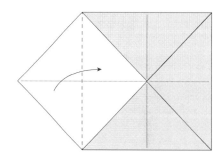

6) Fold the left corner to the center along the dotted line.

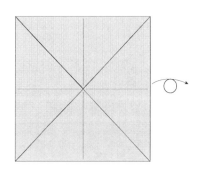

7) Turn the paper over.

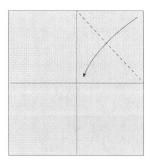

8) Fold the top right corner to the center along the dotted line.

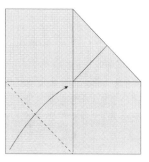

9) Fold the bottom left corner to the center along the dotted line.

Fortune Teller

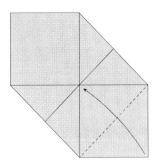

10) Fold the bottom right corner to the center along the dotted line.

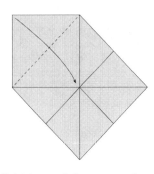

11) Fold the top left corner to the center along the dotted line.

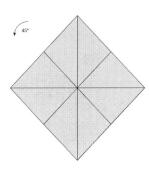

12) Rotate the paper 45 degrees to the left.

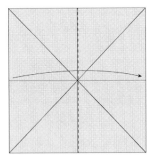

13) Fold the paper in half vertically.

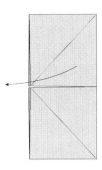

14) Crease this well and then unfold it.

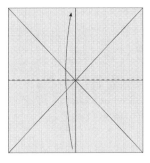

15) Fold the paper in half horizontally and crease it well.

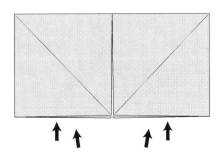

16) Open up the model by putting a finger inside each of the four flaps and pushing along the existing creases.

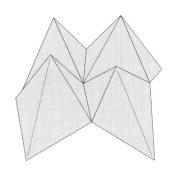

The completed Fortune Teller.

Turtle

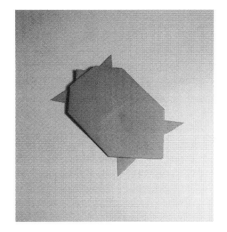

Even though this model requires one small cut it's still technically a traditional origami model.

Techniques Used: Mountain and Valley Folds, Pleat and Scissors.

Before You Start: Begin with a square sheet of paper with the white side facing up.

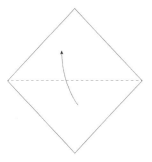

1) Fold the paper in half horizontally along the dotted line.

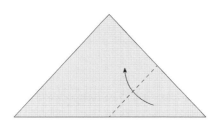

2) Fold the right side of the paper up along the dotted line.

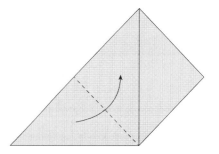

3) Fold the left side of the paper up along the dotted line.

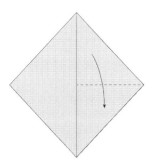

4) Fold the right flap of paper down along the dotted line.

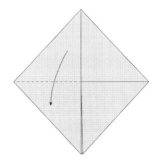

5) Fold the left flap of paper down along the dotted line.

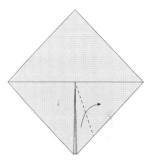

6) Fold the right flap of paper out along the dotted line.

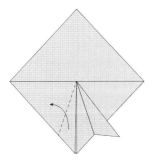

7) Fold the left flap of paper out along the dotted line.

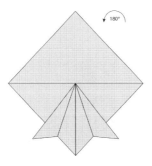

8) Rotate the paper 180 degrees.

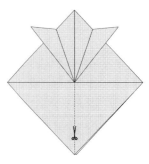

9) Cut the top layer of paper along the dotted line stopping at the middle of the model.

Turtle

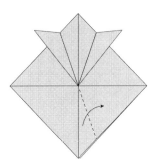

10) Fold the right section of paper out along the dotted line.

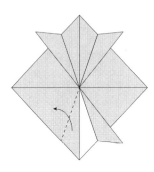

11) Fold the left section of paper out along the dotted line.

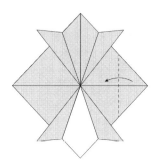

12) Fold the right side of the paper towards the center along the dotted line.

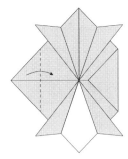

13) Fold the left side of the paper towards the center along the dotted line.

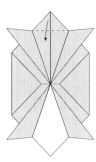

14) Fold the top part of the paper down along the dotted line.

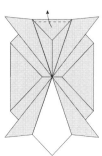

15) Fold the top part of the paper up along the dotted line.

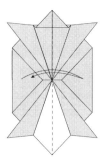

16) Fold the entire model in half along the dotted line. Crease this well and then unfold it.

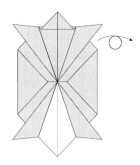

17) Turn the paper over.

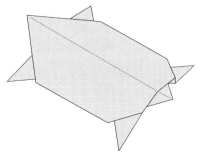

The completed Turtle.

Parakeet

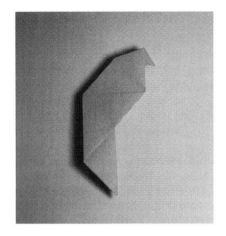

This is an excellent model to practice making Inside Reverse Folds.

Techniques Used: Mountain and Valley Folds and Inside Reverse Fold.

Before You Start: Begin with a square sheet of paper with the white side facing up.

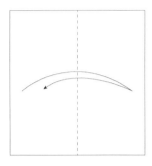

1) Fold the paper in half vertically. Crease it well and then unfold it.

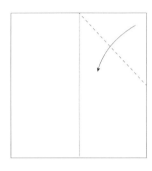

2) Fold the top right corner of the paper to the center along the dotted line.

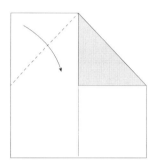

3) Fold the top left corner of the paper to the center along the dotted line.

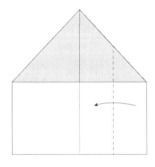

4) Fold the right side of the paper to the center along the dotted line.

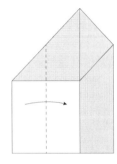

5) Fold the left side of the paper to the center along the dotted line.

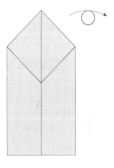

6) Turn the paper over.

7) Fold the paper in half vertically along the dotted line.

8) Fold the bottom of the paper up along the dotted line.

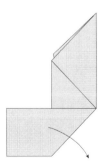

9) Crease this well and then unfold it.

Parakeet

10) Turn the paper over.

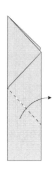

11) Fold the bottom of the paper up along the dotted line. This is the opposite direction of the fold on the other side.

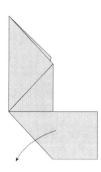

12) Crease this well and then unfold it.

13) Make an Inside Reverse fold using the existing creases.

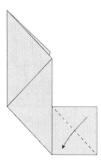

14) Fold the paper down along the dotted line.

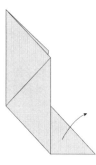

15) Crease this well and then unfold it.

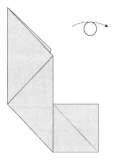

16) Turn the paper over.

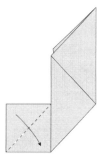

17) Fold the paper down along the dotted line. This is the opposite direction of the fold on the other side.

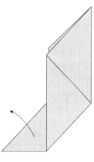

18) Crease this well and then unfold it.

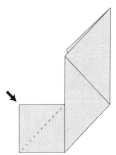

19) Make an Inside Reverse Fold using the existing creases.

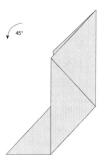

20) Rotate the model 45 degrees to the left.

21) Fold the top of the paper down along the dotted line.

Parakeet

22) Crease this well and then unfold it.

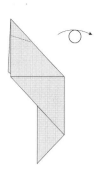

23) Turn the paper over.

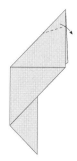

24) Fold the top of the paper down along the dotted line. This is the opposite direction of the fold on the other side.

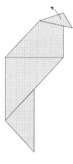

25) Crease this well and then unfold it.

26) Make an Inside Reverse Fold using the existing creases.

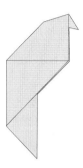

The completed Parakeet

Peacock

This model begins with a Kite Base. If you're already familiar with this base you can skip ahead to step 4.

Techniques Used: Mountain and Valley Folds, Kite Base and Inside Reverse Fold.

Before You Start: Begin with a square sheet of paper rotated 45 degrees with the white side facing up.

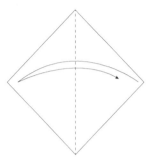

1) Fold the paper in half vertically and then unfold it..

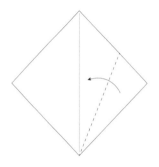

2) Fold the right side of the paper to the center along the dotted line.

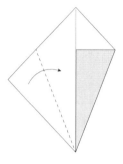

3) Fold the left side of the paper to the center along the dotted line.

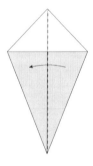

4) Fold the paper in half vertically along the dotted line.

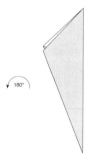

5) Rotate the paper about 180 degrees.

6) Fold the top of the paper down along the dotted line.

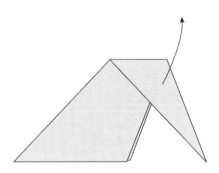

7) Crease this well and then unfold it.

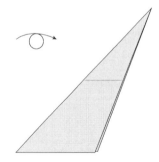

8) Turn the paper over.

9) Fold the top of the paper down along the dotted line. This is the opposite direction of the fold on the other side.

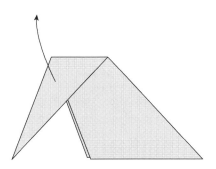

10) Crease this well and then unfold it.

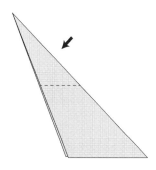

11) Make an Inside Reverse Fold using the existing creases.

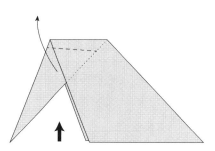

12) Pull the paper up making another Inside Reverse Fold along the thicker dotted line. There aren't any creases here already so this is a little bit tricky.

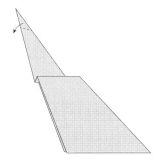

13) Fold the top of the paper down along the dotted line.

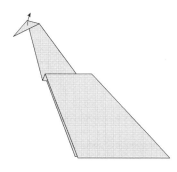

14) Crease this well and then unfold it.

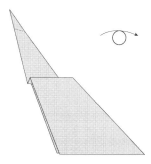

15) Turn the paper over.

16) Fold the top of the paper down along the dotted line. This is the opposite direction of the fold on the other side.

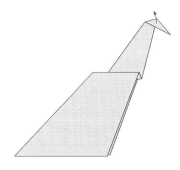

17) Crease this well and then unfold it.

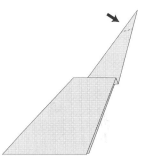

18) Make an Inside Reverse Fold using the existing creases.

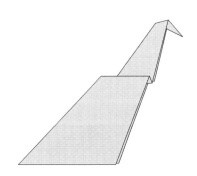

The completed Peacock.

Peacock

Parrot

The first several steps of this parrot are very similar to a Kite Base however the shape is a little bit different.

Techniques Used: Mountain and Valley Folds, Inside Reverse Fold, Outside Reverse Fold and Scissors.

Before You Start: Begin with a square sheet of paper rotated 45 degrees with the white side facing up.

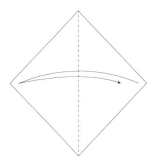

1) Fold the paper in half vertically and then unfold it..

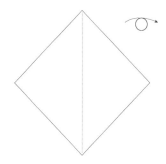

2) Turn the paper over.

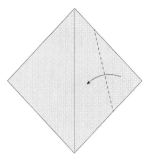

3) Fold the right corner to the center along the dotted line.

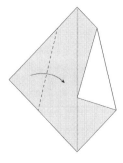

4) Fold the left corner to the center along the dotted line.

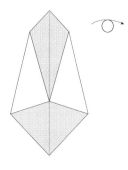

5) Turn the paper over.

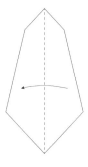

6) Fold the paper in half vertically along the dotted line.

7) Carefully cut through both layers of paper along the dotted line stopping where the dotted line ends.

8) Fold the top layer of paper up and to the left along the dotted line.

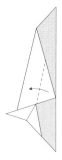

9) Fold the top layer of paper to the left along the dotted line.

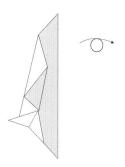 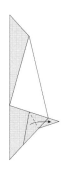 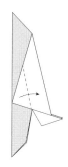

10) Turn the paper over.

11) Fold the top layer of paper up and to the right along the dotted line.

12) Fold the top layer of paper to the right along the dotted line.

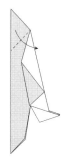  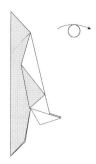

13) Fold the top part of the paper down along the dotted line.

14) Crease this well and then unfold it.

15) Turn the paper over.

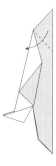  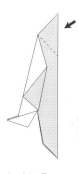

16) Fold the top part of the paper down along the dotted line. This is the opposite direction of the previous crease on the other side.

17) Crease this well and then unfold it.

18) Make an Inside Reverse Fold using the existing creases.

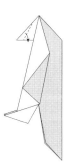 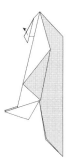 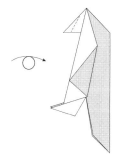

19) Fold the paper down along the dotted line.

20) Crease this well and then unfold it.

21) Turn the paper over.

Parrot

Page 75

22) Fold the paper down along the dotted line. This is the opposite direction of the previous crease on the other side.

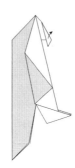

23) Crease this well and then unfold it.

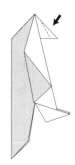

24) Make an Outside Reverse Fold along the existing creases.

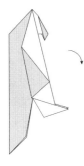

25) Rotate the paper a bit to the right so the parrot is standing upright on its feet.

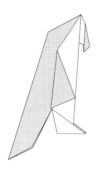

The completed Parrot.

Talking Fish

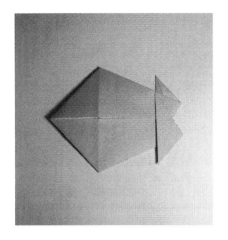

If you pull on the top and bottom of this fish's tail then the mouth moves a little bit, almost like it's talking.

Techniques Used: Mountain and Valley Folds, Kite Base and Swivel Fold.

Before You Start: Begin with a square sheet of paper rotated 45 degrees with the white side facing up.

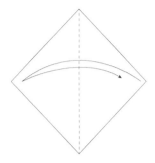

1) Fold the paper in half vertically. Crease it well and then unfold it.

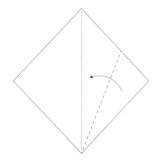

2) Fold the right side of the paper to the center along the dotted line.

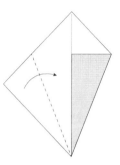

3) Fold the left side of the paper to the center along the dotted line.

4) Fold the top right part of the paper to the center along the dotted line.

5) Crease this well and then unfold it.

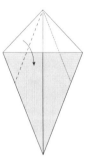

6) Fold the top left part of the paper to the center along the dotted line.

7) Crease this well and then unfold it.

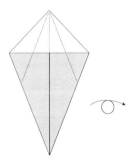

8) Turn the paper over.

9) Fold the paper along the dotted line bringing the top corner to the bottom corner.

Talking Fish

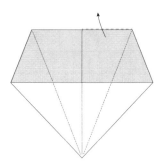 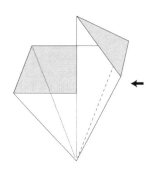 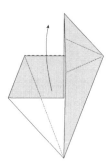

10) Fold the top layer of paper on the right up along the dotted line.

11) As you fold this up make a Swivel Fold on the side using the existing creases.

12) Fold the top layer of paper on the left up along the dotted line.

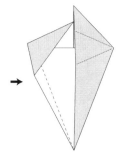  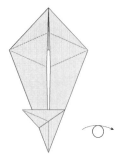

13) As you fold this up make a Swivel Fold on the side using the existing creases.

14) Fold the top flap of paper up and to the left along the dotted line.

15) Turn the paper over.

 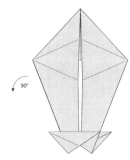 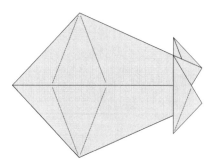

16) Fold the top flap of paper up and to the left along the dotted line.

17) Rotate the model 90 degrees to the left.

The completed Talking Fish.

Crown

This is the first fully 3-dimensional model in this book.

Techniques Used: Mountain and Valley Folds and Blintz Base.

Before You Start: Begin with a square sheet of paper rotated 45 degrees with the white side facing up.

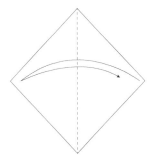

1) Fold the paper in half vertically. Crease it well and then unfold it.

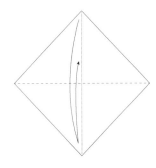

2) Fold the paper in half horizontally. Crease it well and then unfold it.

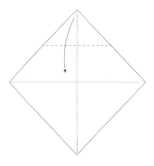

3) Fold the top corner to the center.

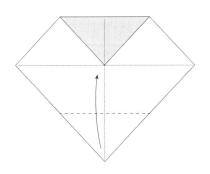

4) Fold the bottom corner to the center.

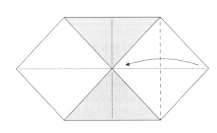

5) Fold the right corner to the center.

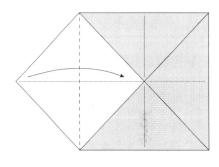

6) Fold the left corner to the center.

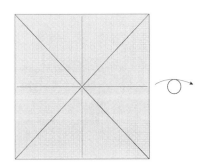

7) Turn the paper over.

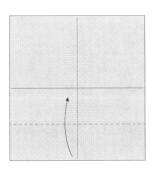

8) Fold the bottom part of the paper up along the dotted line. As you do, let the triangle shaped flap of paper out.

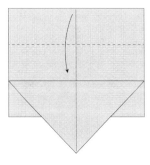

9) Fold the top part of the paper down along the dotted line. As you do, let the triangle shaped flap of paper out.

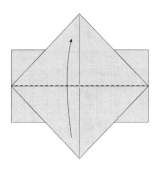

10) Fold the bottom triangle of paper up along the dotted line.

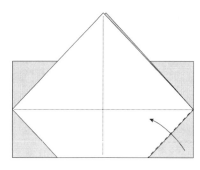

11) Fold the bottom right section of the paper up along the dotted line.

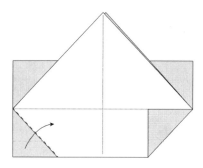

12) Fold the bottom left section of paper up along the dotted line.

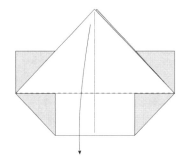

13) Fold the triangle of paper back down along the dotted line.

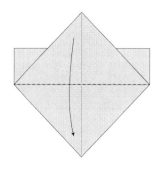

14) Fold the top triangle of paper down along the dotted line.

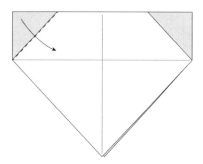

15) Fold the top left section of the paper down along the dotted line.

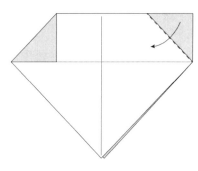

16) Fold the top right section of the paper down along the dotted line.

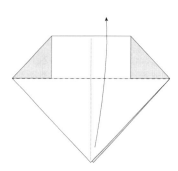

17) Fold the triangle of paper back up along the dotted line.

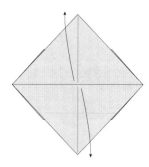

18) Pull the paper apart in the middle to open up the crown and give it a 3D shape.

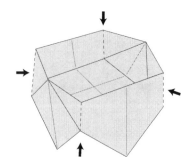

19) Make creases along the four edges in the corners to give the crown a more solid shape.

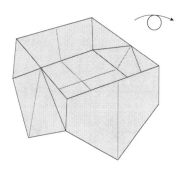

20) Turn the model over.

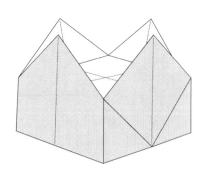

The completed Crown.

Crown

Rooster

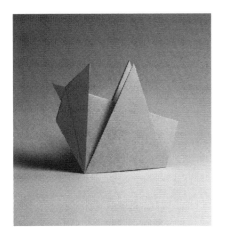

There are a couple of tricky folds near the end of these instructions. If you're having trouble just keep practicing and eventually you'll get it.

Techniques Used: Mountain and Valley Folds, Pleat and Swivel Fold.

Before You Start: Begin with a square sheet of paper rotated 45 degrees with the colored side facing up.

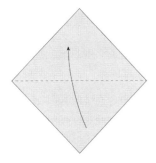

1) Fold the paper in half horizontally.

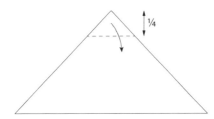

2) Fold the top layer of paper down along the dotted line. This crease should be about one quarter of the way from the top to the bottom.

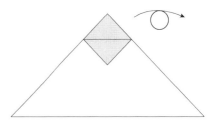

3) Turn the paper over.

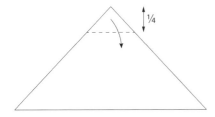

4) Fold the top layer of paper down along the dotted line. This crease should be about one quarter of the way from the top to the bottom.

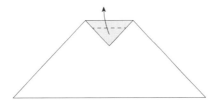

5) Fold the top layer of paper up along the dotted line.

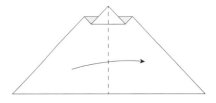

6) Fold the paper in half along the dotted line.

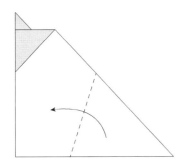

7) Fold the top flap of paper over to the left along the dotted line.

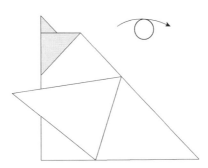

8) Turn the paper over.

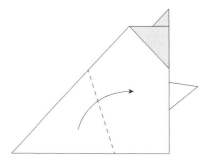

9) Fold the top flap of paper over to the right along the dotted line.

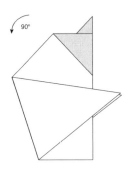

10) Rotate the paper about 90 degrees to the left.

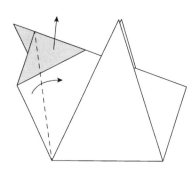

11) Fold the top layer of paper over to the right along the dotted line making a Swivel Fold. The paper on the top will come up.

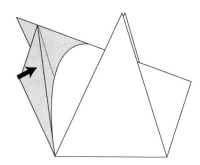

12) Push everything flat.

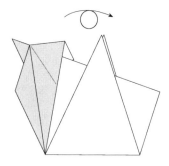

13) Turn the paper over.

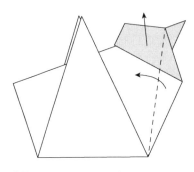

14) Fold the top layer of paper over to the left along the dotted line making a Swivel Fold. The paper on the top will come up.

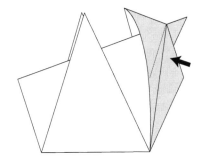

15) Push everything flat.

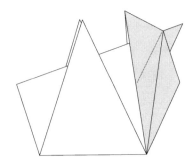

The completed Rooster.

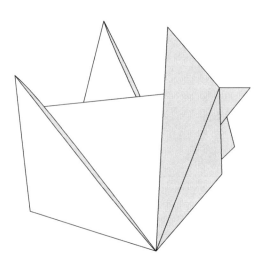

Easy

Angelfish

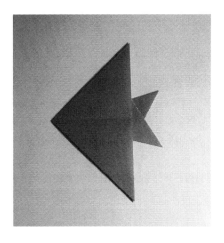

This folding sequence begins with a Water Bomb Base. If you're already familiar with this base you can skip ahead to step 8.

Techniques Used: Mountain and Valley Folds and Water Bomb Base.

Before You Start: Begin with a sheet square of paper with the colored side facing up.

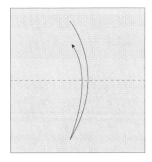

1) Fold the paper in half horizontally. Crease this well and then unfold it.

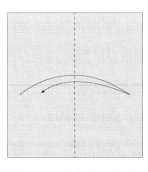

2) Fold the paper in half vertically. Crease this well and then unfold it.

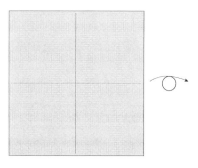

3) Turn the paper over.

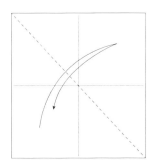

4) Fold the paper in half diagonally. Crease this well and then unfold it.

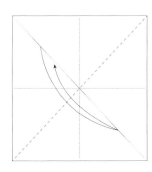

5) Fold the paper in half diagonally the other way. Crease this well and then unfold it.

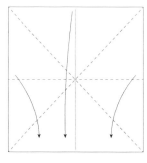

6) Following the existing creases bring the left and right sides of the paper as well as the top edge towards the bottom.

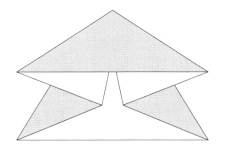

7) The paper will begin to take a shape that looks like this. Push everything flat along the existing creases.

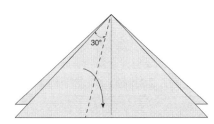

8) Fold the top left flap towards the right along the dotted line. This should roughly be a 30 degree angle but don't worry about getting it completely perfect.

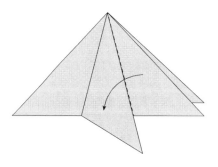

9) Fold the top right flap towards the left along the dotted line.

Angelfish

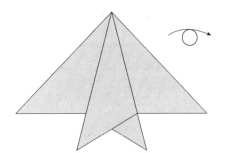 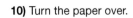 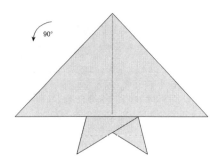 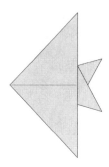

10) Turn the paper over.

11) Rotate the paper 90 degrees to the left.

The completed Angelfish

Butterfly

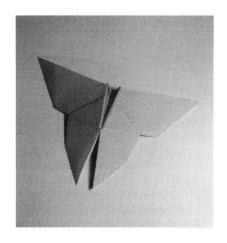

This is a fairly simple origami butterfly but it looks really great. It begins with a Water Bomb Base and if you're already familiar with that base you can skip ahead to step 8.

Techniques Used: Mountain and Valley Folds, Pleat, Water Bomb Base and Squash Fold.

Before You Start: Begin with a square of paper with the colored side up.

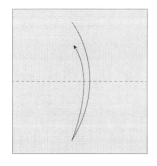

1) Fold the paper in half horizontally. Crease this well and then unfold it.

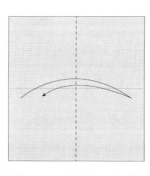

2) Fold the paper in half vertically. Crease this well and then unfold it.

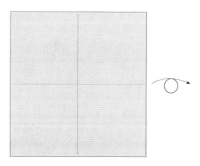

3) Turn the paper over.

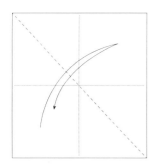

4) Fold the paper in half diagonally. Crease this well and then unfold it.

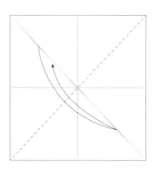

5) Fold the paper in half diagonally the other way. Crease this well and then unfold it.

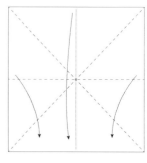

6) Following the existing creases bring the left and right sides of the paper as well as the top edge towards the bottom.

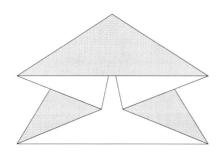

7) The paper will begin to take a shape that looks like this. Push everything flat along the existing creases.

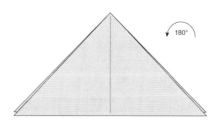

8) Rotate the paper 180 degrees.

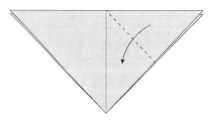

9) Fold the top right flap of paper down along the dotted line.

Butterfly Page **87**

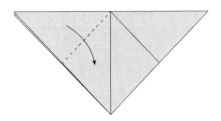

10) Fold the top left flap of paper down along the dotted line.

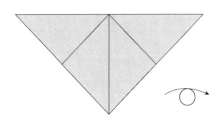

11) Turn the paper over.

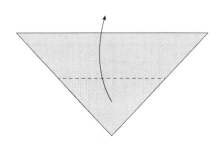

12) Fold all layers of paper up along the dotted line.

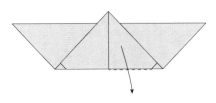

13) Fold the top right flap of paper down along the dotted line.

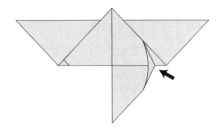

14) As you fold this flap of paper down Squash Fold the paper on the edge flat.

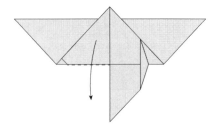

15) Fold the top left flap of paper down along the dotted line.

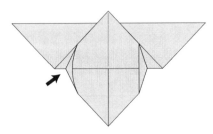

16) As you fold this flap of paper down Squash Fold the paper on the edge flat.

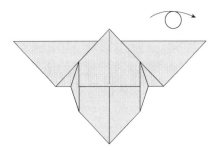

17) Turn the paper over.

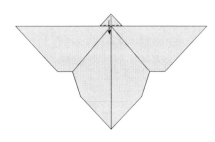

18) Fold the top triangle of paper down along the dotted line and over top of the rest of the paper.

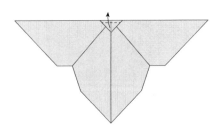

19) Fold this triangle back up along the dotted line making a Pleat.

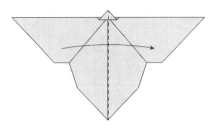

20) Fold the paper in half vertically along the dotted line.

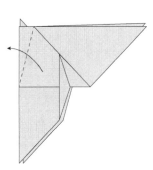

21) Fold the top part of the model over to the left along the dotted line.

Butterfly

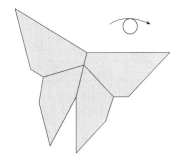

22) Turn the paper over.

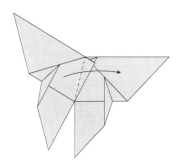

23) Fold the top part of the model over to the right along the dotted line.

24) Bring the back wings over to the left and open up the model.

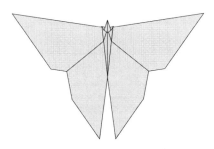

The completed Butterfly.

Butterfly

Goldfish

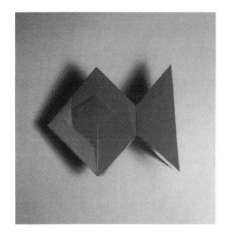

The beginning of this folding sequence is almost exactly the same as the traditional Samurai Helmet on page 63.

Techniques Used: Mountain and Valley Folds, Outside Reverse Fold and Scissors.

Before You Start: Begin with a square sheet of paper rotated 45 degrees with the white side facing up.

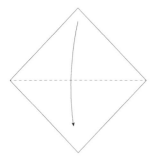

1) Fold the paper in half horizontally.

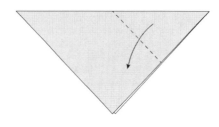

2) Fold the right side of the paper to the center along the dotted line.

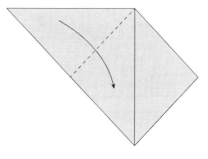

3) Fold the left side of the paper to the center along the dotted line.

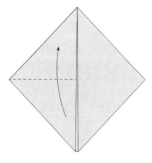

4) Fold the left flap of paper up along the dotted line

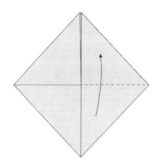

5) Fold the right flap of paper up along the dotted line.

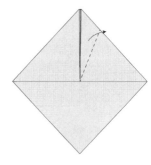

6) Fold the top right flap of paper out along the dotted line.

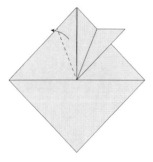

7) Fold the top left flap of paper out along the dotted line.

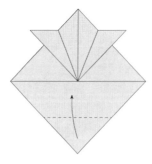

8) Fold the top layer of paper at the bottom up along the dotted line.

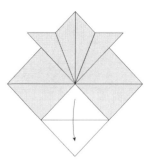

9) Crease this well and then unfold it.

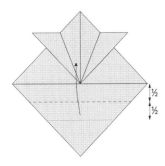

10) Fold the top layer of paper at the bottom up along the dotted line. This crease should be halfway between the previous crease and the middle.

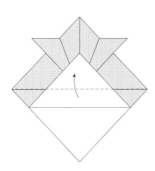

11) Fold the top flap of paper up along the dotted line.

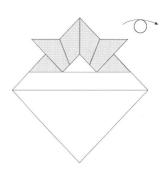

12) Turn the paper over.

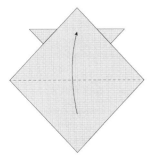

13) Fold the top layer of paper up along the dotted line.

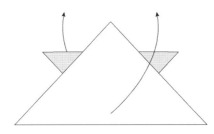

14) Open up the paper pulling the top and bottom apart.

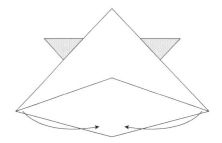

15) As you open the paper bring the left and right corners together closing the paper back up.

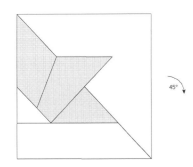

16) Rotate the paper 45 degrees to the right.

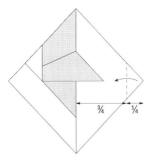

17) Fold the right side of the paper along the dotted line. This crease should be about a quarter of the way from the edge to the middle.

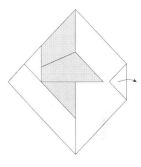

18) Crease this well and then unfold it.

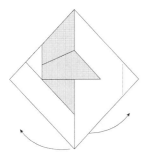

19) Open the paper again bringing it back to the same position as in step 14.

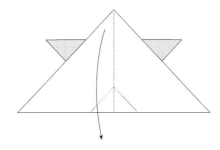

20) Unfold the top layer of paper.

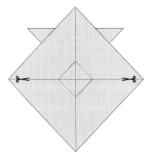

21) Cut the top layer of paper along the dotted lines. Stop cutting at the diamond shaped crease.

Goldfish

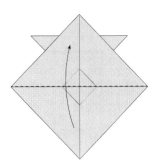

22) Fold the top layer of paper back up.

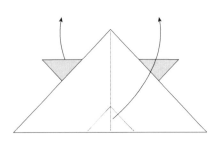

23) Open up the paper pulling the top and bottom apart.

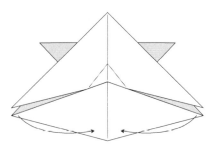

24) As you open the paper bring the left and right corners together closing the paper back up.

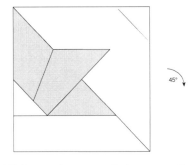

25) Rotate the paper 45 degrees to the right.

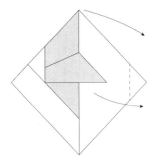

26) Pull back the top layer of paper along the dotted line making an Outside Reverse Fold.

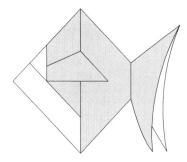

27) Push the tail completely flat.

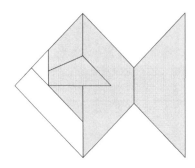

The completed Goldfish.

Piano

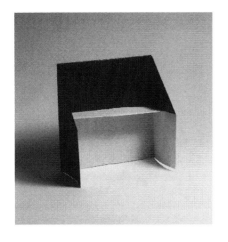

The beginning of this folding sequence is exactly the same as the traditional origami house on page 51.

Techniques Used: Mountain and Valley Folds and Swivel Fold.

Before You Start: Begin with a square sheet of paper with the white side facing up.

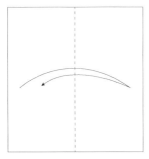

1) Fold the paper in half vertically and then unfold it.

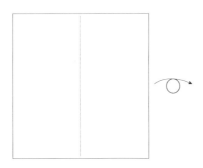

2) Turn the paper over.

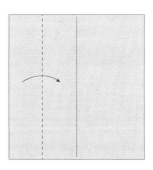

3) Fold the left side of the paper towards the center along the dotted line.

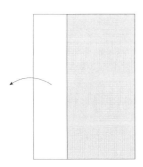

4) Crease this well and then unfold it.

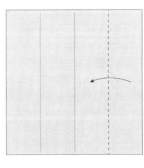

5) Fold the right side of the paper towards the center along the dotted line.

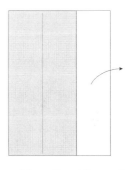

6) Crease this well and then unfold it.

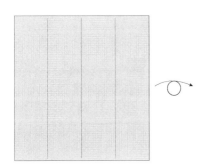

7) Turn the paper over.

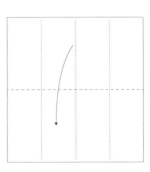

8) Fold the paper in half horizontally along the dotted line.

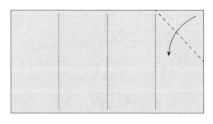

9) Fold the top right corner of paper down along the dotted line.

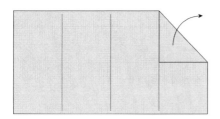

10) Crease this well and then unfold it.

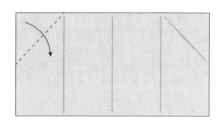

11) Fold the top left corner of paper down along the dotted line.

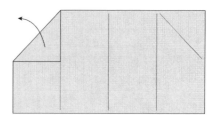

12) Crease this well and then unfold it.

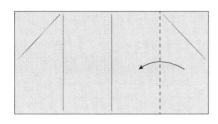

13) Fold the top layer of paper towards the center along the dotted line.

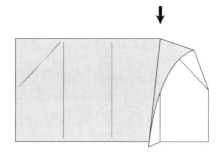

14) As the paper opens Swivel Fold the top down along the existing creases and push everything flat.

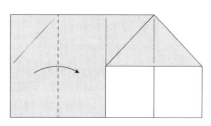

15) Fold the top layer of paper towards the center along the dotted line.

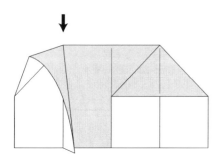

16) As the paper opens Swivel Fold the top down along the existing creases and push everything flat.

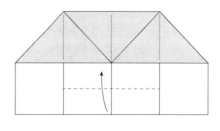

17) Fold the middle flap of paper up along the dotted line.

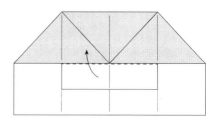

18) Fold this flap of paper up along the dotted line.

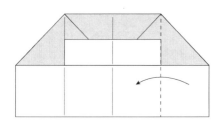

19) Fold the right side of the model towards the center along the dotted line.

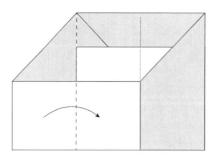

20) Fold the left side of the model towards the center along the dotted line.

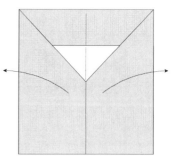

21) Open up both sides of the model a little bit.

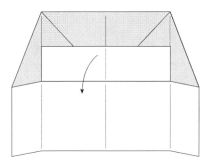
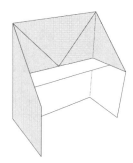

22) Fold the middle flap of paper down and tuck the edges under the colored flaps of paper on the two sides.

The completed piano.

Long Box

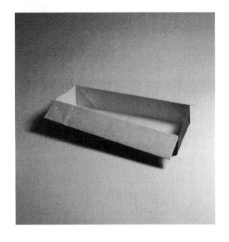

The beginning of this folding sequence is exactly the same as the traditional origami house on page 51.

Techniques Used: Mountain and Valley Folds and Swivel Fold.

Before You Start: Begin with a square sheet of paper with the white side facing up.

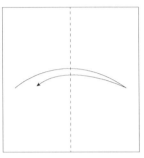

1) Fold the paper in half vertically and then unfold it.

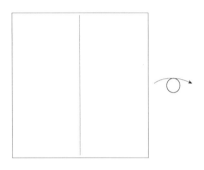

2) Turn the paper over.

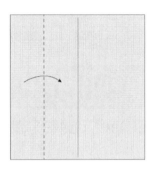

3) Fold the left side of the paper towards the center along the dotted line.

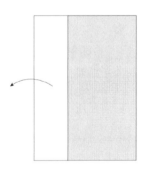

4) Crease this well and then unfold it.

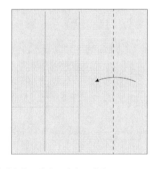

5) Fold the right side of the paper towards the center along the dotted line.

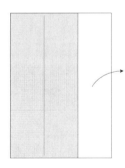

6) Crease this well and then unfold it.

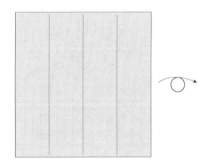

7) Turn the paper over.

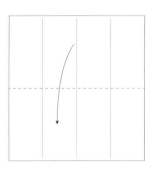

8) Fold the paper in half horizontally along the dotted line.

9) Fold the top right corner of paper down along the dotted line.

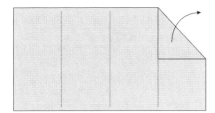

10) Crease this well and then unfold it.

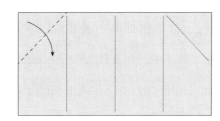

11) Fold the top left corner of paper down along the dotted line.

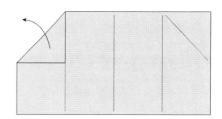

12) Crease this well and then unfold it.

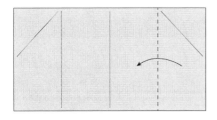

13) Fold the top layer of paper towards the center along the dotted line.

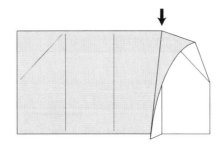

14) As the paper opens Swivel Fold the top down along the existing creases and push everything flat.

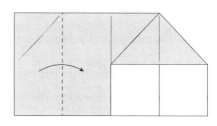

15) Fold the top layer of paper towards the center along the dotted line.

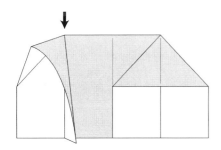

16) As the paper opens Swivel Fold the top down along the existing creases and push everything flat.

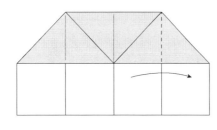

17) Fold the top right flap of paper back over to the right.

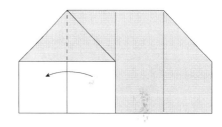

18) Fold the top left flap of paper back over to the left.

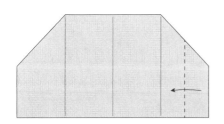

19) Fold the top flap of paper on the right toward the center along the dotted line.

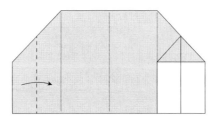

20) Fold the top flap of paper on the left toward the center along the dotted line.

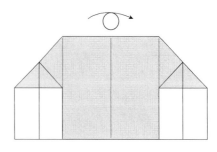

21) Turn the paper over.

Long Box

Page 97

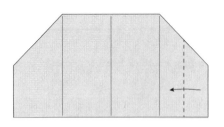

22) Fold the top right flap of paper toward the center along the dotted line.

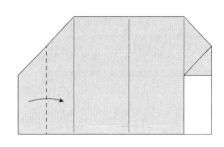

23) Fold the top left flap of paper toward the center along the dotted line.

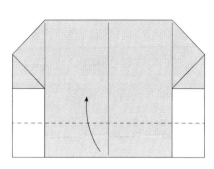

24) Fold the top flap of paper up along the dotted line.

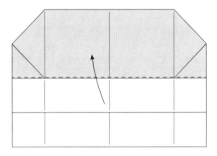

25) Fold the top flap of paper up again along the dotted line.

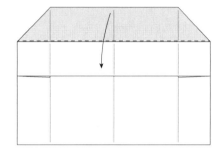

26) Fold the top of the paper down along the dotted line.

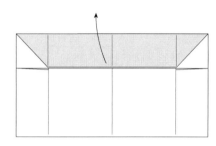

27) Crease this well and then unfold it.

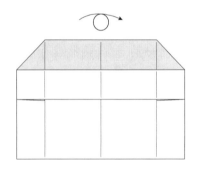

28) Turn the paper over.

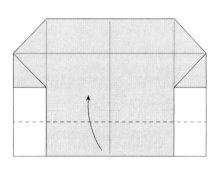

29) Fold the top flap of paper up along the dotted line.

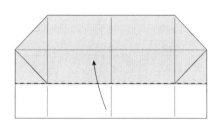

30) Fold the top flap of paper up again along the dotted line.

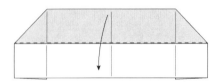

31) Fold the top of the paper down along the dotted line. This is the opposite direction of the crease made on the other side.

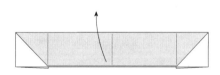

32) Crease this well and then unfold it.

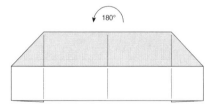

33) Rotate the model 180 degrees.

Long Box

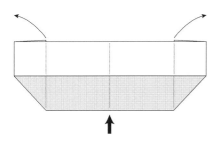 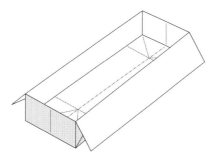

34) Push the bottom up and open up the box forming the shape along the existing creases.

The completed Long Box.

Sailboat

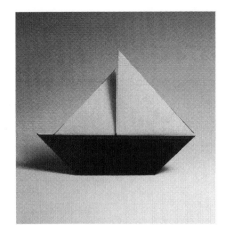

This model begins with a slightly modified Square Base.

Techniques Used: Mountain and Valley Folds and Square Base.

Before You Start: Begin with a square sheet of paper rotated 45 degrees with the colored side facing up.

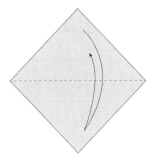

1) Fold the paper in half horizontally. Crease it well and then unfold it.

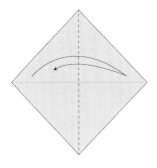

2) Fold the paper in half vertically. Crease it well and then unfold it.

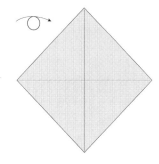

3) Turn the paper over and rotate it 45 degrees.

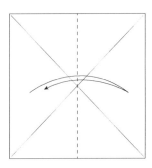

4) Fold the paper in half vertically. Crease it well and then unfold it.

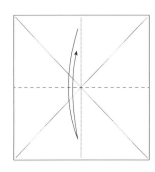

5) Fold the paper in half horizontally. Crease it well and then unfold it.

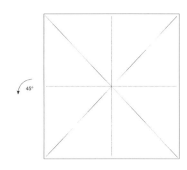

6) Rotate the paper 45 degrees.

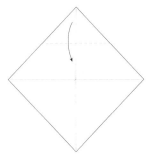

7) Fold the top of the paper towards the center along the dotted line.

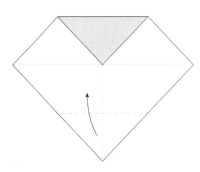

8) Fold the bottom of the paper towards the center along the dotted line.

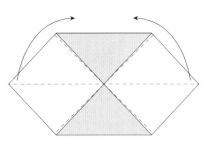

9) Using the existing creases fold the left and right corners up into a slightly modified Square Base.

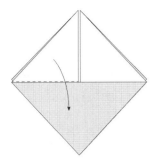

10) Fold the top left section of paper down along the dotted line.

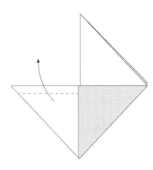

11) Fold this section of paper up along the dotted line.

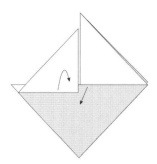

12) Tuck this flap of paper inside of the model.

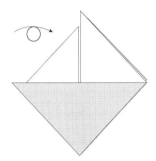

13) Turn the paper over.

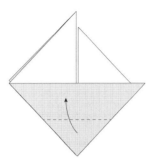

14) Fold the bottom of the paper up along the dotted line.

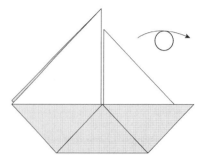

15) Turn the paper over.

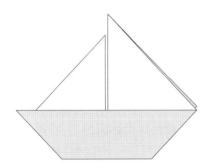

The completed Sailboat.

Chick

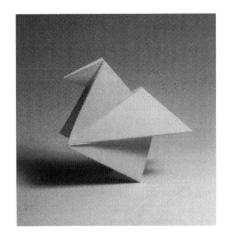

This is another excellent model to practice Inside Reverse Folds.

Techniques Used: Mountain and Valley Folds and Inside Reverse Fold.

Before You Start: Begin with a square sheet of paper rotated 45 degrees with the white side up.

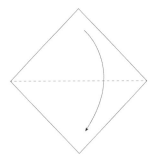

1) Fold the paper in half horizontally along the dotted line.

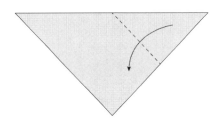

2) Fold the right side of the paper to the center along the dotted line.

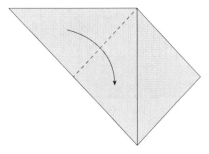

3) Fold the left side of the paper to the center along the dotted line.

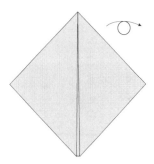

4) Turn the paper over.

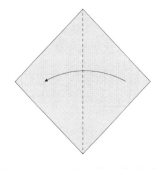

5) Fold the paper in half vertically from right to left along the dotted line.

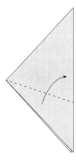

6) For the top layer of paper up along the dotted line.

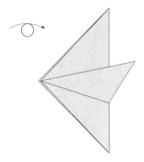

7) Turn the paper over.

8) Fold the top layer of paper up along the dotted line.

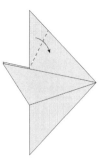

9) Fold the top of the paper down along the dotted line.

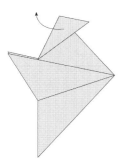

10) Crease this well and then unfold it.

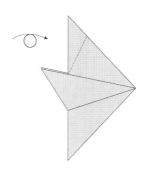

11) Turn the paper over.

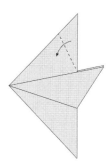

12) Fold the top of the paper down along the dotted line. This is the opposite direction of the crease you made on the other side.

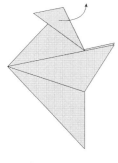

13) Crease this well and then unfold it.

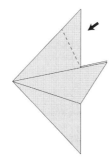

14) Make an Inside Reverse fold along the dotted line using the creases you made previously.

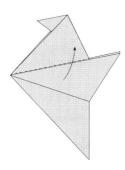

15) Fold the wing up.

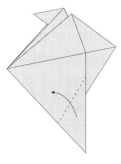

16) Fold the bottom of the paper towards the left along the dotted line.

17) Crease this well and then unfold it.

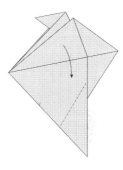

18) Fold the wing back down.

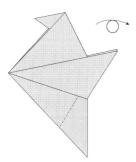

19) Turn the paper over.

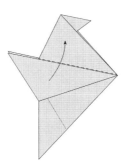

20) Fold the wing up.

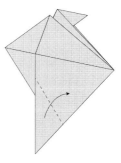

21) Fold the bottom of the paper towards the right along the dotted line.

Chick

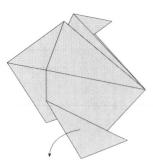

22) Crease this well and then unfold it. This is the opposite direction of the crease you made on the other side.

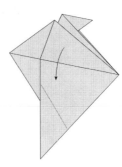

23) Fold the wing back down.

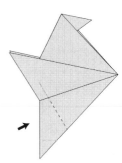

24) Make an Inside Reverse fold along the dotted line using the creases you made previously.

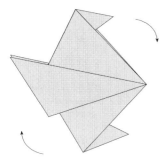

25) Rotate the model so it's standing on the foot at the bottom.

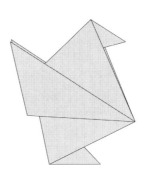

The completed chick.

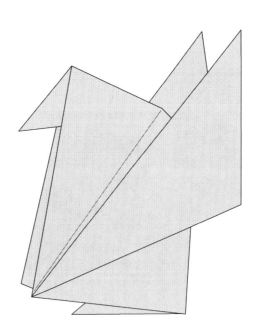

Penguin

This model has a couple of folds where there aren't any guides. Just try to match the instructions here best you can, these folds don't have to be 100% perfect.

Techniques Used: Mountain and Valley Folds and Outside Reverse Fold.

Before You Start: Begin with a square sheet of paper rotated 45 degrees with the colored side up.

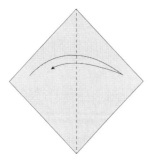

1) Fold the paper in half vertically and then unfold it.

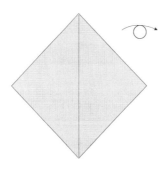

2) Turn the paper over.

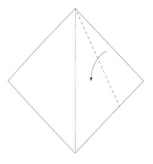

3) Fold the right side of the paper towards the center along the dotted line.

4) Fold the left side of the paper towards the center along the dotted line.

5) Turn the paper over.

6) Fold the left side of the paper towards the center along the dotted line.

7) Fold the right side of the paper towards the center along the dotted line.

8) Fold the bottom of the paper up along the dotted line.

9) Fold the paper in half vertically.

10) Fold the top of the paper down along the dotted line.

11) Crease this well and then unfold it.

12) Turn the model over.

13) Fold the top of the paper down along the dotted line. This is the opposite side of the fold from step 10.

14) Crease this well and then unfold it.

15) Make an Outside Reverse Fold along the existing creases.

The completed Penguin.

Duck

This model begins with a Kite Base. If you're already familiar with this base you can skip ahead to step 4.

Techniques Used: Mountain and Valley Folds, Kite Base and Inside Reverse Fold.

Before You Start: Begin with a square sheet of paper rotated 45 degrees with the white side facing up.

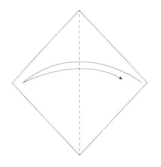

1) Fold the paper in half vertically and then unfold it.

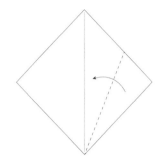

2) Fold the right side of the paper towards the center along the dotted line.

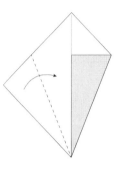

3) Fold the left side of the paper towards the center along the dotted line.

4) Fold the top right section of paper down along the dotted line.

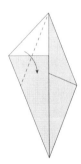

5) Fold the top left section of paper down along the dotted line.

6) Rotate the paper 90 degrees to the left.

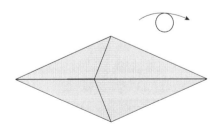

7) Turn the paper over.

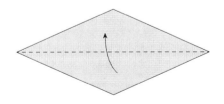

8) Fold the paper in half horizontally along the dotted line.

9) Fold the left part of the paper up along the dotted line.

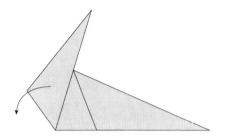

10) Crease this well and then unfold it.

11) Turn the paper over.

12) Fold the right part of the paper up along the dotted line. This is the opposite direction of the previous fold.

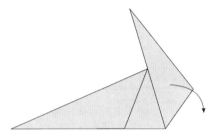

13) Crease this well and then unfold it.

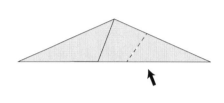

14) Make an Inside Reverse Fold along the existing creases.

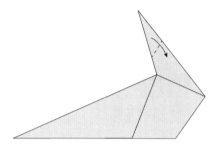

15) Fold the top part of the paper down along the dotted line.

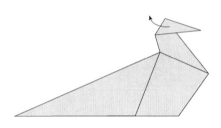

16) Crease this well and then unfold it.

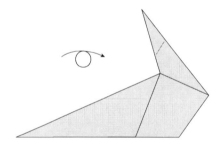

17) Turn the paper over.

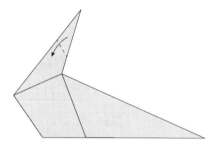

18) Fold the top part of the paper down along the dotted line. This is the opposite direction of the previous fold.

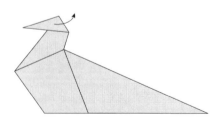

19) Crease this well and then unfold it.

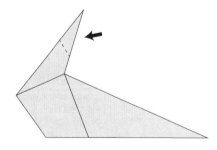

20) Make an Inside Reverse Fold along the existing creases.

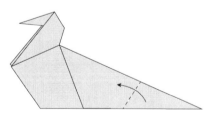

21) Fold the right part of the paper up along the dotted line.

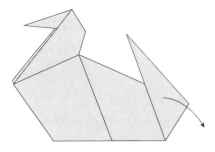

22) Crease this well and then unfold it.

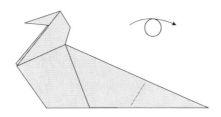

23) Turn the paper over.

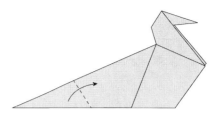

24) Fold the left part of the paper up along the dotted line. This is the opposite direction of the previous fold.

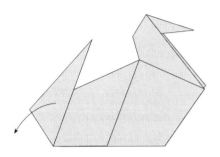

25) Crease this well and then unfold it.

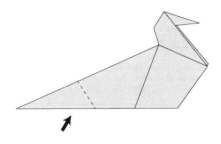

26) Make an Inside Reverse Fold along the existing creases.

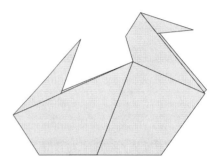

The completed Duck.

Duck

Pajarita (Little Bird)

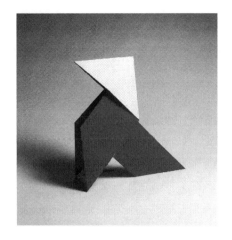

This model originated in Spain. Pajarita means "Little Bird" in Spanish and the Spanish Origami Association uses a Pajarita in its logo.

Techniques Used: Mountain and Valley Folds and Outside Reverse Fold.

Before You Start: Begin with a square sheet of paper rotated 45 degrees with the white side facing up.

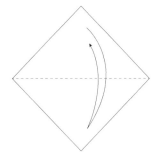

1) Fold the paper in half horizontally along the dotted line. Crease it well and then unfold it.

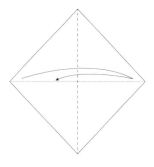

2) Fold the paper in half vertically. Crease it well and then unfold it.

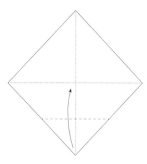

3) Fold the bottom of the paper towards the center along the dotted line.

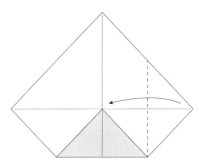

4) Fold the right side of the paper towards the center along the dotted line.

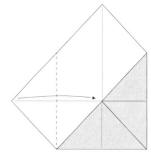

5) Fold the left side of the paper towards the center along the dotted line.

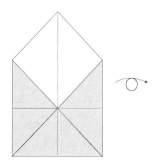

6) Turn the paper over.

7) Fold the top of the paper towards the center along the dotted line.

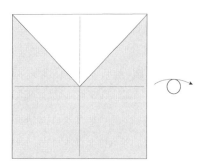

8) Turn the paper over.

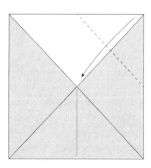

9) Fold the top right corner towards the center along the dotted line.

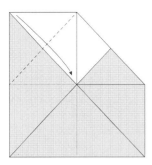

10) Fold the top left corner towards the center along the dotted line.

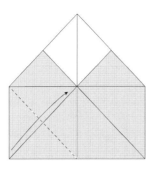

11) Fold the bottom left corner towards the center along the dotted line.

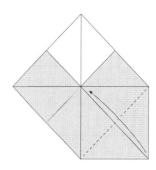

12) Fold the bottom right corner towards the center along the dotted line.

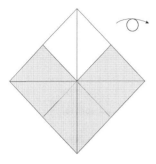

13) Turn the paper over.

14) Fold the model in half along the dotted line bringing the bottom corner to the top.

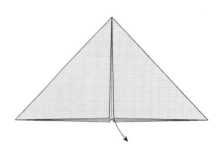

15) Pull out the layer of paper from the inside of the right side of the model.

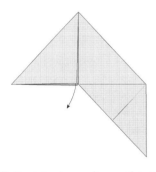

16) Pull out the layer of paper from the inside of the left side of the model.

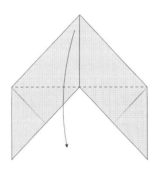

17) Fold the top layer of paper down along the dotted line.

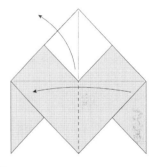

18) Fold the model in half vertically along the dotted line. As you do, bring the top white layer of paper up and outside into an Outside Reverse Fold.

19) Pull out the layer of paper from the inside of the back of the model.

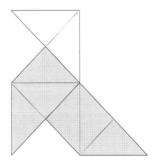

The completed Pajarita.

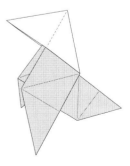

Pajarita (Little Bird)

Pinwheel

This model requires you to make a large amount of initial creases before using them to collapse the paper into a certain shape. This sort of sequence is fairly common in more complex origami.

Techniques Used: Mountain and Valley Folds

Before You Start: Begin with a square sheet of paper with the white side facing up.

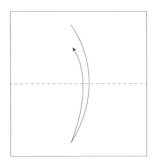

1) Fold the paper in half horizontally. Crease this well and then unfold it.

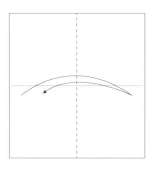

2) Fold the paper in half vertically. Crease it well and then unfold it.

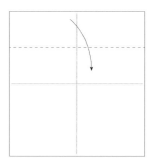

3) Fold the top of the paper down towards the center along the dotted line.

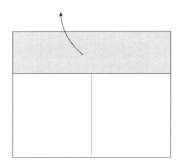

4) Crease this well and then unfold it.

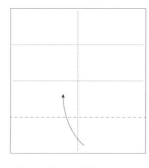

5) Fold the bottom of the paper up towards the center along the dotted line.

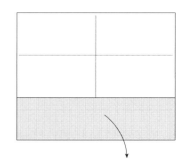

6) Crease this well and then unfold it.

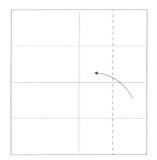

7) Fold the right side of the paper towards the center along the dotted line.

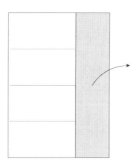

8) Crease this well and then unfold it.

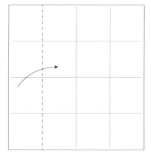

9) Fold the left side of the paper towards the center along the dotted line.

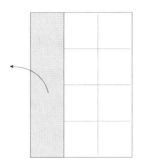

10) Crease this well and then unfold it.

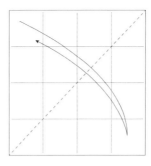

11) Fold the paper in half diagonally. Crease it well and then unfold it.

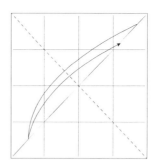

12) Fold the paper in half diagonally the other way. Crease it well and then unfold it.

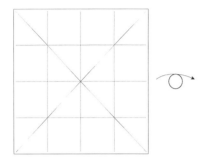

13) Turn the paper over.

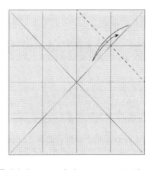

14) Fold the top right corner to the center along the dotted line. Crease this well and then unfold it.

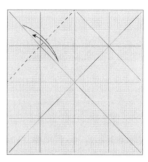

15) Fold the top left corner to the center along the dotted line. Crease this well and then unfold it.

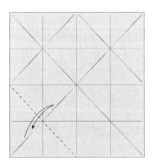

16) Fold the bottom left corner to the center along the dotted line. Crease this well and then unfold it.

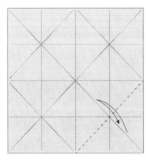

17) Fold the bottom right corner to the center along the dotted line. Crease this well and then unfold it.

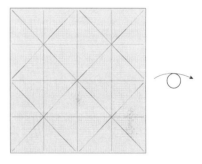

18) Turn the paper over.

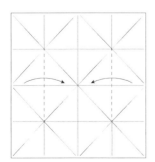

19) Fold both sides towards the center along the dotted lines. These are already existing creases. Only fold along the part with the dotted line.

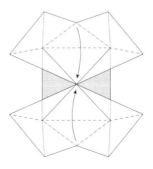

20) This should result in something that looks like what you see here. Fold the top and bottom along the dotted lines towards the center.

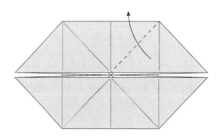

21) Fold the top right flap of paper up along the dotted line.

Pinwheel

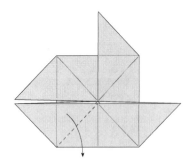 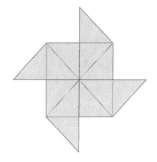

22) Fold the bottom left flap of paper down along the dotted line.

The completed Pinwheel.

Angelfish

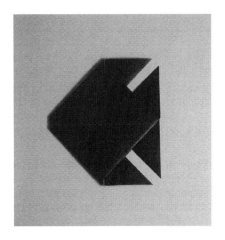

This Angelfish is folded from the same beginning sequence as the traditional origami Pinwheel on page 112.

Techniques Used: Mountain and Valley Folds

Before You Start: Begin with a square sheet of paper with the white side facing up.

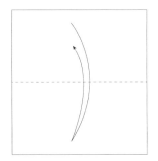

1) Fold the paper in half horizontally. Crease this well and then unfold it.

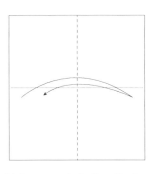

2) Fold the paper in half vertically. Crease it well and then unfold it.

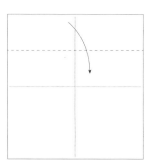

3) Fold the top of the paper down towards the center along the dotted line.

4) Crease this well and then unfold it.

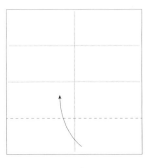

5) Fold the bottom of the paper up towards the center along the dotted line.

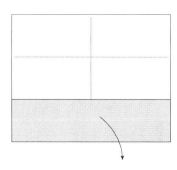

6) Crease this well and then unfold it.

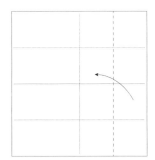

7) Fold the right side of the paper towards the center along the dotted line.

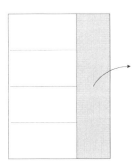

8) Crease this well and then unfold it.

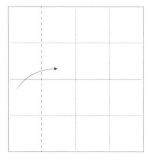

9) Fold the left side of the paper towards the center along the dotted line.

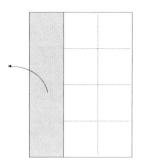

10) Crease this well and then unfold it.

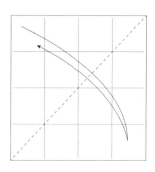

11) Fold the paper in half diagonally. Crease it well and then unfold it.

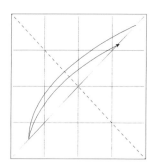

12) Fold the paper in half diagonally the other way. Crease it well and then unfold it.

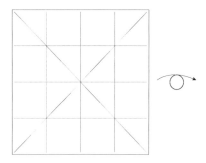

13) Turn the paper over.

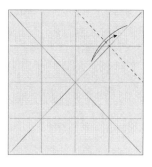

14) Fold the top right corner to the center along the dotted line. Crease this well and then unfold it.

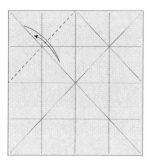

15) Fold the top left corner to the center along the dotted line. Crease this well and then unfold it.

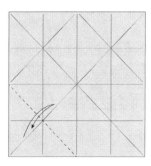

16) Fold the bottom left corner to the center along the dotted line. Crease this well and then unfold it.

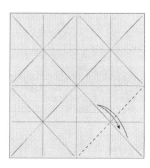

17) Fold the bottom right corner to the center along the dotted line. Crease this well and then unfold it.

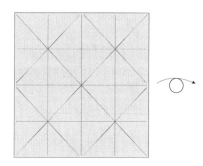

18) Turn the paper over.

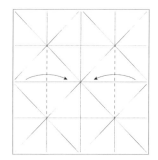

19) Fold both sides towards the center along the dotted lines. These are already existing creases. Only fold along the part with the dotted line.

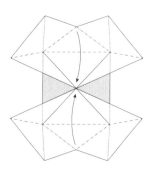

20) This should result in something that looks like what you see here. Fold the top and bottom along the dotted lines towards the center.

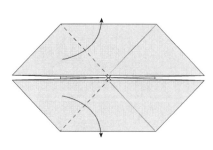

21) Fold the two left flaps out along the dotted lines.

Angelfish

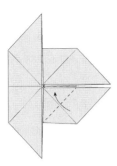
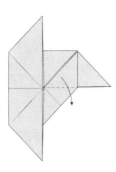
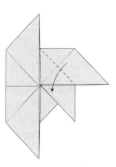

22) Fold the bottom right flap up along the dotted line.

23) Fold this flap down along the dotted line.

24) Fold the top right flap down along the dotted line.

25) Fold this flap up along the dotted line.

26) Fold the top left flap down along the dotted line.

27) Fold the bottom left flap up along the dotted line.

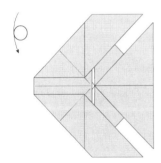
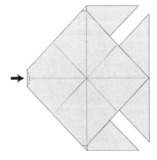
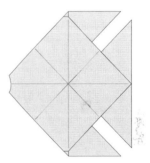

28) Press everything as flat as possible and turn the model over.

29) Push in a little bit at the front of the model to form the mouth.

The completed Angelfish.

Crab

This crab is also folded using the same beginning sequence as the traditional Pinwheel. It's technically missing some legs but still looks very crab-like.

Techniques Used: Mountain and Valley Folds

Before You Start: Begin with a square sheet of paper with the white side facing up.

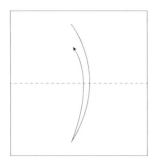

1) Fold the paper in half horizontally. Crease this well and then unfold it.

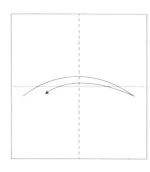

2) Fold the paper in half vertically. Crease it well and then unfold it.

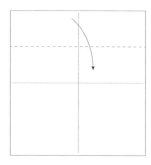

3) Fold the top of the paper down towards the center along the dotted line.

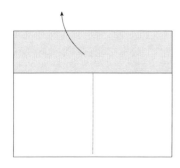

4) Crease this well and then unfold it.

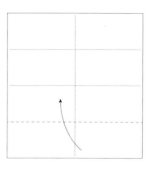

5) Fold the bottom of the paper up towards the center along the dotted line.

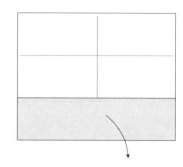

6) Crease this well and then unfold it.

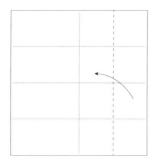

7) Fold the right side of the paper towards the center along the dotted line.

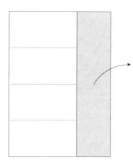

8) Crease this well and then unfold it.

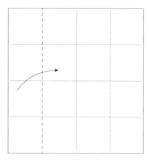

9) Fold the left side of the paper towards the center along the dotted line.

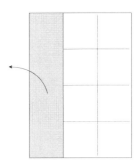

10) Crease this well and then unfold it.

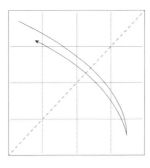

11) Fold the paper in half diagonally. Crease it well and then unfold it.

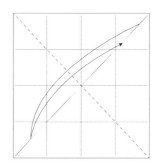

12) Fold the paper in half diagonally the other way. Crease it well and then unfold it.

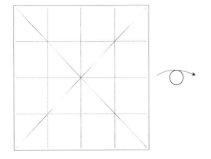

13) Turn the paper over.

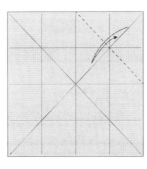

14) Fold the top right corner to the center along the dotted line. Crease this well and then unfold it.

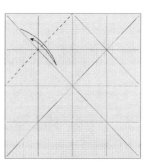

15) Fold the top left corner to the center along the dotted line. Crease this well and then unfold it.

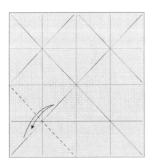

16) Fold the bottom left corner to the center along the dotted line. Crease this well and then unfold it.

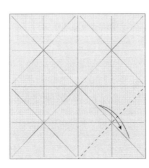

17) Fold the bottom right corner to the center along the dotted line. Crease this well and then unfold it.

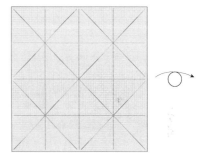

18) Turn the paper over.

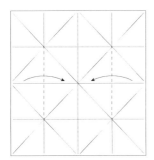

19) Fold both sides towards the center along the dotted lines. These are already existing creases. Only fold along the part with the dotted line.

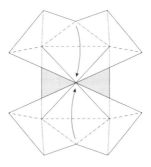

20) This should result in something that looks like what you see here. Fold the top and bottom along the dotted lines towards the center.

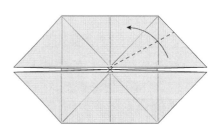

21) Fold the top right flap of paper up along the dotted line.

Crab

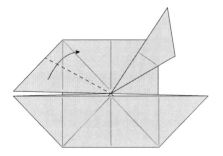

22) Fold the top left flap of paper up along the dotted line.

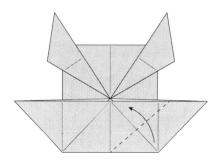

23) Fold the bottom right flap of paper up along the dotted line.

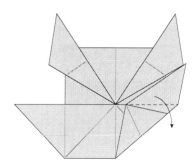

24) Fold the top part of this flap down along the dotted line.

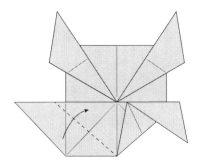

25) Fold the bottom left flap of paper up along the dotted line.

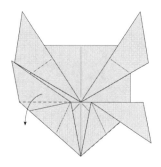

26) Fold the top part of this flap down along the dotted line.

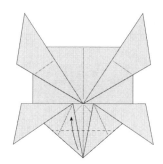

27) Fold the bottom of the paper up along the dotted line.

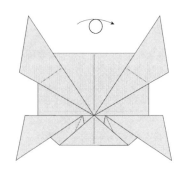

28) Turn the paper over.

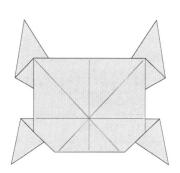

The completed Crab.

Bird

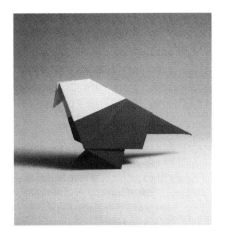

This is one of the most famous traditional origami birds.

Techniques Used: Mountain and Valley Folds, Kite Base, Inside Reverse Fold, Pleat and Swivel Fold.

Before You Start: Begin with a square sheet of paper rotated 45 degrees with the white side facing up.

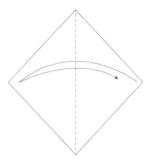

1) Fold the paper in half vertically and then unfold it.

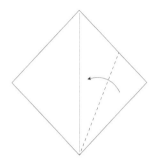

2) Fold the right side of the paper towards the center along the dotted line.

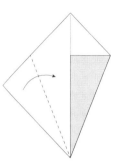

3) Fold the left side of the paper towards the center along the dotted line.

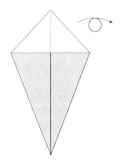

4) Turn the paper over.

5) Fold the top triangle of paper down along the dotted line.

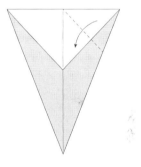

6) Fold the top right corner of paper towards the center along the dotted line.

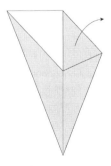

7) Crease this well and then unfold it.

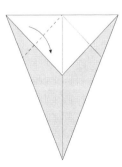

8) Fold the top left corner of paper towards the center along the dotted line.

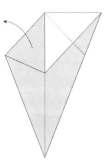

9) Crease this well and then unfold it.

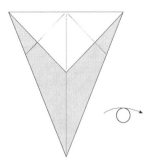

10) Turn the paper over.

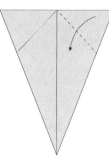

11) Fold the top right corner of paper towards the center along the dotted line. This is the opposite direction of the fold from step 6.

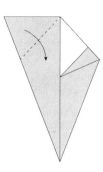

12) Fold the top left corner of paper towards the center along the dotted line. This is the opposite direction of the fold from step 8.

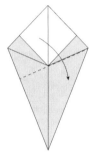

13) Fold everything down and to the right along the dotted line.

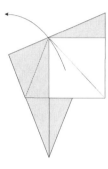

14) Crease this well and then unfold it.

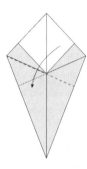

15) Fold everything down and to the left along the dotted line.

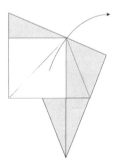

16) Crease this well and then unfold it.

17) Unfold the two corners at the top.

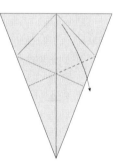

18) Open the right flap by folding the top layer of paper down along the dotted line.

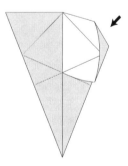

19) Swivel Fold the paper flat along the existing creases.

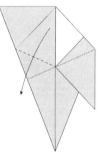

20) Open the left flap by folding the top layer of paper down along the dotted line.

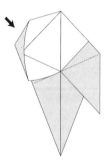

21) Swivel Fold the paper flat along the existing creases.

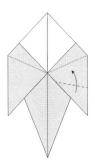
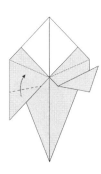
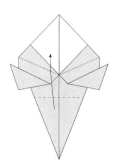

22) Fold the triangle of paper on the right up along the dotted line.

23) Fold the triangle of paper on the left up along the dotted line.

24) Fold the bottom part of the paper up along the dotted line.

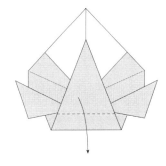
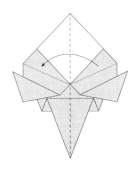

25) Fold the bottom part of the paper down along the dotted line.

26) Fold the model in half vertically along the dotted line.

27 Rotate the paper to the left approximately 90 degrees.

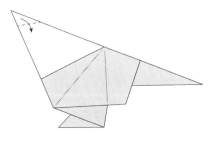
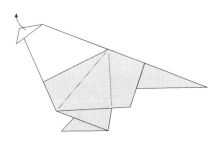
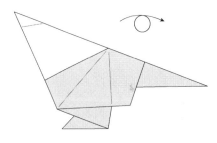

28) Fold the top left corner of paper down along the dotted line.

29) Crease this well and then unfold it.

30) Turn the paper over.

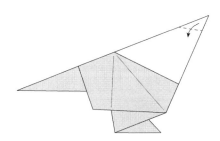
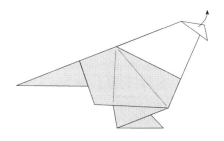
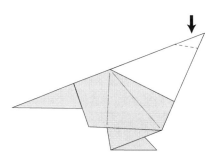

31) Fold the top right corner of paper down along the dotted line. This is the opposite direction of the fold on the other side.

32) Crease this well and then unfold it.

33) Make an Inside Reverse Fold using the existing creases.

Bird

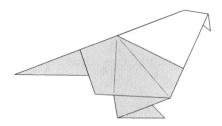

The completed Bird.

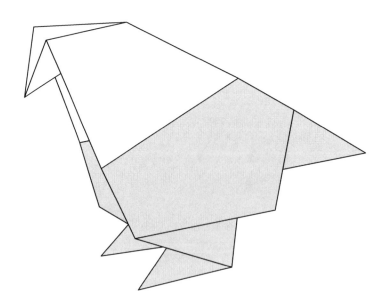

Pig

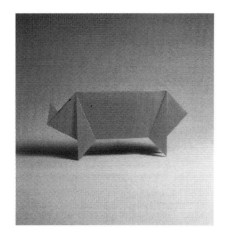

This is an excellent model for practicing Swivel Folds.

Techniques Used: Mountain and Valley Folds, Inside Reverse Fold and Swivel Fold.

Before You Start: Begin with a square sheet of paper with the colored side facing up.

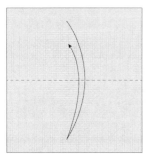

1) Fold the paper in half horizontally and then unfold it.

2) Turn the paper over.

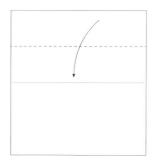

3) Fold the top part of the paper down to the center.

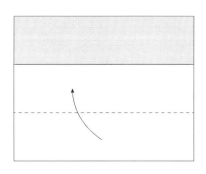

4) Fold the bottom part of the paper up to the center.

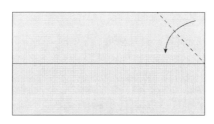

5) Fold the top right corner down along the dotted line.

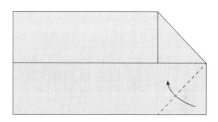

6) Fold the bottom right corner up along the dotted line.

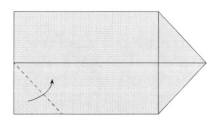

7) Fold the bottom left corner up along the dotted line.

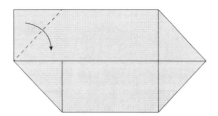

8) Fold the top left corner down along the dotted line.

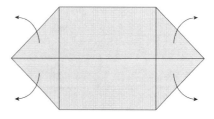

9) Unfold all four corners.

Pig

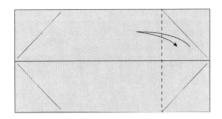

10) Fold the right side of the paper towards the center along the dotted line. Crease it well and then unfold it.

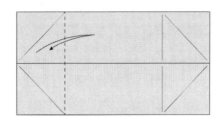

11) Fold the left side of the paper towards the center along the dotted line. Crease it well and then unfold it

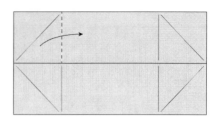

12) Fold the top layer of paper towards the center along the dotted line opening the paper up.

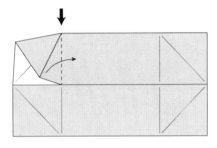

13) As the paper opens up make a Swivel Fold along the existing creases.

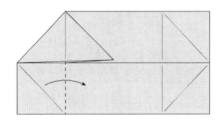

14) Fold the top layer of paper towards the center along the dotted line opening the paper up.

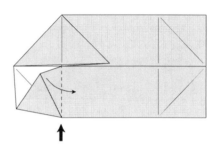

15) As the paper opens up make a Swivel Fold along the existing creases.

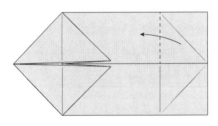

16) Fold the top layer of paper towards the center along the dotted line opening the paper up.

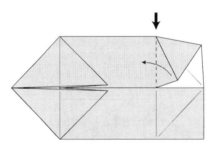

17) As the paper opens up make a Swivel Fold along the existing creases.

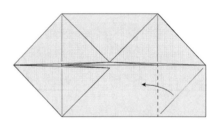

18) Fold the top layer of paper towards the center along the dotted line opening the paper up.

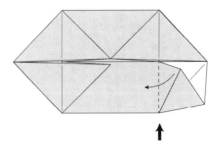

19) As the paper opens up make a Swivel Fold along the existing creases.

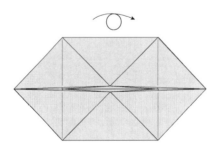

20) Turn the paper over.

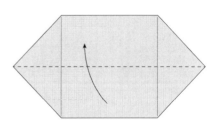

21) Fold the paper in half horizontally along the dotted line.

22) Fold the flap of paper on the left down along the dotted line.

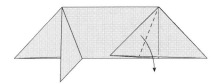

23) Fold the flap of paper on the right down along the dotted line.

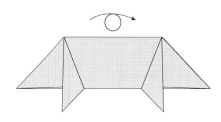

24) Turn the paper over.

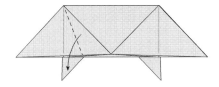

25) Fold the flap of paper on the left down along the dotted line.

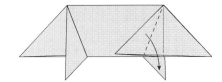

26) Fold the flap of paper on the right down along the dotted line.

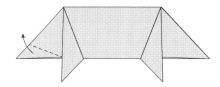

27 Fold the paper up along the dotted line.

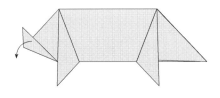

28) Crease this well and then unfold it.

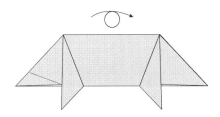

29) Turn the paper over.

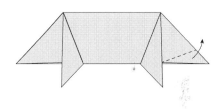

30) Fold the paper up along the dotted line. This is the opposite direction of the previous fold on the other side.

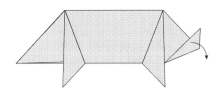

31) Crease this well and then unfold it.

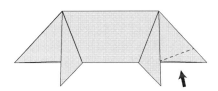

32) Make an Inside Reverse Fold along the existing creases.

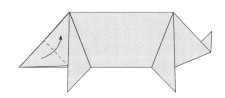

33) Fold the paper up along the dotted line.

Pig

Page 127

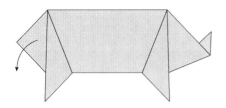

34) Crease this well and then unfold it.

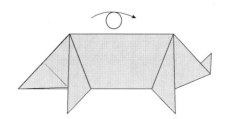

35) Turn the paper over.

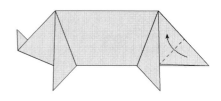

36) Fold the paper up along the dotted line. This is the opposite direction of the fold on the other side.

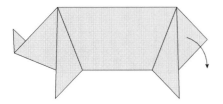

37) Crease this well and then unfold it.

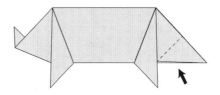

38) Make an Inside Reverse Fold along the existing creases.

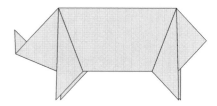

The completed Pig.

Lantern

This model begins with a Blintz Base. If you're already familiar with this base you can skip ahead to step 7.

Techniques Used: Mountain and Valley Folds, Blintz Base and Swivel Fold.

Before You Start: Begin with a square sheet of paper rotated 45 degrees with the white side facing up.

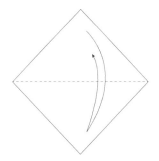

1) Fold the paper in half horizontally along the dotted line. Crease it well and then unfold it.

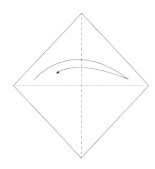

2) Fold the paper in half vertically along the dotted line. Crease it well and then unfold it.

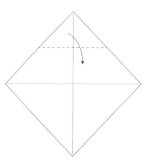

3) Fold the top of the paper down towards the center along the dotted line.

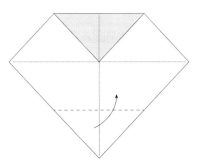

4) Fold the bottom of the paper up towards the center along the dotted line.

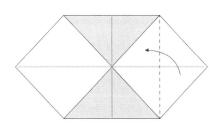

5) Fold the right side of the paper towards the center along the dotted line.

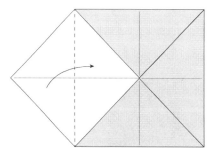

6) Fold the left side of the paper towards the center along the dotted line.

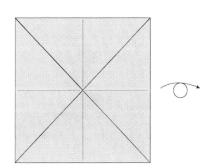

7) Turn the paper over.

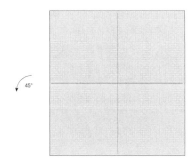

8) Rotate the paper 45 degrees.

9) Fold the top part of the paper down towards the center along the dotted line.

Lantern

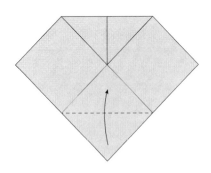

10) Fold the bottom part of the paper up towards the center along the dotted line.

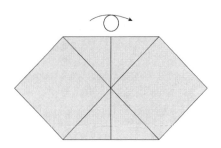

11) Turn the paper over.

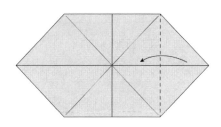

12) Fold the right side of the paper towards the center along the dotted line.

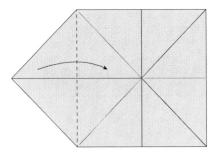

13) Fold the left side of the paper towards the center along the dotted line.

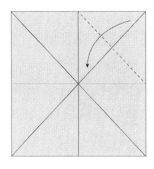

14) Fold the top right corner to the center along the dotted line.

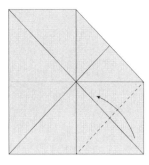

15) Fold the bottom right corner to the center along the dotted line.

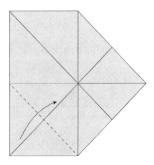

16) Fold the bottom left corner to the center along the dotted line.

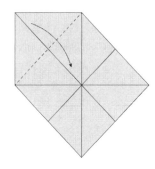

17) Fold the top left corner to the center along the dotted line.

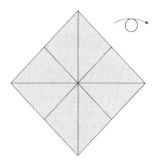

18) Turn the paper over.

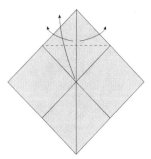

19) Open up the two flaps of paper at the top while also lifting up along the dotted line.

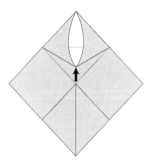

20) As you open this up make a Swivel Fold and push everything flat.

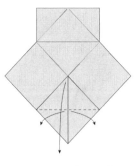

21) Open up the two flaps of paper at the bottom while also lifting down along the dotted line.

Lantern

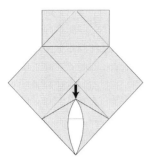 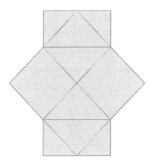

22) As you open this up make a Swivel Fold and push everything flat.

The completed Lantern.

Yakko-San

Yakko were servants who worked for samurai back in Feudal Japan. They wore a typical uniform with square sleeves.

Techniques Used: Mountain and Valley Folds, Blintz Base and Swivel Fold.

Before You Start: Begin with a square sheet of paper rotated 45 degrees with the white side facing up.

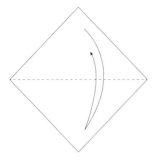

1) Fold the paper in half horizontally along the dotted line and then unfold.

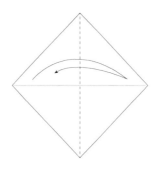

2) Fold the paper in half vertically along the dotted line and then unfold it.

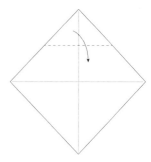

3) Fold the top corner of the paper down towards the center.

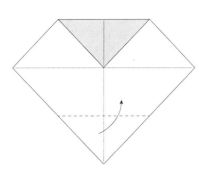

4) Fold the bottom corner of the paper up towards the center.

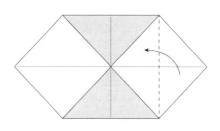

5) Fold the right corner of the paper towards the center.

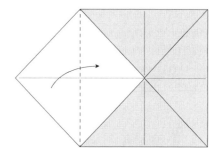

6) Fold the left corner of the paper towards the center.

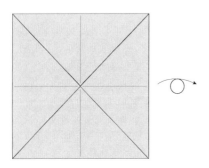

7) Turn the paper over.

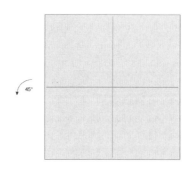

8) Rotate the paper 45 degrees.

9) Fold the top corner of the paper down towards the center.

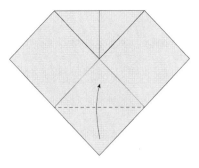

10) Fold the bottom corner of the paper up towards the center.

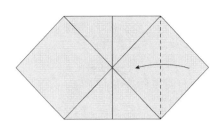

11) Fold the right corner of the paper towards the center.

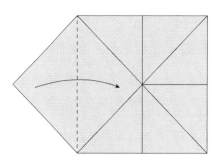

12) Fold the left corner of the paper towards the center.

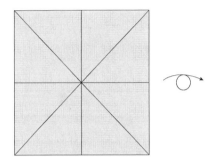

13) Turn the paper over.

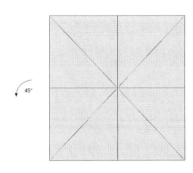

14) Rotate the paper 45 degrees.

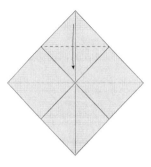

15) Fold the top corner of the paper down towards the center.

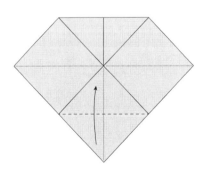

16) Fold the bottom corner of the paper up towards the center.

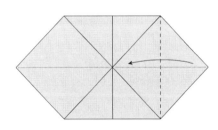

17) Fold the right corner of the paper towards the center.

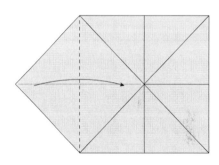

18) Fold the left corner of the paper towards the center.

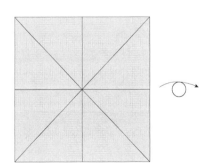

19) Turn the paper over.

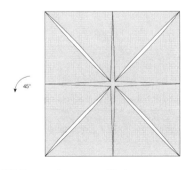

20) Rotate the paper 45 degrees.

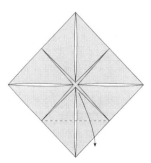

21) Open up the paper on the bottom and make a Swivel Fold along the dotted line and existing creases.

Yakko-San

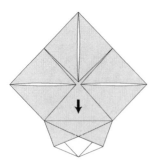

22) Push the Swivel Fold flat.

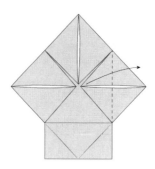

23) Open up the paper on the right and make a Swivel Fold along the dotted line and existing creases.

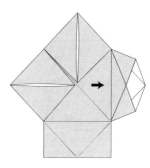

24) Push the Swivel Fold flat.

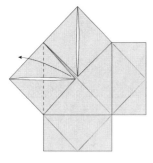

25) Open up the paper on the left and make a Swivel Fold along the dotted line and existing creases.

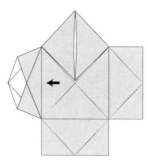

26) Push the Swivel Fold flat.

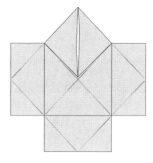

The completed Yakko-San

Chair

The folding sequence for this origami chair is very similar to the lantern and Yakko-San.

Techniques Used: Mountain and Valley Folds, Blintz Base and Swivel Fold.

Before You Start: Begin with a square sheet of paper rotated 45 degrees with the white side facing up.

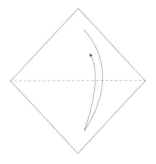

1) Fold the paper in half horizontally along the dotted line and then unfold.

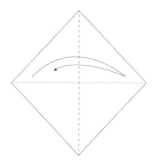

2) Fold the paper in half vertically along the dotted line and then unfold it.

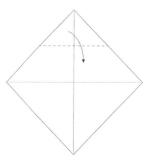

3) Fold the top corner of the paper down towards the center.

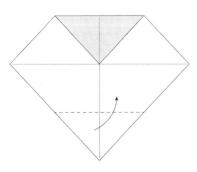

4) Fold the bottom corner of the paper up towards the center.

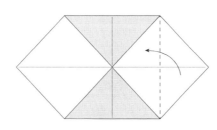

5) Fold the right corner of the paper towards the center.

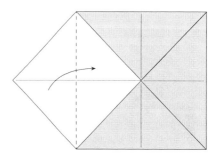

6) Fold the left corner of the paper towards the center.

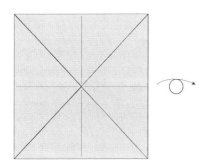

7) Turn the paper over.

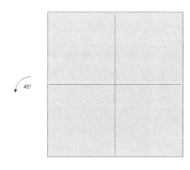

8) Rotate the paper 45 degrees.

9) Fold the top corner of the paper down towards the center.

Chair

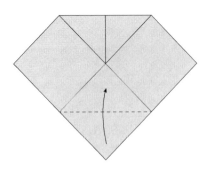

10) Fold the bottom corner of the paper up towards the center.

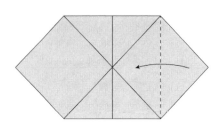

11) Fold the right corner of the paper towards the center.

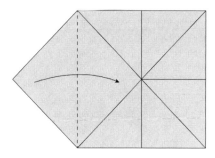

12) Fold the left corner of the paper towards the center.

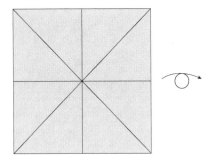

13) Turn the paper over.

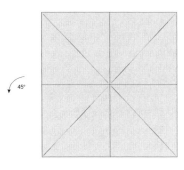

14) Rotate the paper 45 degrees.

15) Fold the top corner of the paper down towards the center.

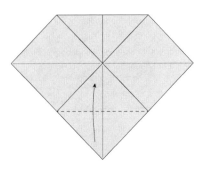

16) Fold the bottom corner of the paper up towards the center.

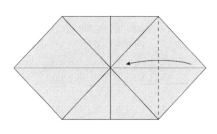

17) Fold the right corner of the paper towards the center.

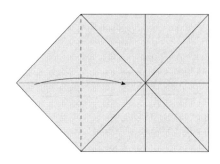

18) Fold the left corner of the paper towards the center.

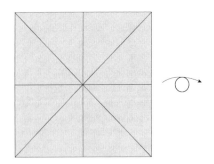

19) Turn the paper over.

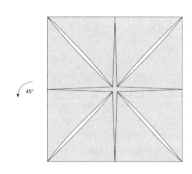

20) Rotate the paper 45 degrees.

21) Open up the paper on the bottom and make a Swivel Fold along the dotted line and existing creases.

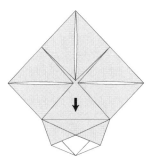

22) Push the Swivel Fold flat.

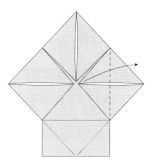

23) Open up the paper on the right and make a Swivel Fold along the dotted line and existing creases.

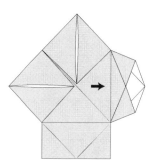

24) Push the Swivel Fold flat.

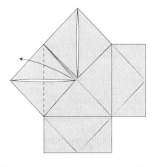

25) Open up the paper on the left and make a Swivel Fold along the dotted line and existing creases.

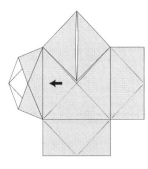

26) Push the Swivel Fold flat.

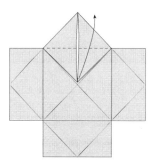

27) Open up the paper on the top and make a Swivel Fold along the dotted line and existing creases.

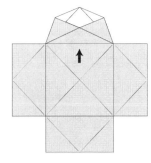

28) Push the Swivel Fold flat.

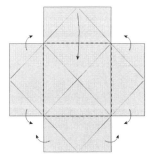

29) The flap on the top will be the back of the chair. Fold it up towards the middle of the model. The remaining 3 flaps will be the legs of the chair, fold them underneath the model.

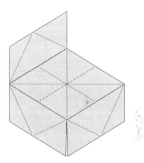

The completed chair.

Beetle

This is an excellent origami insect that looks more complex than it actually is.

Techniques Used: Mountain and Valley Folds, Inside Reverse Fold and Squash Fold.

Before You Start: Begin with a square sheet of paper with the white side facing up.

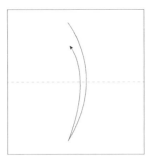

1) Fold the paper in half horizontally and then unfold it.

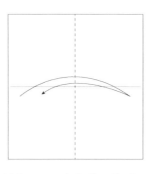

2) Fold the paper in half vertically and then unfold it.

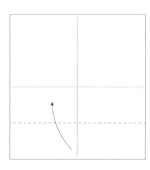

3) Fold the bottom quarter of the paper up along the dotted line towards the center.

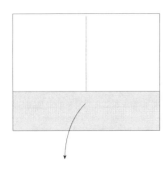

4) Crease this well and then unfold it.

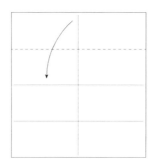

5) Fold the top quarter of the paper down along the dotted line towards the center.

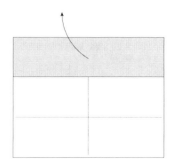

6) Crease this well and then unfold it.

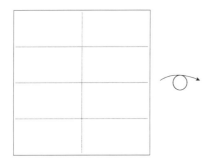

7) Turn the paper over.

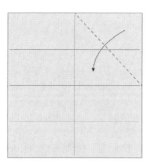

8) Fold the top right corner of paper towards the center along the dotted line.

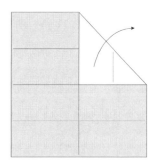

9) Crease this well and then unfold it.

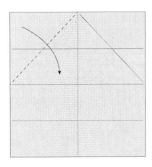

10) Fold the top left corner of paper towards the center along the dotted line.

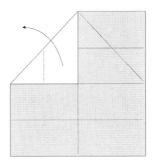

11) Crease this well and then unfold it.

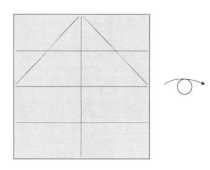

12) Turn the paper over.

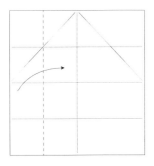

13) Fold the left quarter of the paper towards the center along the dotted line.

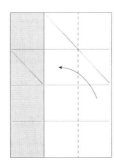

14) Fold the right quarter of the paper towards the center along the dotted line.

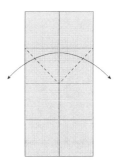

15) Open up the paper along the dotted lines. These are already existing creases.

16) As you open the paper up Squash Fold it down along the dotted line.

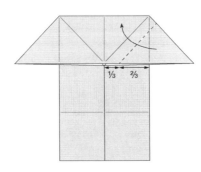

17) Fold the flap on the right up along the dotted line. The bottom of this crease should start about one third of the way from the center of the model to the edge.

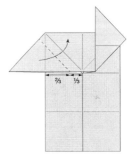

18) Fold the flap on the left up along the dotted line. The bottom of this crease should start about one third of the way from the center of the model to the edge.

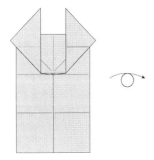

19) Turn the paper over.

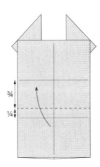

20) Fold the bottom of the paper up along the dotted line. This fold should be about one quarter of the way up between the two creases in the middle.

21) Turn the paper over.

Beetle

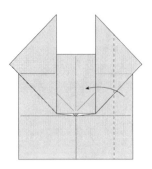

22) Fold all of the layers of paper on the right along the dotted line towards the center.

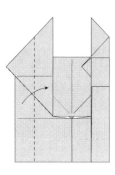

23) Fold all of the layers of paper on the left along the dotted line towards the center.

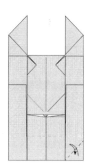

24) Fold the bottom right corner up along the dotted line. Crease it well and unfold it.

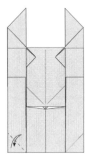

25) Fold the bottom left corner up along the dotted line. Crease it well and unfold it.

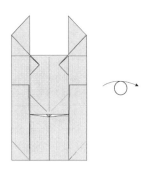

26) Turn the paper over.

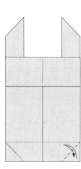

27) Fold the bottom right corner up along the dotted line. This is the opposite direction of the fold from step 24. Crease it well and unfold it.

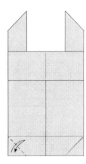

28) Fold the bottom left corner up along the dotted line. The is the opposite direction of the fold from step 25. Crease it well and unfold it.

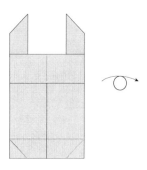

29) Turn the paper over.

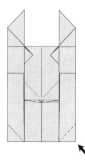

30) Make an Inside Reverse Fold on the bottom right corner using the existing creases.

31) Make an Inside Reverse Fold on the bottom left corner using the existing creases.

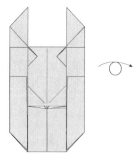

32) Turn the paper over.

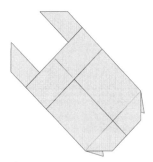

The completed Beetle.

Sitting Dog

This model requires you to reshape a couple of folds by pulling the paper out a little bit. The best way to figure out how to do this is with practice.

Techniques Used: Mountain and Valley Folds, Kite Base, Outside Reverse Fold and Pleat.

Before You Start: Begin with a square sheet of paper rotated 45 degrees with the white side facing up.

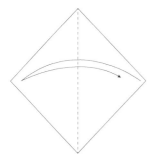

1) Fold the paper in half vertically and then unfold it.

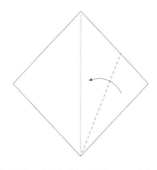

2) Fold the right side of the model towards the center along the dotted line.

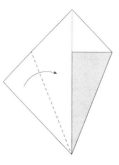

3) Fold the left side of the model towards the center along the dotted line.

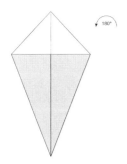

4) Rotate the paper 180 degrees.

5) Turn the paper over.

6) Fold the top of the paper down along the dotted line.

7) Fold the top flap of paper up along the dotted line.

8) Turn the paper over.

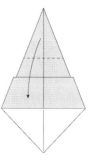

9) Fold the top of the paper down along the dotted line.

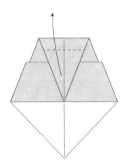

10) Fold the top of the paper up along the dotted line.

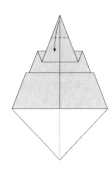

11) Fold the top of the paper down along the dotted line.

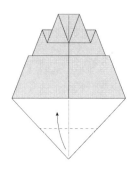

12) Fold the bottom of the paper up along the dotted line.

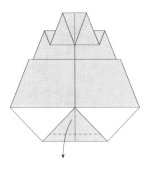

13) Fold the bottom of the paper down along the dotted line.

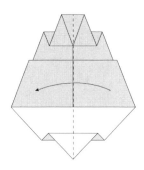

14) Fold the paper in half vertically.

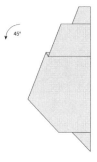

15) Rotate the paper 45 degrees to the left.

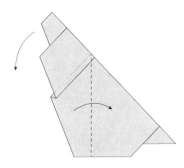

16) Make an Outside Reverse Fold along the vertical dotted line bringing the paper on both sides to the right. As you make this fold the head will rotate down.

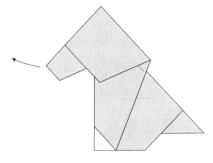

17) Pull a little bit of paper out and up to shape the nose.

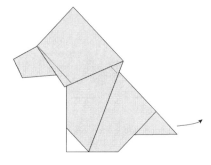

18) Pull a little bit of paper out and up to shape the tail.

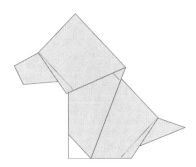

19) Flatten all of the folds on the nose and tail.

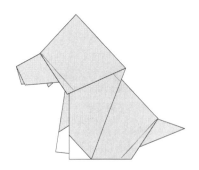

The completed Sitting Dog.

Sitting Elephant

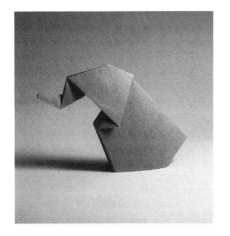

This model uses a very similar folding sequence to the Sitting Dog on page 141.

Techniques Used: Mountain and Valley Folds, Kite Base, Inside Reverse Fold and Outside Reverse Fold.

Before You Start: Begin with a square sheet of paper rotated 45 degrees with the white side facing up.

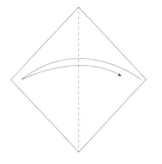

1) Fold the paper in half vertically and then unfold it.

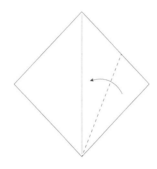

2) Fold the right side of the model towards the center along the dotted line.

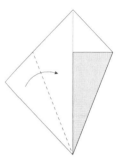

3) Fold the left side of the model towards the center along the dotted line.

4) Rotate the paper 180 degrees.

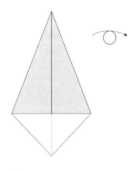

5) Turn the paper over.

6) Fold the top of the paper down along the dotted line.

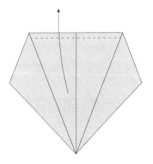

7) Fold the top flap of paper up along the dotted line.

8) Turn the paper over.

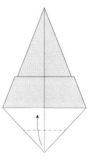

9) Fold the bottom of the paper up along the dotted line.

Sitting Elephant

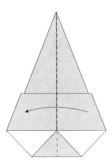

10) Fold the paper in half vertically along the dotted line.

11) Pull the flaps of paper on the inside down along the thicker dotted line essentially making an Outside Reverse Fold inside the model.

12) Fold the paper down along the dotted line.

13) Crease this well and then unfold it.

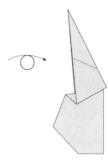

14) Turn the paper over.

15) Fold the paper down along the dotted line.

16) Crease this well and then unfold it.

17) Make an Inside Reverse Fold along the existing creases.

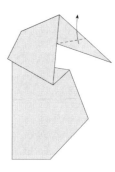

18) Fold the paper up along the dotted line.

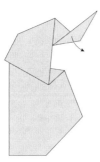

19) Crease this well and then unfold it.

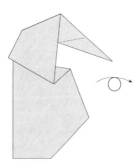

20) Turn the paper over.

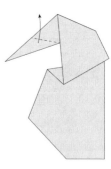

21) Fold the paper up along the dotted line. This is the opposite direction of the fold on the other side.

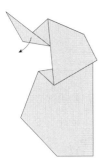

22) Crease this well and then unfold it.

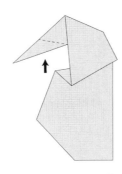

23) Make an Inside Reverse Fold along the existing creases.

24) Make a tiny Inside Reverse Fold at the very tip of the trunk.

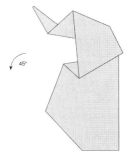

25) Rotate the model 45 degrees down and to the left.

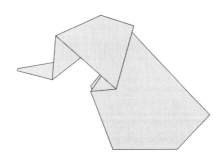

The completed Sitting Elephant.

Talking Crow

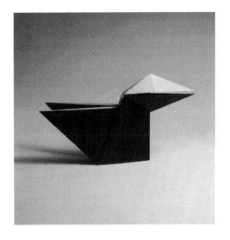

This is a really great action origami model. By pulling on the two wings you can make the crow's mouth open and close.

Techniques Used: Mountain and Valley Folds and Rabbit Ear Fold.

Before You Start: Begin with a square sheet of paper rotated 45 degrees with the white side facing up.

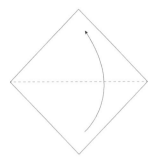

1) Fold the paper in half horizontally.

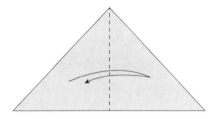

2) Fold the paper in half vertically. Crease it well and then unfold it.

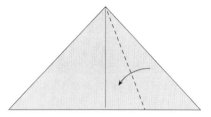

3) Fold the right side of the paper towards the center along the dotted line.

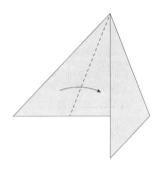

4) Fold the left side of the paper towards the center along the dotted line.

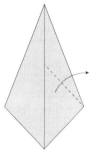

5) Fold the right side of the paper up along the dotted line.

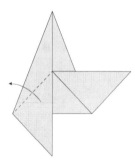

6) Fold the left side of the paper up along the dotted line.

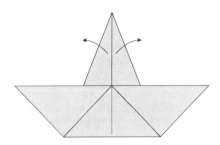

7) Open up the paper.

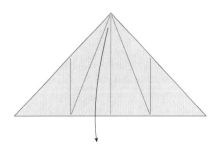

8) Pull the top layer of the paper down.

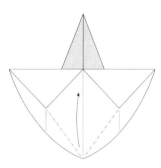

9) Re-fold the top section using the existing creases. Re-fold the bottom section using the existing creases and bring it up and in front.

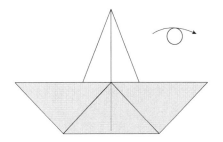

10) Turn the paper over.

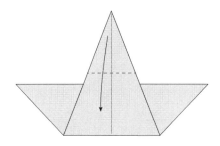

11) Fold the top layer of paper down along the dotted line.

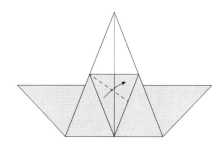

12) Fold the bottom triangle of paper along the dotted line.

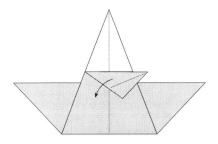

13) Crease this well and then unfold it.

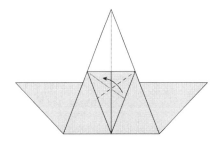

14) Fold the bottom triangle of paper along the dotted line.

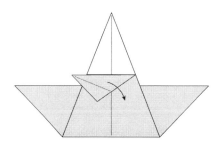

15) Crease this well and then unfold it.

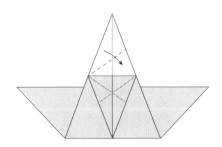

16) Fold the top triangle of paper along the dotted line.

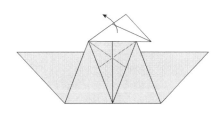

17) Crease this well and then unfold it.

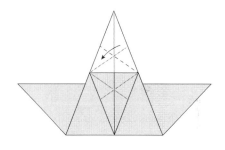

18) Fold the top triangle of paper along the dotted line.

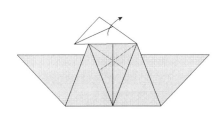

19) Crease this well and then unfold it.

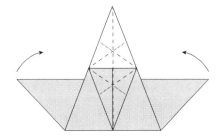

20) Fold the model in half bringing the left and right corners to the back. Two Rabbit Ear Folds should take place along the existing creases.

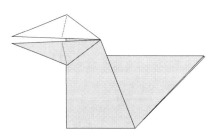

21) Flatten all the creases.

Talking Crow

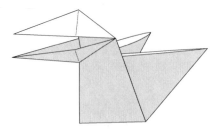

The completed Talking Crow.

Carp

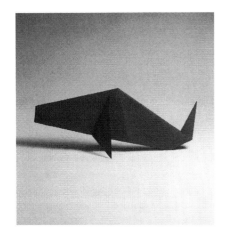

This model begins with a Fish Base. If you're already familiar with this base you can skip ahead to step 14.

Techniques Used: Mountain and Valley Folds, Inside Reverse Fold, Rabbit Ear Fold and Fish Base.

Before You Start: Begin with a square of paper rotated 45 degrees with the white side facing up.

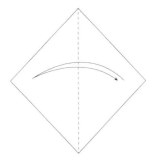

1) Fold the paper in half vertically. Crease this well and then unfold it.

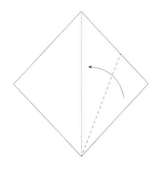

2) Fold the bottom right side of the paper to the center along the dotted line.

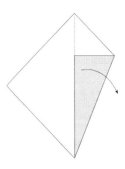

3) Crease this well and then unfold it.

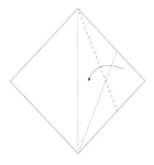

4) Fold the top right side of the paper to the center along the dotted line.

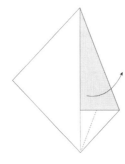

5) Crease this well and then unfold it.

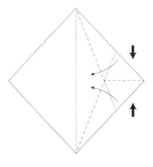

6) Using the two creases you just created make a Rabbit Ear Fold.

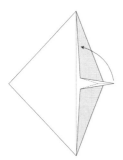

7) Fold the triangle flap of paper towards the top.

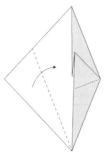

8) Fold the bottom left side of the paper to the center along the dotted line.

9) Crease this well and then unfold it.

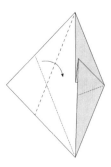

10) Fold the top left side of the paper to the center along the dotted line.

11) Crease this well and then unfold it.

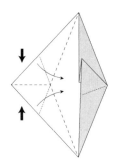

12) Using the two creases you just created make a Rabbit Ear Fold.

13) Fold the triangle flap of paper towards the top.

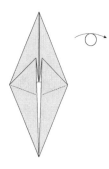

14) Turn the paper over.

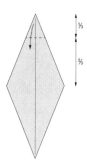

15) Fold the top of the paper down along the dotted line. This should be about one third of the way from the top to the center of the paper.

16) Fold the paper in half vertically along the dotted line.

17) Fold the top flap of paper down along the dotted line.

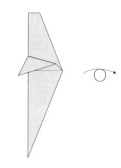

18) Turn the paper over.

19) Fold the top flap of paper down along the dotted line.

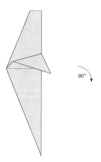

20) Rotate the paper 90 degrees to the right.

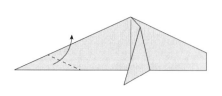

21) Fold the left side of the paper up along the dotted line.

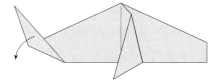

22) Crease this well and then unfold it.

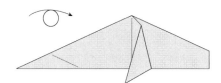

23) Turn the paper over.

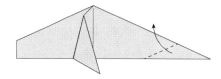

24) Fold the right side of the paper up along the dotted line. This is the opposite direction of the previous crease.

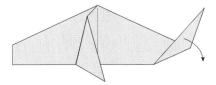

25) Crease this well and then unfold it.

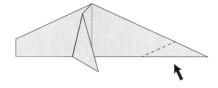

26) Make an Inside Reverse Fold along the existing creases.

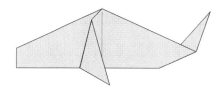

The completed Carp.

Whale

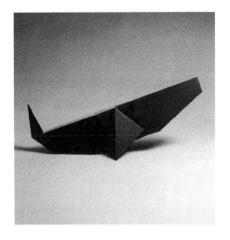

This model begins with a Fish Base. If you're already familiar with this base you can skip ahead to step 14.

Techniques Used: Mountain and Valley Folds, Outside Reverse Fold, Rabbit Ear Fold and Fish Base.

Before You Start: Begin with a square sheet of paper rotated 45 degrees with the white side facing up.

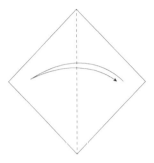

1) Fold the paper in half and then unfold it.

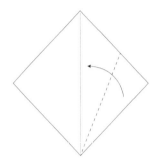

2) Fold the bottom right side of the paper towards the center along the dotted line.

3) Crease this well and then unfold it.

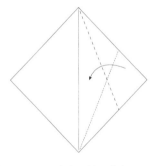

4) Fold the top right side of the paper towards the center along the dotted line.

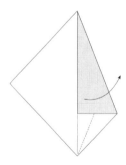

5) Crease this well and then unfold it.

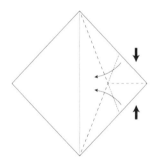

6) Using the existing creases on the right side make a Rabbit Ear Fold.

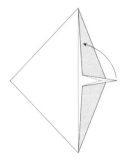

7) Fold the triangle flap of paper up towards the top.

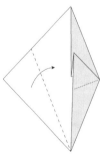

8) Fold the bottom left side of the paper towards the center along the dotted line.

9) Crease this well and then unfold it.

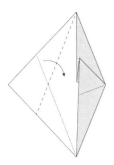

10) Fold the top left side of the paper towards the center along the dotted line.

11) Crease this well and then unfold it.

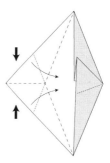

12) Using the existing creases on the left side make a Rabbit Ear Fold.

13) Fold the triangle flap of paper up towards the top.

14) Flatten everything well.

15) Fold the top of the paper down along the dotted line.

16) Crease this well and then unfold it.

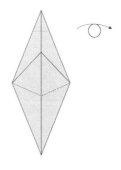

17) Turn the paper over.

18) Fold the top of the paper down along the dotted line. This is the opposite side of the crease you made in step 16.

19) Fold the left side of the paper towards the center along the dotted line.

20) Fold the right side of the paper towards the center along the dotted line.

21) Fold the paper in half vertically along the dotted line.

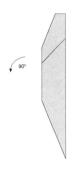  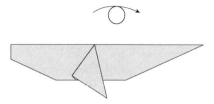

22) Rotate the model 90 degrees to the left.

23) Fold the top flap of paper down and to the right along the dotted line.

24) Turn the paper over.

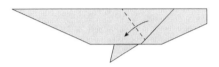 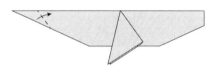 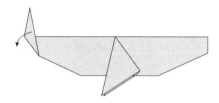

25) Fold the top flap of paper down and to the left along the dotted line.

26) Fold the back of the model up along the dotted line.

27) Crease this well and then unfold it.

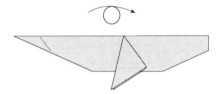 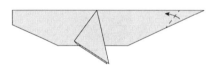 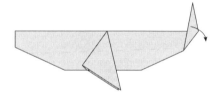

28) Turn the paper over.

29) Fold the back of the model up along the dotted line. This is the opposite direction of the previous crease.

30) Crease this well and then unfold it.

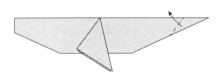 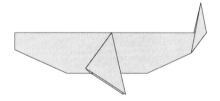

31) Make an Outside Reverse Fold along the existing crease.

32) The completed Whale.

Page **154**   **Whale**

Seal

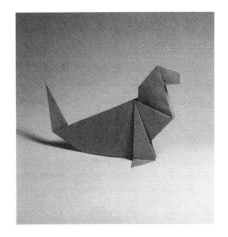

This model also begins with a Fish Base even though it's technically not a fish.

Techniques Used: Mountain and Valley Folds, Inside Reverse Fold, Rabbit Ear Fold and Fish Base.

Before You Start: Begin with a square of paper rotated 45 degrees with the white side facing up.

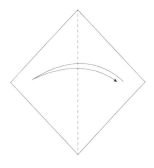

1) Fold the paper in half vertically. Crease this well and then unfold it.

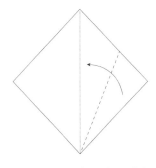

2) Fold the bottom right side of the paper to the center along the dotted line.

3) Crease this well and then unfold it.

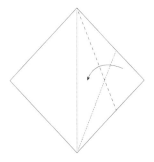

4) Fold the top right side of the paper to the center along the dotted line.

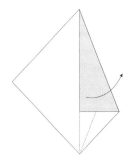

5) Crease this well and then unfold it.

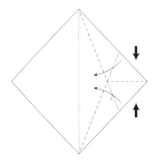

6) Using the two creases you just created make a Rabbit Ear Fold.

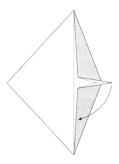

7) Fold the triangle flap of paper towards the bottom.

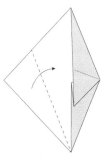

8) Fold the bottom left side of the paper to the center along the dotted line.

9) Crease this well and then unfold it.

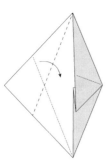

10) Fold the top left side of the paper to the center along the dotted line.

11) Crease this well and then unfold it.

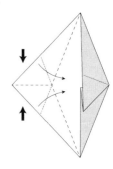

12) Using the two creases you just created make a Rabbit Ear Fold.

13) Fold the triangle flap of paper towards the bottom.

14) Rotate the paper 90 degrees to the right.

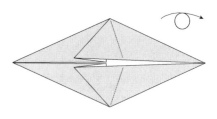

15) Turn the paper over.

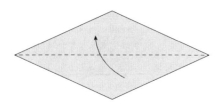

16) Fold the paper in half horizontally along the dotted line.

17) Fold the left part of the paper up along the dotted line.

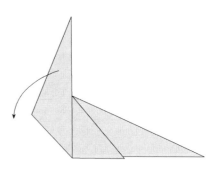

18) Crease this well and then unfold it.

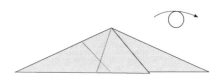

19) Turn the paper over.

20) Fold the right part of the paper up along the dotted line. This is the opposite direction of the previous fold on the other side.

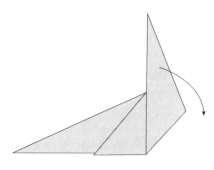

21) Crease this well and then unfold it.

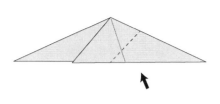

22) Make an Inside Reverse Fold using the existing creases.

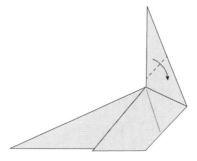

23) Fold the top part of the paper down along the dotted line.

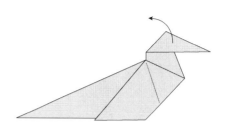

24) Crease this well and then unfold it.

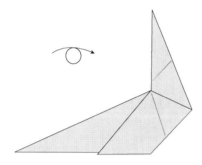

25) Turn the paper over.

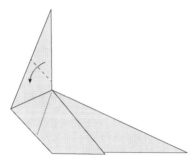

26) Fold the top part of the paper down along the dotted line. This is the opposite direction of the previous fold on the other side.

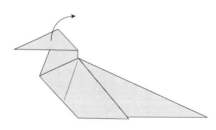

27) Crease this well and then unfold it.

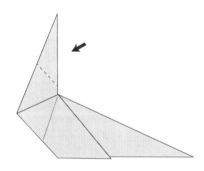

28) Make an Inside Reverse Fold along the existing creases.

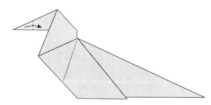

29) Fold the tip of the paper to the right along the dotted line.

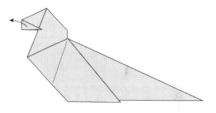

30) Crease this well and then unfold it.

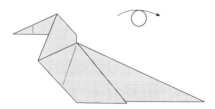

31) Turn the paper over.

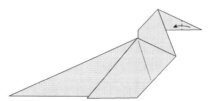

32) Fold the tip of the paper to the left along the dotted line. This is the opposite direction of the previous fold on the other side.

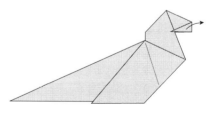

33) Crease this well and then unfold it.

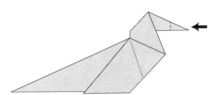

34) Make an Inside Reverse Fold along the existing creases.

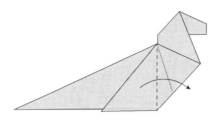

35) Fold the flap of paper to the right along the dotted line.

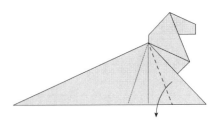

36) Fold the flap of paper down along the dotted line.

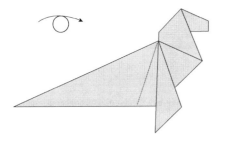

37) Turn the paper over.

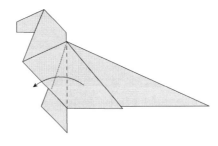

38) Fold the flap of paper to the left along the dotted line.

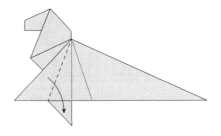

39) Fold the flap of paper down along the dotted line.

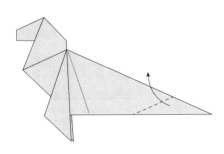

40) Fold the right section of paper up along the dotted line.

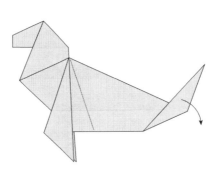

41) Crease this well and then unfold it.

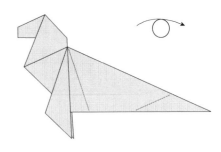

42) Turn the paper over.

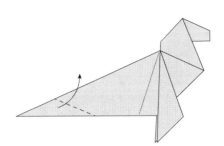

43) Fold the left section of paper up along the dotted line. This is the opposite direction of the previous fold on the other side.

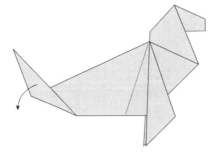

44) Crease this well and then unfold it.

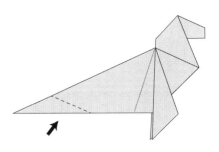

45) Make an Inside Reverse Fold along the existing creases.

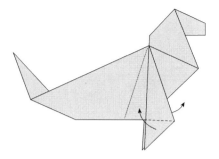 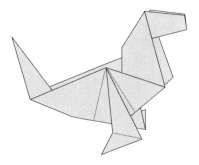

46) Fold the bottom part of the flippers up on each side.

The completed Seal.

Rabbit

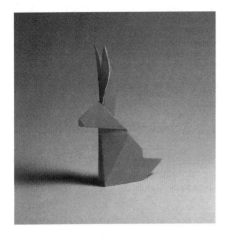

This model has a tricky double Outside Reverse Fold. Try to use the next diagram in the sequence as a guide for making this fold.

Techniques Used: Mountain and Valley Folds, Inside Reverse Fold, Outside Reverse Fold, Crimp and Squash Fold.

Before You Start: Begin with a square sheet of paper rotated 45 degrees with the white side facing up.

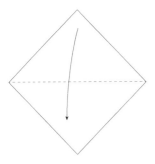

1) Fold the paper in half horizontally along the dotted line.

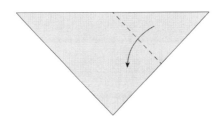

2) Fold the right side of the paper towards the center along the dotted line bringing the corner on the right to the corner on the bottom.

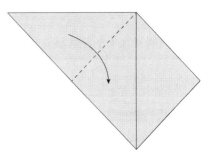

3) Fold the left side of the paper towards the center along the dotted line bringing the corner on the left to the corner on the bottom.

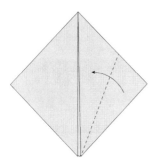

4) Fold the right side of the paper towards the center along the dotted line.

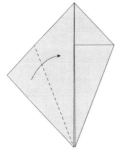

5) Fold the left side of the paper towards the center along the dotted line.

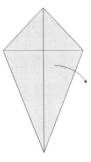

6) Pull out the right flap of paper a little bit.

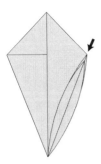

7) Squash Fold this flap of paper making sure both sides are symmetrical.

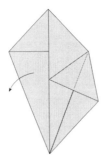

8) Pull out the left flap of paper a little bit.

9) Squash Fold this flap of paper making sure both sides are symmetrical.

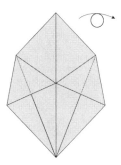

10) Turn the paper over.

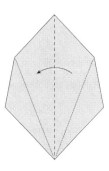

11) Fold the paper in half vertically along the dotted line.

12) Rotate the model to the left 45 degrees.

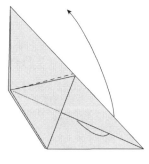

13) Fold the long flap at the top of the model up and inside along the dotted line.

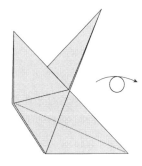

14) Turn the paper over.

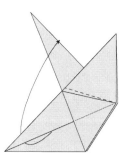

15) Fold the long flap at the top of the model up and inside along the dotted line.

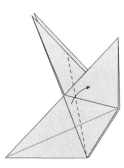

16) Fold the top layers of paper towards the right along the dotted line.

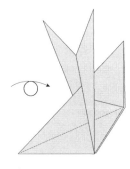

17) Turn the paper over.

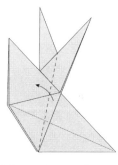

18) Fold the top layers of paper towards the left along the dotted line.

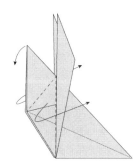

19) Make an Outside Reverse Fold on both sides along the vertical dotted line. As you do, make an Outside Reverse Fold along the diagonal dotted line.

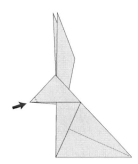

20) Make a small Inside Reverse Fold along the dotted line.

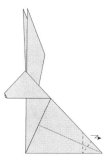

21) Make a Crimp to form the rabbit's tail by making two Inside Reverse Folds, first along the vertical dotted line then on the diagonal dotted line.

Rabbit

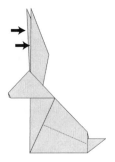

22) Open up both the ears making them round.

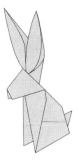

The completed rabbit

Intermediate

Mandarin Duck

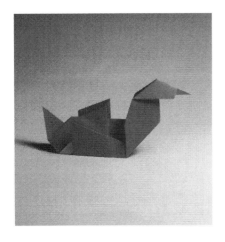

This model requires a Crimp fold on the underside of the head. The diagrams will change perspective for these steps.

Techniques Used: Mountain and Valley Folds, Kite Base, Inside Reverse Fold, Outside Reverse Fold, Pleat and Crimp.

Before You Start: Begin with a square sheet of paper rotated 45 degrees with the white side facing up.

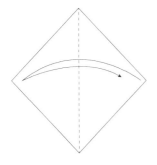

1) Fold the paper in half vertically and then unfold it.

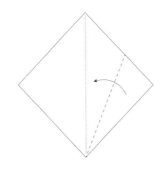

2) Fold the right side of the paper towards the center along the dotted line.

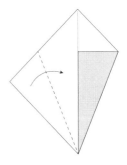

3) Fold the left side of the paper towards the center along the dotted line.

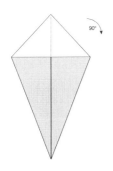

4) Rotate the paper 90 degrees to the right.

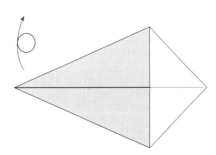

5) Turn the paper over.

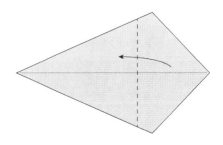

6) Fold the right side of the paper over to the left along the dotted line.

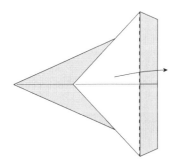

7) Fold the white triangle of paper over to the right along the dotted line.

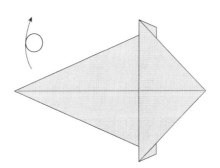

8) Turn the paper over.

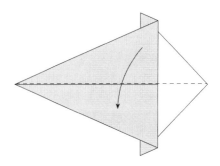

9) Fold the paper in half horizontally along the dotted line.

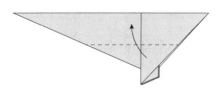

10) Fold the top flap of paper up along the dotted line.

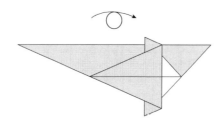

11) Turn the paper over.

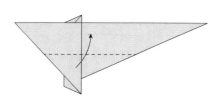

12) Fold the paper up along the dotted line.

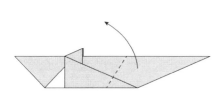

13) Fold the right section of paper up along the dotted line.

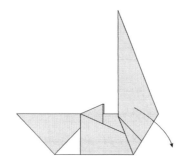

14) Crease this well and then unfold it.

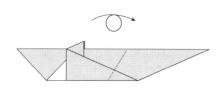

15) Turn the paper over.

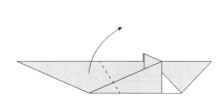

16) Fold the left section of paper up along the dotted line. This is the opposite direction of the previous crease on the other side.

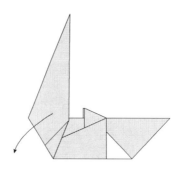

17) Crease this well and then unfold it.

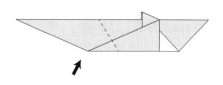

18) Make an Outside Reverse Fold along the existing creases.

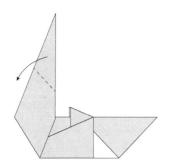

19) Fold the top section of paper down along the dotted line.

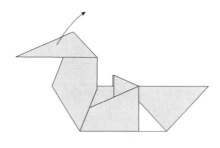

20) Crease this well and then unfold it.

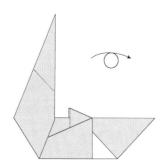

21) Turn the paper over.

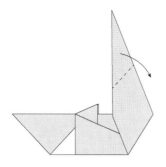

22) Fold the top section of paper down along the dotted line. This is the opposite direction of the previous crease on the other side.

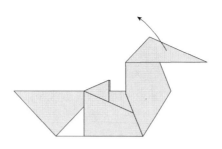

23) Crease this well and then unfold it.

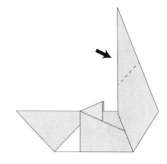

24) Make an Outside Reverse Fold along the existing creases.

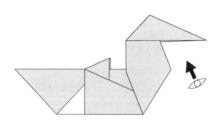

25) The next steps take place underneath this flap of paper. Open the paper up a little bit and look underneath where the arrow indicates.

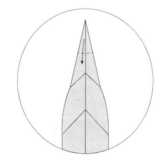

26) Fold the tip of the paper down along the dotted line.

27) Fold the tip of the paper back up along the dotted line.

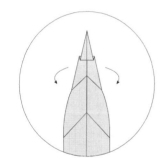

28) Close this flap of paper back up.

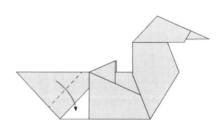

29) Fold the left side of the paper down along the dotted line.

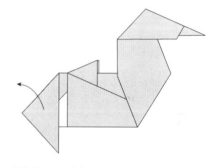

30) Crease this well and then unfold it.

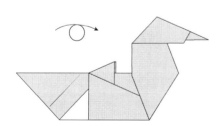

31) Turn the paper over.

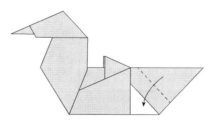

32) Fold the right side of the paper down along the dotted line. This is the opposite direction of the previous fold on the other side.

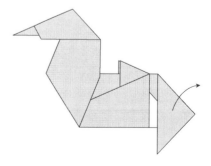

33) Crease this well and then unfold it.

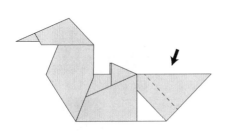

34) Make an Inside Reverse Fold along the existing creases.

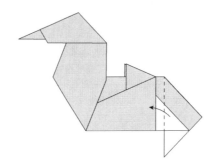

35) Open up the paper along the dotted line.

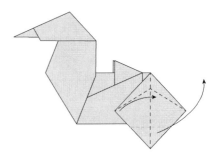

36) Lift the paper up along the dotted lines and fold it back making a Crimp.

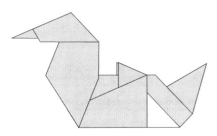

The completed Mandarin Duck.

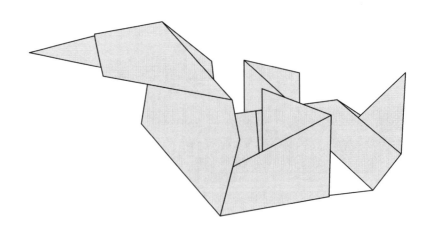

Chicken

Normally you use the colored side of the paper for the outside of the model but this chicken is the opposite.

Techniques Used: Mountain and Valley Folds, Inside Reverse Fold, Outside Reverse Fold and Swivel Fold.

Before You Start: Begin with a square sheet of paper rotated 45 degrees with the colored side facing up.

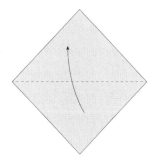

1) Fold the paper in half horizontally along the dotted line.

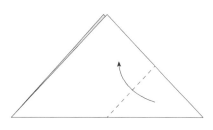

2) Fold the right side of the paper up along the dotted line.

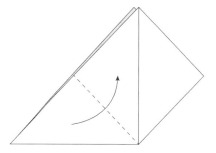

3) Fold the left side of the paper up along the dotted line.

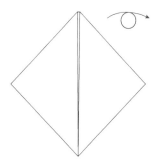

4) Turn the paper over.

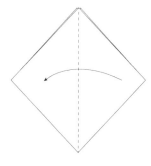

5) Fold the paper in half vertically along the dotted line.

6) Fold the top flap of paper down along the dotted line and prepare to make a Swivel Fold.

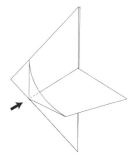

7) As you fold this flap down make a Swivel Fold and push everything flat.

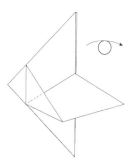

8) Turn the paper over.

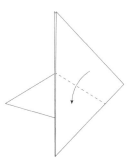

9) Fold the top flap of paper down along the dotted line and prepare to make a Swivel Fold.

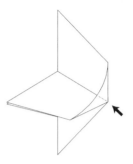

10) As you fold this flap down make a Swivel Fold and push everything flat.

11) Fold this flap of paper up along the dotted line.

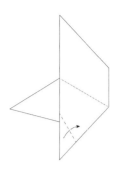

12) Fold the bottom of the paper along the dotted line.

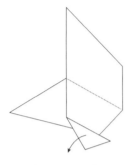

13) Crease this well and then unfold it.

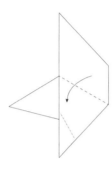

14) Fold the top flap of paper back down along the dotted line.

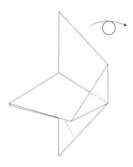

15) Turn the paper over.

16) Fold the top flap up along the dotted line.

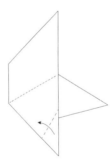

17) Fold the bottom of the paper along the dotted line. This is the opposite direction of the previous fold.

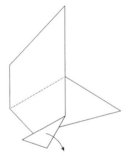

18) Crease this well and then unfold it.

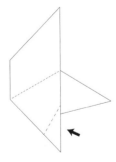

19) Make an Inside Reverse Fold using the existing creases.

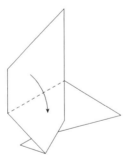

20) Fold the top flap back down along the dotted line.

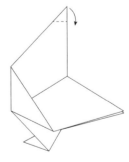

21) Fold back the top layer of paper at the top along the dotted line making an Outside Reverse Fold. Open the paper a bit to make this fold a little easier.

Chicken

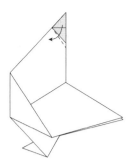 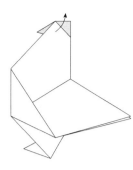 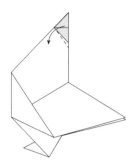

22) Fold the inside layer of paper down along the dotted line. This fold will take place inside the top layer of paper.

23) Crease this well and then unfold it.

24) Fold the inside layer of paper down along the dotted line but in the other direction. This fold will also take place inside the top layer of paper.

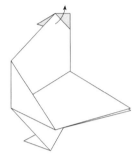 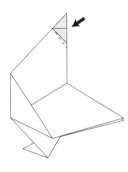 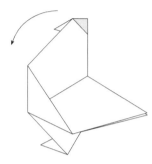

25) Crease this well and then unfold it.

26) Make an Inside Reverse Fold using the existing creases on the inside layer of paper.

27) Rotate the model a little bit so it's standing upright.

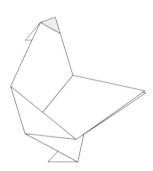

The completed Chicken.

Catamaran

This is an excellent model to practice making the Open Sink fold.

Techniques Used: Mountain and Valley Folds and Open Sink.

Before You Start: Begin with a square sheet of paper with the white side facing up.

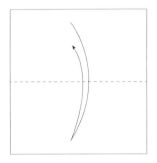

1) Fold the paper in half horizontally along the dotted line. Crease it well and then unfold it.

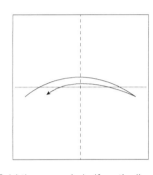

2) Fold the paper in half vertically along the dotted line. Crease it well and then unfold it.

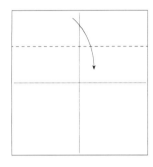

3) Fold the top quarter of the paper towards the center along the dotted line.

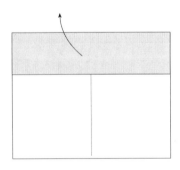

4) Crease this well and then unfold it.

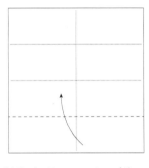

5) Fold the bottom quarter of the paper towards the center along the dotted line.

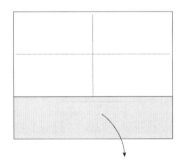

6) Crease this well and then unfold it.

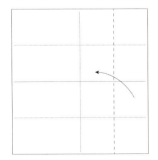

7) Fold the right quarter of the paper towards the center along the dotted line.

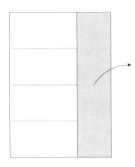

8) Crease this well and then unfold it.

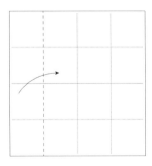

9) Fold the left quarter of the paper towards the center along the dotted line.

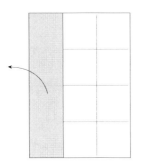

10) Crease this well and then unfold it.

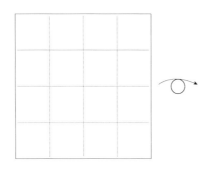

11) Turn the paper over.

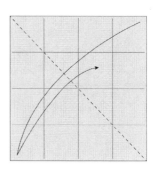

12) Fold the paper in half diagonally. Crease it well and then unfold it.

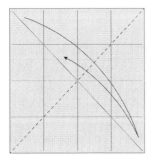

13) Fold the paper in half diagonally the other way. Crease it well and then unfold it.

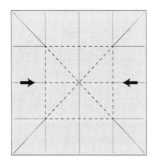

14) Make an open sink along the dotted lines in the middle. These are already existing creases.

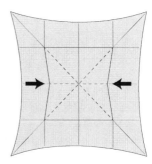

15) Push in the left and right sides while pushing the center of the paper down along the existing creases.

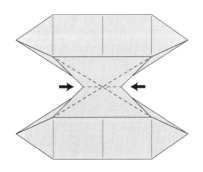

16) Continue making the Open Sink.

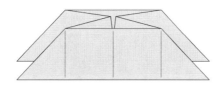

17) The completed Open Sink. Push everything completely flat.

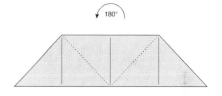

18) The thin dotted line shows the path of the paper inside the model. Rotate the paper 180 degrees.

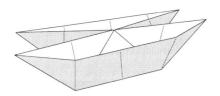

The completed Catamaran.

Catamaran

Fish

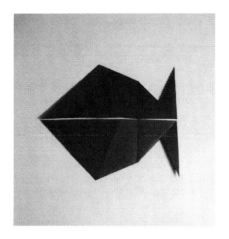

This model is kind of similar to the Talking Fish but it's a little more complicated.

Techniques Used: Mountain and Valley Folds, Rabbit Ear Fold and Fish Base.

Before You Start: Begin with a square of paper rotated 45 degrees with the white side facing up.

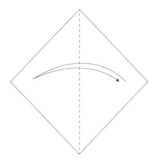

1) Fold the paper in half vertically. Crease this well and then unfold it.

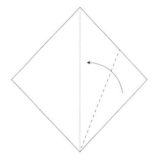

2) Fold the bottom right side of the paper to the center along the dotted line.

3) Crease this well and then unfold it.

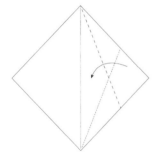

4) Fold the top right side of the paper to the center along the dotted line.

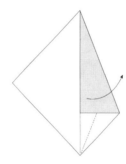

5) Crease this well and then unfold it.

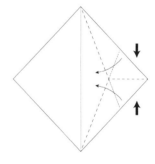

6) Using the two creases you just created make a Rabbit Ear Fold.

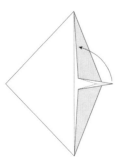

7) Fold the triangle flap of paper towards the top.

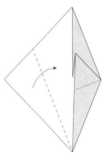

8) Fold the bottom left side of the paper to the center along the dotted line.

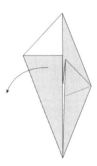

9) Crease this well and then unfold it.

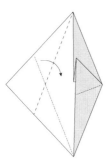

10) Fold the top left side of the paper to the center along the dotted line.

11) Crease this well and then unfold it.

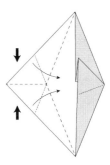

12) Using the two creases you just created make a Rabbit Ear Fold.

13) Fold the triangle flap of paper towards the top.

14) Turn the paper over.

15) Fold the top flap of paper down along the dotted line.

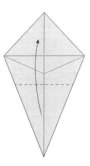

16) Fold the top flap of paper up along the dotted line.

17) Fold the top triangle of paper to the right along the dotted line.

18) Crease this well and then unfold it.

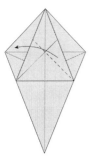

19) Fold the top triangle of paper to the left along the dotted line.

20) Crease this well and then unfold it.

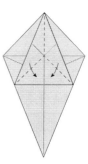

21) Make a Rabbit Ear Fold using the existing creases.

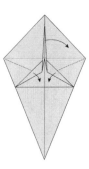

22) Finish folding the rabbit ear by folding the top flap over to the right and pushing everything flat along the existing creases.

23) Fold the top flap of paper down along the dotted line.

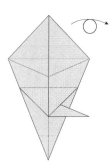

24) Turn the paper over.

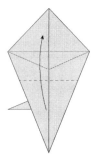

25) Fold the top flap of paper up along the dotted line.

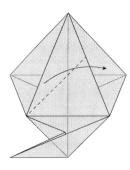

26) Fold the top triangle of paper to the right along the dotted line.

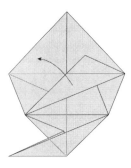

27) Crease this well and then unfold it.

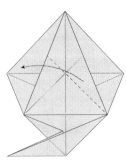

28) Fold the top triangle of paper to the left along the dotted line.

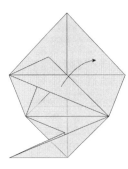

29) Crease this well and then unfold it.

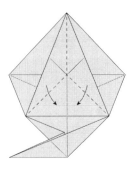

30) Make a Rabbit Ear Fold using the existing creases.

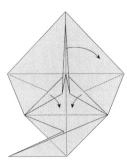

31) Finish folding the rabbit ear by folding the top flap over to the right and pushing everything flat along the existing creases.

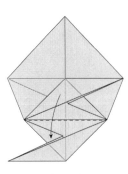

32) Fold the top flap of paper down along the dotted line.

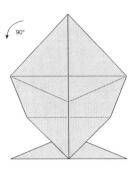

33) Rotate the paper 90 degrees to the left.

Fish

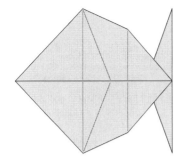

The completed Fish.

Dolphin

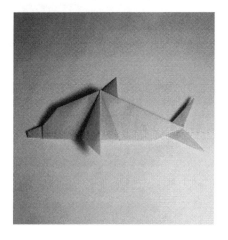

This Dolphin has a somewhat complicated series of folds on the back. Don't worry if they're not perfect, since they're on the back no one will see them.

Techniques Used: Mountain and Valley Folds, Inside Reverse Fold, Pleat, Swivel Fold, Rabbit Ear Fold, Fish Base and Scissors.

Before You Start: Begin with a square of paper rotated 45 degrees with the white side facing up.

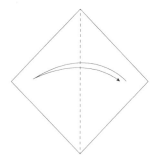

1) Fold the paper in half vertically. Crease this well and then unfold it.

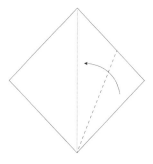

2) Fold the bottom right side of the paper to the center along the dotted line.

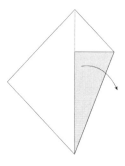

3) Crease this well and then unfold it.

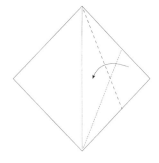

4) Fold the top right side of the paper to the center along the dotted line.

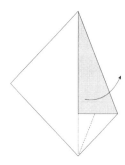

5) Crease this well and then unfold it.

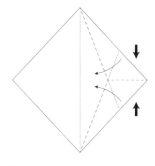

6) Using the two creases you just created make a Rabbit Ear Fold.

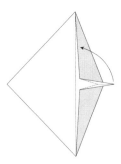

7) Fold the triangle flap of paper towards the top.

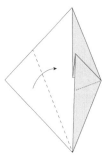

8) Fold the bottom left side of the paper to the center along the dotted line.

9) Crease this well and then unfold it.

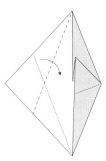

10) Fold the top left side of the paper to the center along the dotted line.

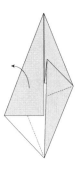

11) Crease this well and then unfold it.

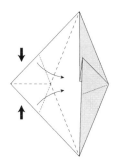

12) Using the two creases you just created make a Rabbit Ear Fold.

13) Fold the triangle flap of paper towards the top.

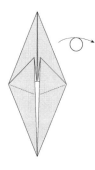

14) Turn the paper over.

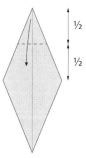

15) Fold the top part of the paper down along the dotted line. This should be exactly halfway between the center of the model and the top.

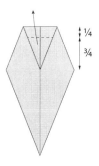

16) Fold the paper back up along the dotted line. This should be about one quarter of the distance from the top of the model to the center.

17) Fold the right corner down along the dotted line.

18) Crease this well and then unfold it.

19) Make an Inside Reverse Fold along the existing crease.

20) Fold the left corner down along the dotted line.

21) Crease this well and then unfold it.

Dolphin

22) Make an Inside Reverse Fold along the existing crease.

23) Fold the top of the paper down along the dotted line. This should be about one third of the way from the tip of the triangle to the bottom.

24) Fold the paper in half vertically along the dotted line.

25) Fold the top flap of paper down along the dotted line.

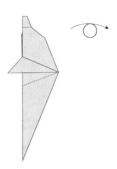

26) Turn the paper over.

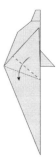

27) Fold the top layer of paper down along the dotted line.

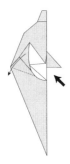

28) Continue folding the top layer of paper down, opening up the paper and making a Swivel Fold.

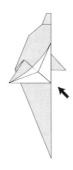

29) Push everything flat.

30) Fold the bottom part of the paper up along the dotted line.

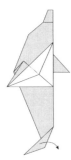

31) Crease this well and then unfold it.

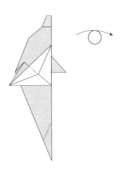

32) Turn the paper over.

33) Fold the bottom part of the paper up along the dotted line. This is the opposite direction from the previous crease.

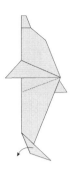

34) Crease this well and then unfold it.

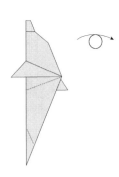

35) Turn the paper over.

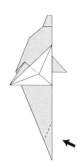

36) Make an Inside Reverse Fold using the existing creases.

37) Carefully cut along the top of the Inside Reverse Fold.

38) Unfold the top half of the Inside Reverse Fold.

39) Fold the top part of the bottom of the paper along the dotted line.

40) Fold the top layer of paper back along the dotted line.

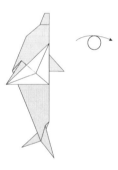

41) Turn the paper over.

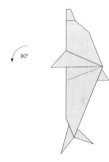

42) Rotate the model 90 degrees to the left.

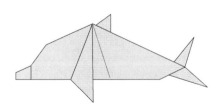

The completed Dolphin.

Dolphin

Flapping Bird

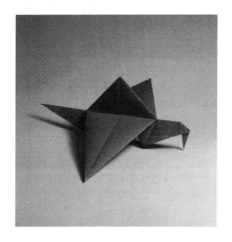

If you pull on the neck and tail of this bird you can make the wings flap.

Techniques Used: Mountain and Valley Folds, Inside Reverse Fold, Square Base, Petal Fold and Bird Base.

Before You Start: Begin with a square sheet of paper with the white side facing up.

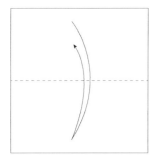

1) Fold the paper in half horizontally. Crease it well and then unfold.

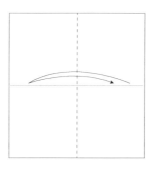

2) Fold the paper in half vertically. Crease it well and then unfold it.

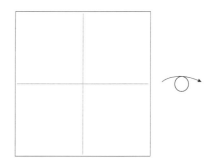

3) Turn the paper over.

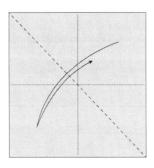

4) Fold the paper in half diagonally. Crease it well and then unfold it.

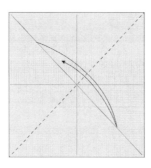

5) Fold the paper in half diagonally the other way. Crease it well and then unfold it.

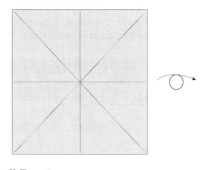

6) Turn the paper over.

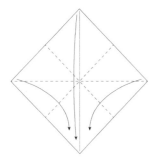

7) Fold the paper along the existing creases bringing the left, right and top corners to the bottom into a Square base.

8) Fold the flap of paper on the right to the center along the dotted line.

9) Crease this well and then unfold it.

10) Fold the flap of paper on the left to the center along the dotted line.

11) Crease this well and then unfold it.

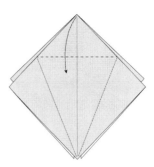

12) Fold the top of the model down along the dotted line. The ends of this dotted line will line up with the previous two creases you made.

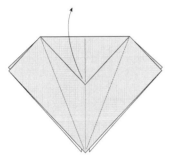

13) Crease this well and then unfold it.

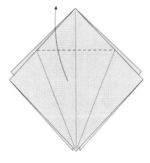

14) Lift up the top flap of paper along the horizontal crease you just made.

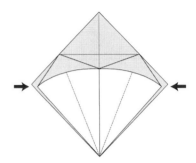

15) As you lift the paper up fold in both sides along the existing creases making a Petal Fold.

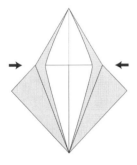

16) Push everything flat along the existing creases.

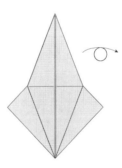

17) Turn the paper over.

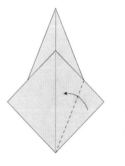

18) Fold the flap of paper on the right to the center along the dotted line.

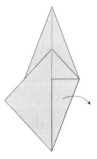

19) Crease this well and then unfold it.

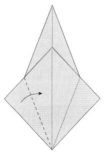

20) Fold the flap of paper on the left to the center along the dotted line.

21) Crease this well and then unfold it.

Flapping Bird

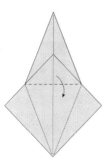

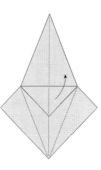

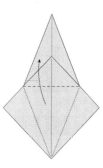

22) Fold the top of the model down along the dotted line. The ends of this dotted line will line up with the previous two creases you made.

23) Crease this well and then unfold it.

24) Lift up the top flap of paper along the horizontal crease you just made.

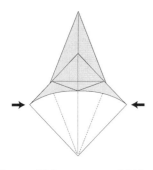

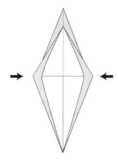

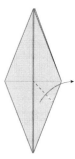

25) As you lift the paper up fold in both sides along the existing creases making a Petal Fold.

26) Push everything flat along the existing creases.

27) Fold the bottom right flap of paper up and to the right along the dotted line.

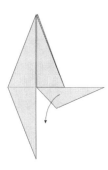

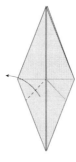

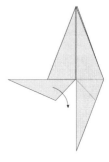

28) Crease this well and then unfold it.

29) Fold the bottom left flap of paper up and to the left along the dotted line.

30) Crease this well and then unfold it.

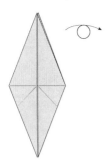

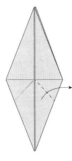

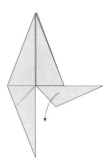

31) Turn the paper over.

32) Fold the bottom right flap of paper up and to the right along the dotted line. This is the opposite direction of the crease on the other side.

33) Crease this well and then unfold it.

Flapping Bird

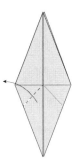

34) Fold the bottom left flap of paper up and to the left along the dotted line. This is the opposite direction of the crease on the other side.

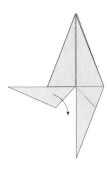

35) Crease this well and then unfold it.

36) Make an Inside Reverse Fold along the existing creases.

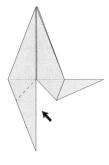

37) Make an Inside Reverse Fold along the existing creases.

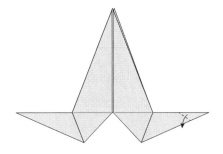

38) Fold the right section of paper down along the dotted line.

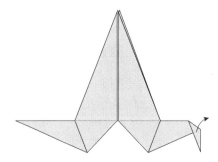

39) Crease this well and then unfold it.

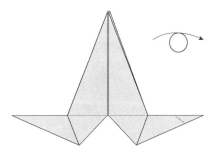

40) Turn the paper over.

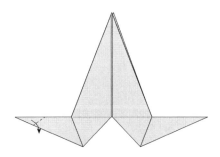

41) Fold the left section of paper down along the dotted line. This is the opposite direction of the previous fold.

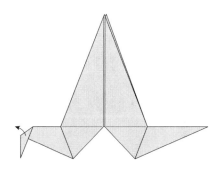

42) Crease this well and then unfold it.

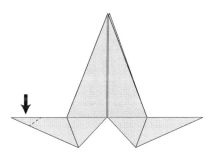

43) Make an Inside Reverse Fold along the existing creases.

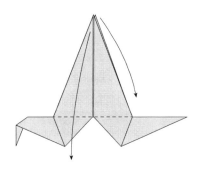

44) Fold both of the wings down.

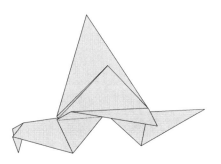

The completed Flapping Bird.

Crane

Legends say that if you fold one thousand of these you get good luck.

Techniques Used: Mountain and Valley Folds, Inside Reverse Fold, Square Base, Petal Fold and Bird Base.

Before You Start: Begin with a square sheet of paper with the white side facing up.

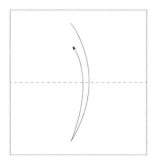

1) Fold the paper in half horizontally. Crease it well and then unfold.

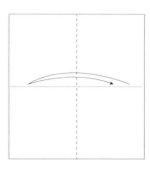

2) Fold the paper in half vertically. Crease it well and then unfold it.

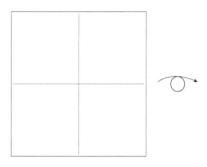

3) Turn the paper over.

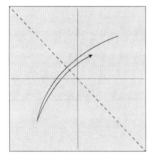

4) Fold the paper in half diagonally. Crease it well and then unfold it.

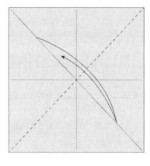

5) Fold the paper in half diagonally the other way. Crease it well and then unfold it.

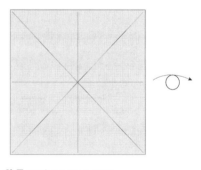

6) Turn the paper over.

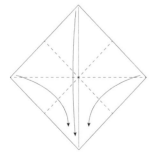

7) Fold the paper along the existing creases bringing the left, right and top corners to the bottom into a Square base.

8) Fold the flap of paper on the right to the center along the dotted line.

9) Crease this well and then unfold it.

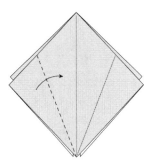

10) Fold the flap of paper on the left to the center along the dotted line.

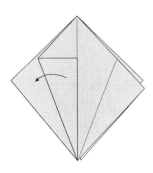

11) Crease this well and then unfold it.

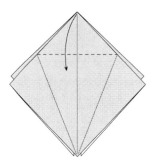

12) Fold the top of the model down along the dotted line. The ends of this dotted line will line up with the previous two creases you made.

13) Crease this well and then unfold it.

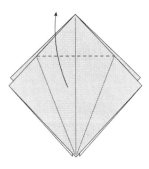

14) Lift up the top flap of paper along the horizontal crease you just made.

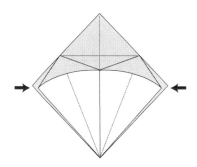

15) As you lift the paper up fold in both sides along the existing creases making a Petal Fold.

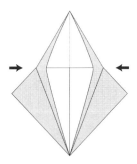

16) Push everything flat along the existing creases.

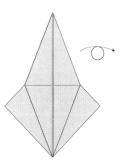

17) Turn the paper over.

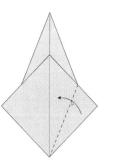

18) Fold the flap of paper on the right to the center along the dotted line.

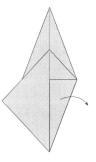

19) Crease this well and then unfold it.

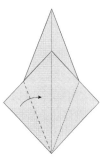

20) Fold the flap of paper on the left to the center along the dotted line.

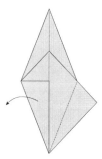

21) Crease this well and then unfold it.

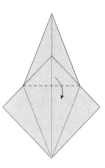
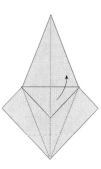
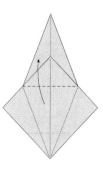

22) Fold the top of the model down along the dotted line. The ends of this dotted line will line up with the previous two creases you made.

23) Crease this well and then unfold it.

24) Lift up the top flap of paper along the horizontal crease you just made.

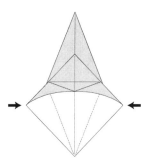
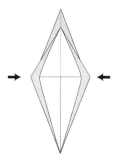
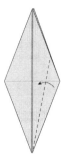

25) As you lift the paper up fold in both sides along the existing creases making a Petal Fold.

26) Push everything flat along the existing creases.

27) Fold the top layer of paper on the right towards the center along the dotted line.

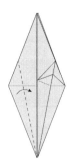
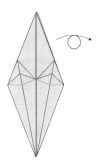

28) Fold the top layer of paper on the left towards the center along the dotted line.

29) Turn the paper over.

30) Fold the top layer of paper on the right towards the center along the dotted line.

31) Fold the top layer of paper on the left towards the center along the dotted line.

32) Fold the bottom right section of paper up along the dotted line.

33) Crease this well and then unfold it.

34) Fold the bottom left section of paper up along the dotted line.

35) Crease this well and then unfold it.

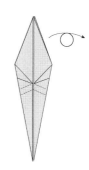

36) Turn the paper over.

37) Fold the bottom right section of paper up along the dotted line.

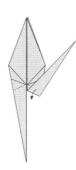

38) Crease this well and then unfold it.

39) Fold the bottom left section of paper up along the dotted line.

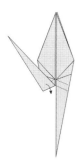

40) Crease this well and then unfold it.

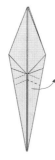

41) Make an Inside Reverse Fold along the dotted line on the right.

42) The Inside Reverse Fold in progress.

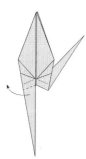

43) Make an Inside Reverse Fold along the dotted line on the left.

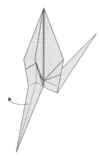

44) The Inside Reverse Fold in progress.

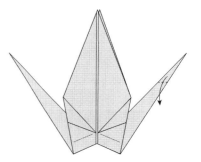

45) Fold the end of the paper on the right down along the dotted line.

Crane

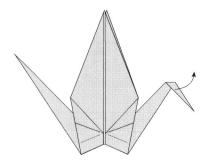

46) Crease this well and then unfold it.

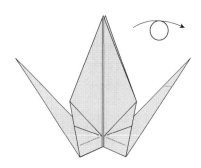

47) Turn the paper over.

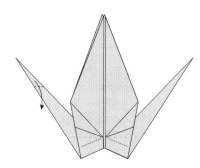

48) Fold the end of the paper on the left down along the dotted line. This is the opposite direction of the previous fold.

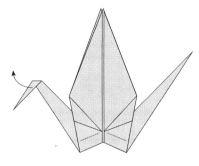

49) Crease this well and then unfold it.

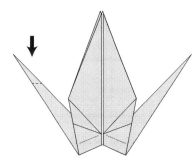

50) Make an Inside Reverse Fold along the existing crease.

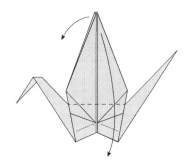

51) Fold both of the wings down.

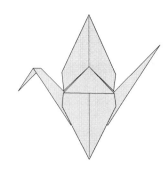

The completed Crane.

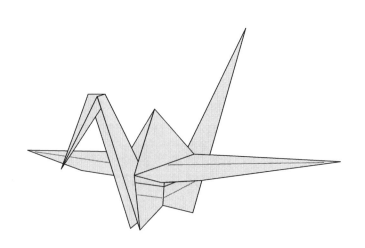

Crow

This model begins with a Bird Base. If you're already familiar with this base you can skip ahead to step 27.

Techniques Used: Mountain and Valley Folds, Inside Reverse Fold, Square Base, Petal Fold and Bird Base.

Before You Start: Begin with a square sheet of paper with the white side facing up.

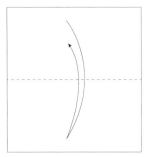

1) Fold the paper in half horizontally. Crease it well and then unfold.

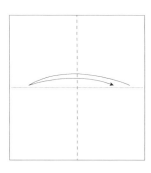

2) Fold the paper in half vertically. Crease it well and then unfold it.

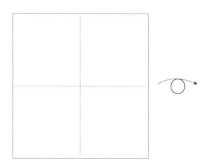

3) Turn the paper over.

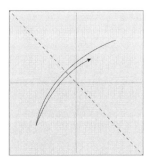

4) Fold the paper in half diagonally. Crease it well and then unfold it.

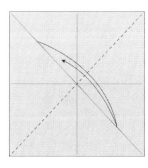

5) Fold the paper in half diagonally the other way. Crease it well and then unfold it.

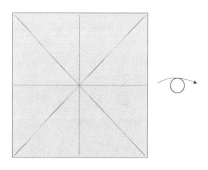

6) Turn the paper over.

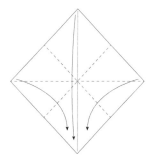

7) Fold the paper along the existing creases bringing the left, right and top corners to the bottom into a Square base.

8) Fold the flap of paper on the right to the center along the dotted line.

9) Crease this well and then unfold it.

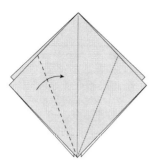

10) Fold the flap of paper on the left to the center along the dotted line.

11) Crease this well and then unfold it.

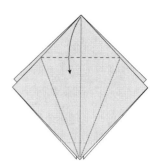

12) Fold the top of the model down along the dotted line. The ends of this dotted line will line up with the previous two creases you made.

13) Crease this well and then unfold it.

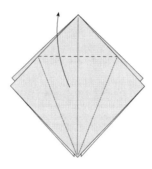

14) Lift up the top flap of paper along the horizontal crease you just made.

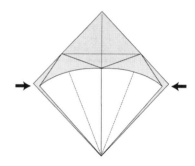

15) As you lift the paper up fold in both sides along the existing creases making a Petal Fold.

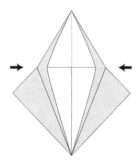

16) Push everything flat along the existing creases.

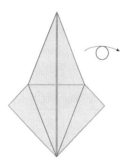

17) Turn the paper over.

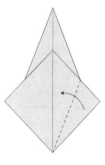

18) Fold the flap of paper on the right to the center along the dotted line.

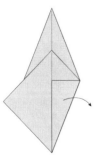

19) Crease this well and then unfold it.

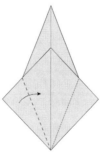

20) Fold the flap of paper on the left to the center along the dotted line.

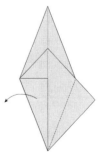

21) Crease this well and then unfold it.

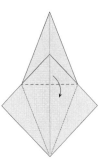

22) Fold the top of the model down along the dotted line. The ends of this dotted line will line up with the previous two creases you made.

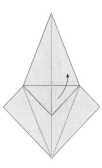

23) Crease this well and then unfold it.

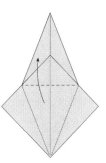

24) Lift up the top flap of paper along the horizontal crease you just made.

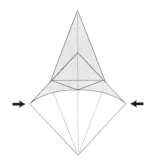

25) As you lift the paper up fold in both sides along the existing creases making a Petal Fold.

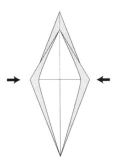

26) Push everything flat along the existing creases.

27) Fold the bottom right section of paper up along the dotted line.

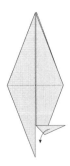

28) Crease this well and then unfold it.

29) Fold the bottom left section of paper up along the dotted line.

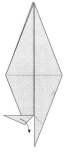

30) Crease this well and then unfold it.

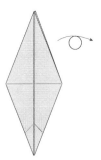

31) Turn the paper over.

32) Fold the bottom right section of paper up along the dotted line.

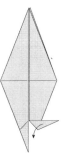

33) Crease this well and then unfold it.

Crow

34) Fold the bottom left section of paper up along the dotted line.

35) Crease this well and then unfold it.

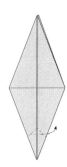

36) Make an Inside Reverse Fold along the existing creases on the right.

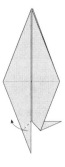

37) Make an Inside Reverse Fold along the existing creases on the left.

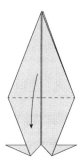

38) Fold the top layer of paper down along the dotted line.

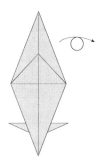

39) Turn the paper over.

40) Fold the paper in half vertically along the dotted line.

41) Fold the top part of the paper down along the dotted line.

42) Crease this well and then unfold it.

43) Turn the paper over.

44) Fold the top part of the paper down along the dotted line. This is the opposite direction of the previous fold.

45) Crease this well and then unfold it.

46) Make an Inside Reverse Fold along the existing creases.

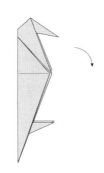

47) Rotate the model down so it's standing on the feet.

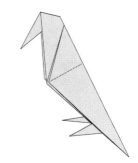

The completed Crow.

Heron

This model begins with a Bird Base. If you're already familiar with this base you can skip ahead to step 27.

Techniques Used: Mountain and Valley Folds, Inside Reverse Fold, Crimp, Square Base, Petal Fold and Bird Base.

Before You Start: Begin with a square sheet of paper with the white side facing up.

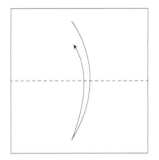

1) Fold the paper in half horizontally. Crease it well and then unfold.

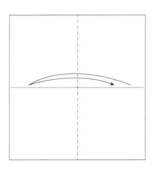

2) Fold the paper in half vertically. Crease it well and then unfold it.

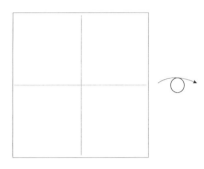

3) Turn the paper over.

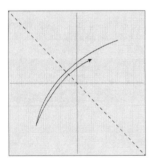

4) Fold the paper in half diagonally. Crease it well and then unfold it.

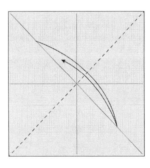

5) Fold the paper in half diagonally the other way. Crease it well and then unfold it.

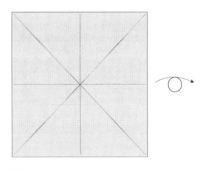

6) Turn the paper over.

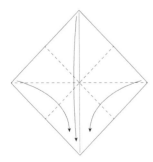

7) Fold the paper along the existing creases bringing the left, right and top corners to the bottom into a Square base.

8) Fold the flap of paper on the right to the center along the dotted line.

9) Crease this well and then unfold it.

10) Fold the flap of paper on the left to the center along the dotted line.

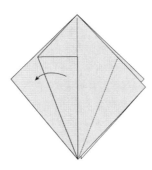

11) Crease this well and then unfold it.

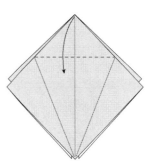

12) Fold the top of the model down along the dotted line. The ends of this dotted line will line up with the previous two creases you made.

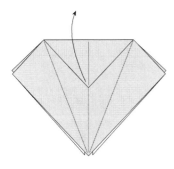

13) Crease this well and then unfold it.

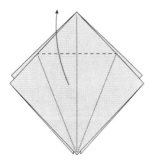

14) Lift up the top flap of paper along the horizontal crease you just made.

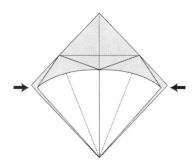

15) As you lift the paper up fold in both sides along the existing creases making a Petal Fold.

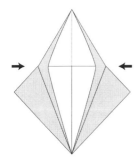

16) Push everything flat along the existing creases.

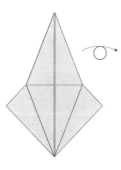

17) Turn the paper over.

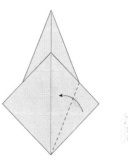

18) Fold the flap of paper on the right to the center along the dotted line.

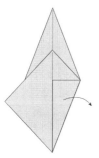

19) Crease this well and then unfold it.

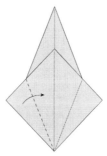

20) Fold the flap of paper on the left to the center along the dotted line.

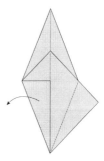

21) Crease this well and then unfold it.

Heron

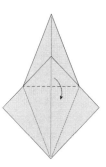
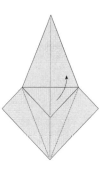
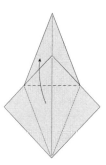

22) Fold the top of the model down along the dotted line. The ends of this dotted line will line up with the previous two creases you made.

23) Crease this well and then unfold it.

24) Lift up the top flap of paper along the horizontal crease you just made.

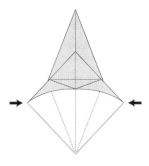
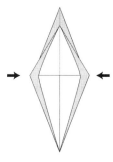
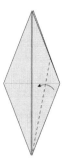

25) As you lift the paper up fold in both sides along the existing creases making a Petal Fold.

26) Push everything flat along the existing creases.

27) Fold the top right flap of paper to the center along the dotted line.

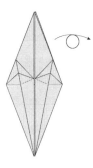

28) Fold the top left flap of paper to the center along the dotted line.

29) Turn the paper over.

30) Fold the top right flap of paper to the center along the dotted line.

31) Fold the top left flap of paper to the center along the dotted line.

32) Fold the left section of paper up along the dotted line.

33) Crease this well and then unfold it.

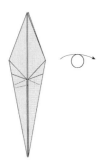

34) Turn the paper over.

35) Fold the right section of paper up along the dotted line. This is the opposite direction of the previous fold on the other side.

36) Crease this well and then unfold it.

37) Make an Inside Reverse Fold along the existing creases.

38) Fold the top of the paper down along the dotted line.

39) Crease this well and then unfold it.

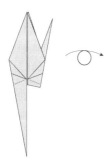

40) Turn the paper over.

41) Fold the top of the paper down along the dotted line.

42) Crease this well and then unfold it.

43) Make an Inside Reverse Fold along the existing creases.

44) Fold the bottom section of paper up along the dotted line.

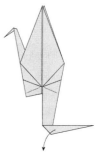

45) Crease this well and then unfold it.

Heron

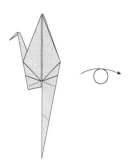

46) Turn the paper over.

47) Fold the bottom section of paper up along the dotted line. This is the opposite direction of the previous fold on the other side.

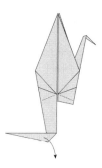

48) Crease this well and then unfold it.

49) Make an Inside Reverse Fold along the existing creases.

50) Make another Inside Reverse Fold pushing the paper to the right making a Crimp. There are no existing creases to help this time so do your best.

51) Fold the top left flap of paper over to the center along the dotted line. The bottom of the model will get a bit messy but that's okay.

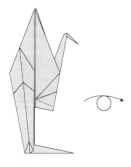

52) Turn the paper over.

53) Fold the top right flap of paper over to the center along the dotted line.

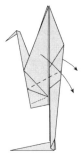

54) Fold both of the wings down.

The completed Heron.

Horse

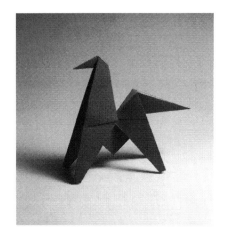

This model requires you to make a Bird Base and then to unfold it and use those creases for different folds.

Techniques Used: Mountain and Valley Folds, Inside Reverse Fold, Square Base, Petal Fold, Bird Base and Scissors.

Before You Start: Begin with a square sheet of paper with the white side facing up.

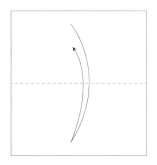

1) Fold the paper in half horizontally. Crease it well and then unfold.

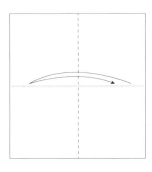

2) Fold the paper in half vertically. Crease it well and then unfold it.

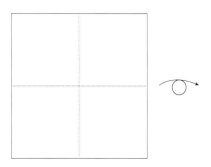

3) Turn the paper over.

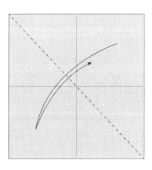

4) Fold the paper in half diagonally. Crease it well and then unfold it.

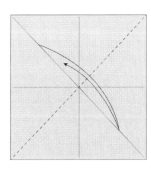

5) Fold the paper in half diagonally the other way. Crease it well and then unfold it.

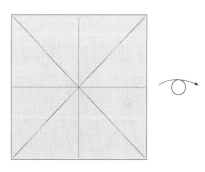

6) Turn the paper over.

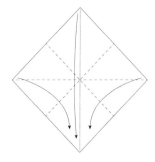

7) Fold the paper along the existing creases bringing the left, right and top corners to the bottom into a Square base.

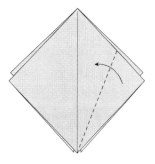

8) Fold the flap of paper on the right to the center along the dotted line.

9) Crease this well and then unfold it.

Horse Page **201**

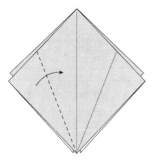

10) Fold the flap of paper on the left to the center along the dotted line.

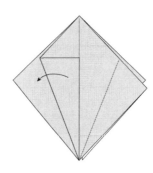

11) Crease this well and then unfold it.

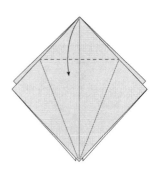

12) Fold the top of the model down along the dotted line. The ends of this dotted line will line up with the previous two creases you made.

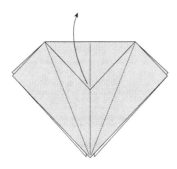

13) Crease this well and then unfold it.

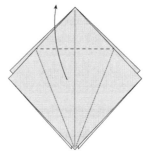

14) Lift up the top flap of paper along the horizontal crease you just made.

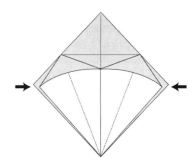

15) As you lift the paper up fold in both sides along the existing creases making a Petal Fold.

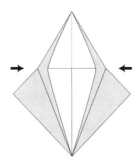

16) Push everything flat along the existing creases.

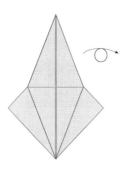

17) Turn the paper over.

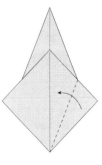

18) Fold the flap of paper on the right to the center along the dotted line.

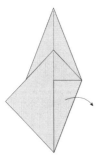

19) Crease this well and then unfold it.

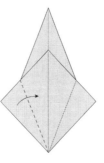

20) Fold the flap of paper on the left to the center along the dotted line.

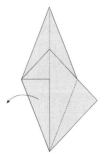

21) Crease this well and then unfold it.

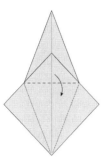
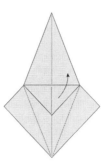
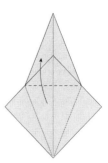

22) Fold the top of the model down along the dotted line. The ends of this dotted line will line up with the previous two creases you made.

23) Crease this well and then unfold it.

24) Lift up the top flap of paper along the horizontal crease you just made.

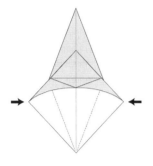
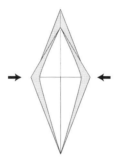

25) As you lift the paper up fold in both sides along the existing creases making a Petal Fold.

26) Push everything flat along the existing creases.

27) Open up the paper and unfold the Petal Fold.

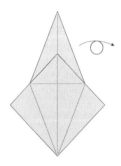
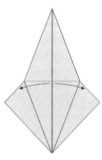

28) Turn the paper over.

29) Open up the paper and unfold the Petal Fold.

30) Cut the top layer of paper along the dotted line stopping at the horizontal crease near the top.

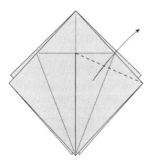
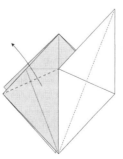
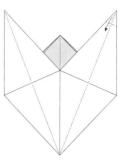

31) Fold the right side of the paper up along the dotted line.

32) Fold the left side of the paper up along the dotted line.

33) Fold the right tip of paper down along the dotted line.

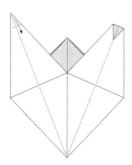

34) Fold the left tip of paper down along the dotted line.

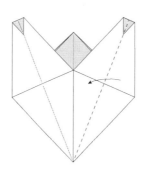

35) Fold the right side of the paper along the dotted line.

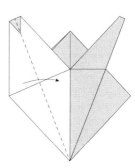

36) Fold the left side of the paper along the dotted line.

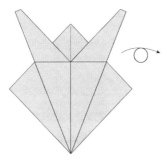

37) Turn the paper over.

38) Cut the top layer of paper along the dotted line stopping at the horizontal crease near the top.

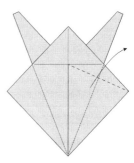

39) Fold the right side of the paper up along the dotted line.

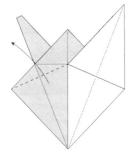

40) Fold the left side of the paper up along the dotted line.

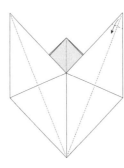

41) Fold the right tip of paper down along the dotted line.

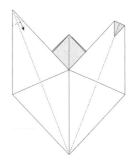

42) Fold the left tip of paper down along the dotted line.

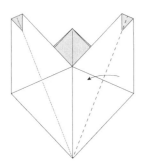

43) Fold the right side of the paper along the dotted line.

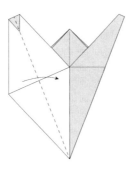

44) Fold the left side of the paper along the dotted line.

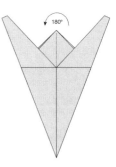

45) Rotate the paper 180 degrees.

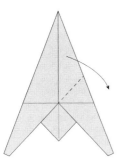

46) Fold the right flap of paper down along the dotted line.

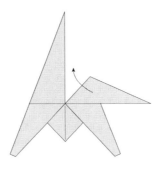

47) Crease this well and then unfold it.

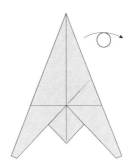

48) Turn the paper over.

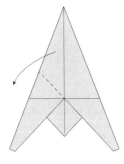

49) Fold the left flap of paper down along the dotted line. This is the opposite direction of the previous fold.

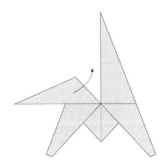

50) Crease this well and then unfold it.

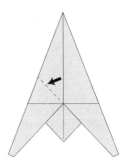

51) Make an Inside Reverse Fold along the existing creases.

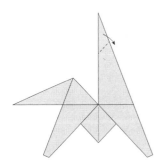

52) Fold the right flap of paper down along the dotted line.

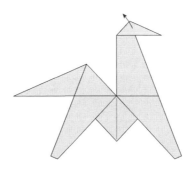

53) Crease this well and then unfold it.

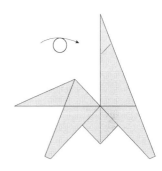

54) Turn the paper over.

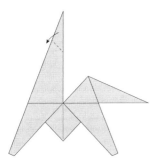

55) Fold the left flap of paper down along the dotted line. This is the opposite direction of the previous fold.

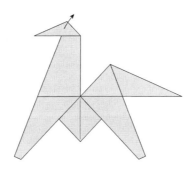

56) Crease this well and then unfold it.

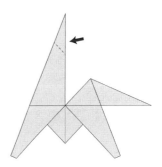

57) Make an Inside Reverse Fold along the existing creases.

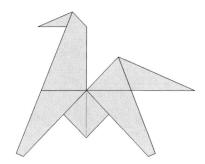

The completed Horse.

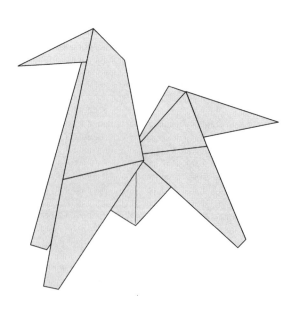

Horse

Swallow

This model begins with a Bird Base. If you're already familiar with this base you can skip ahead to step 27.

Techniques Used: Mountain and Valley Folds, Inside Reverse Fold, Pleat, Square Base, Petal Fold, Bird Base and Scissors.

Before You Start: Begin with a square sheet of paper with the white side facing up.

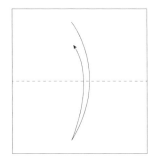

1) Fold the paper in half horizontally. Crease it well and then unfold.

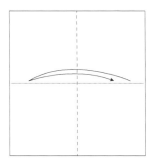

2) Fold the paper in half vertically. Crease it well and then unfold it.

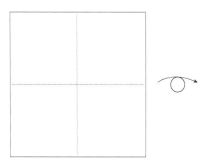

3) Turn the paper over.

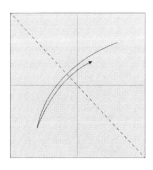

4) Fold the paper in half diagonally. Crease it well and then unfold it.

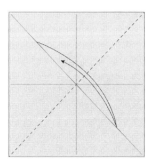

5) Fold the paper in half diagonally the other way. Crease it well and then unfold it.

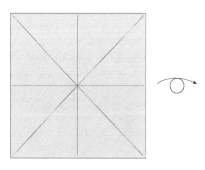

6) Turn the paper over.

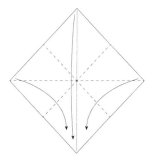

7) Fold the paper along the existing creases bringing the left, right and top corners to the bottom into a Square base.

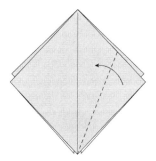

8) Fold the flap of paper on the right to the center along the dotted line.

9) Crease this well and then unfold it.

Swallow

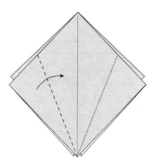

10) Fold the flap of paper on the left to the center along the dotted line.

11) Crease this well and then unfold it.

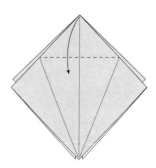

12) Fold the top of the model down along the dotted line. The ends of this dotted line will line up with the previous two creases you made.

13) Crease this well and then unfold it.

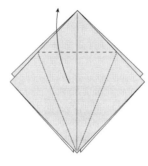

14) Lift up the top flap of paper along the horizontal crease you just made.

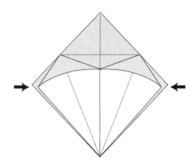

15) As you lift the paper up fold in both sides along the existing creases making a Petal Fold.

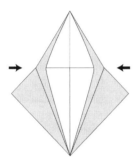

16) Push everything flat along the existing creases.

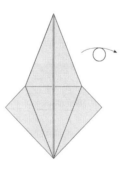

17) Turn the paper over.

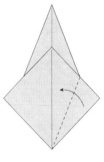

18) Fold the flap of paper on the right to the center along the dotted line.

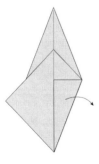

19) Crease this well and then unfold it.

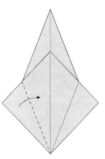

20) Fold the flap of paper on the left to the center along the dotted line.

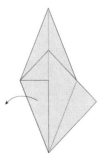

21) Crease this well and then unfold it.

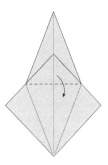

22) Fold the top of the model down along the dotted line. The ends of this dotted line will line up with the previous two creases you made.

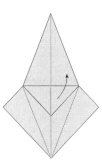

23) Crease this well and then unfold it.

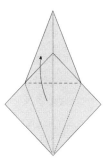

24) Lift up the top flap of paper along the horizontal crease you just made.

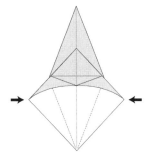

25) As you lift the paper up fold in both sides along the existing creases making a Petal Fold.

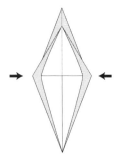

26) Push everything flat along the existing creases.

27) Fold the top right flap of paper to the center along the dotted line.

28) Fold the top left flap of paper to the center along the dotted line.

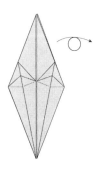

29) Turn the paper over.

30) Fold the right flap of paper to the center along the dotted line.

31) Fold the left flap of paper to the center along the dotted line.

32) Fold the top right flap of paper over to the left along the dotted line.

33) Turn the paper over.

Swallow

34) Fold the top right flap of paper over the left along the dotted line.

35) Pull the top right section of paper down and out along the dotted line making an Inside Reverse Fold.

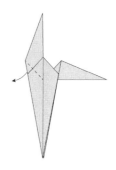

36) Pull the top left section of paper down and out along the dotted line making an Inside Reverse Fold.

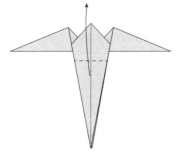

37) Fold the top flap of paper up along the dotted line.

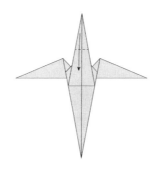

38) Fold the top flap of paper down along the dotted line.

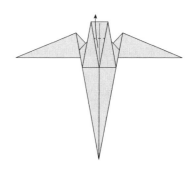

39) Fold the top flap of paper up along the dotted line.

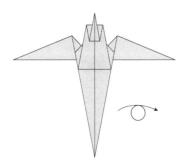

40) Turn the paper over.

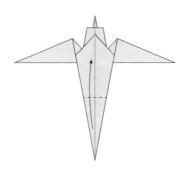

41) Fold the paper up along the dotted line.

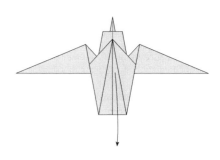

42) Fold the paper back down.

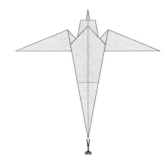

43) Cut this flap of paper down the middle stopping at the horizontal crease you just made.

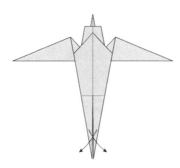

44) Twist the two pieces of paper to the left and right.

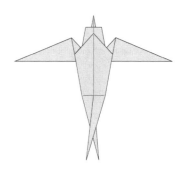

45) The competed swallow.

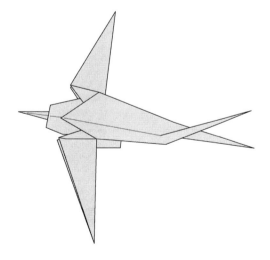

Rabbit

Even though this is a rabbit and not a bird it still begins with a Bird Base. If you're already familiar with this base you can skip ahead to step 27.

Techniques Used: Mountain and Valley Folds, Inside Reverse Fold, Outside Reverse Fold, Crimp, Square Base, Petal Fold and Bird Base.

Before You Start: Begin with a square sheet of paper with the white side facing up.

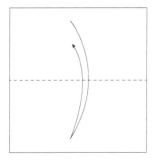

1) Fold the paper in half horizontally. Crease it well and then unfold.

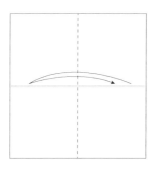

2) Fold the paper in half vertically. Crease it well and then unfold it.

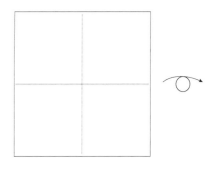

3) Turn the paper over.

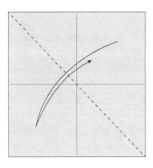

4) Fold the paper in half diagonally. Crease it well and then unfold it.

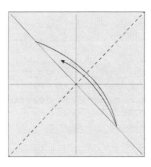

5) Fold the paper in half diagonally the other way. Crease it well and then unfold it.

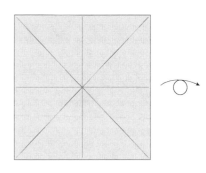

6) Turn the paper over.

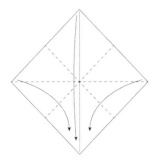

7) Fold the paper along the existing creases bringing the left, right and top corners to the bottom into a Square base.

8) Fold the flap of paper on the right to the center along the dotted line.

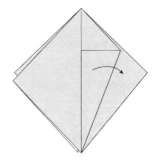

9) Crease this well and then unfold it.

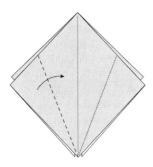

10) Fold the flap of paper on the left to the center along the dotted line.

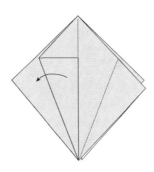

11) Crease this well and then unfold it.

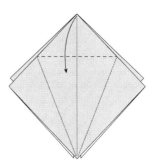

12) Fold the top of the model down along the dotted line. The ends of this dotted line will line up with the previous two creases you made.

13) Crease this well and then unfold it.

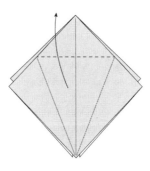

14) Lift up the top flap of paper along the horizontal crease you just made.

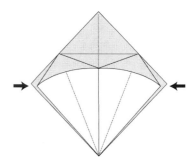

15) As you lift the paper up fold in both sides along the existing creases making a Petal Fold.

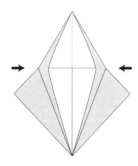

16) Push everything flat along the existing creases.

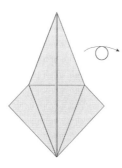

17) Turn the paper over.

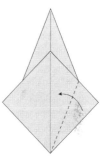

18) Fold the flap of paper on the right to the center along the dotted line.

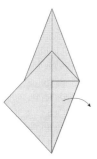

19) Crease this well and then unfold it.

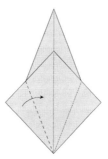

20) Fold the flap of paper on the left to the center along the dotted line.

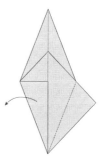

21) Crease this well and then unfold it.

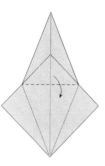
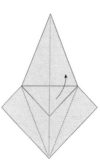
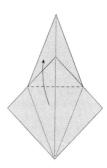

22) Fold the top of the model down along the dotted line. The ends of this dotted line will line up with the previous two creases you made.

23) Crease this well and then unfold it.

24) Lift up the top flap of paper along the horizontal crease you just made.

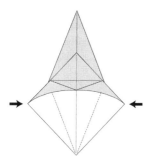
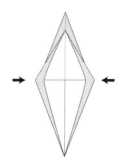

25) As you lift the paper up fold in both sides along the existing creases making a Petal Fold.

26) Push everything flat along the existing creases.

27) Fold the top flap of paper down along the dotted line.

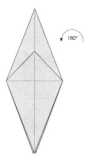

28) Rotate the paper 180 degrees.

29) Fold the paper in half vertically along the dotted line.

30) Fold all the layers of paper down along the dotted line.

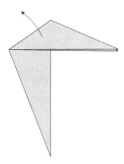

31) Crease this well and then unfold it.

32) Turn the paper over.

33) Fold all the layers of paper down along the dotted line. This is the opposite direction of the previous fold made on the other side.

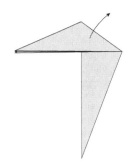

34) Crease this well and then unfold it.

35) Make an Outside Reverse Fold along the existing creases.

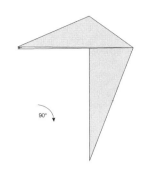

36) Rotate the paper 90 degrees to the right.

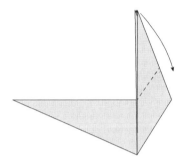

37) Fold the top flap of paper down along the dotted line making an Outside Reverse Fold.

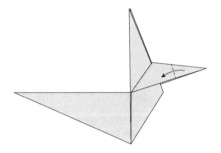

38) Fold the tip of the paper along the dotted line.

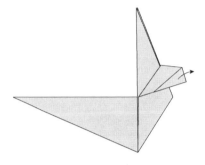

39) Crease this well and then unfold it.

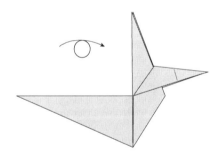

40) Turn the paper over.

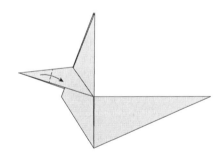

41) Fold the tip of the paper along the dotted line. This is the opposite direction of the previous fold made on the other side.

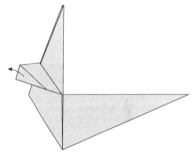

42) Crease this well and then unfold it.

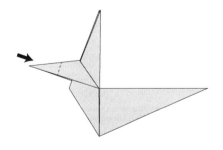

43) Make an Inside Reverse Fold along the existing creases.

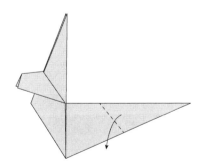

44) Fold the paper down along the dotted line.

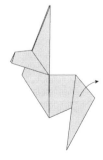

45) Crease this well and then unfold it.

Rabbit

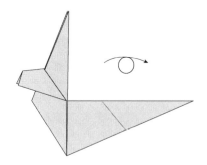

46) Turn the paper over.

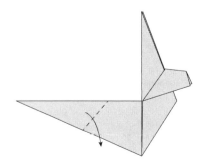

47) Fold the paper down along the dotted line. This is the opposite direction of the previous fold made on the other side.

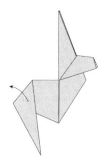

48) Crease this well and then unfold it.

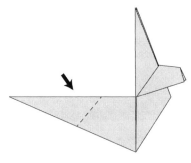

49) Make an Inside Reverse Fold along the existing creases.

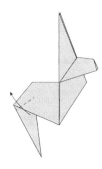

50) Pull the paper up along the dotted line making another Inside Reverse Fold resulting in a Crimp.

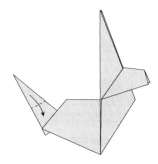

51) Fold the paper down along the dotted line.

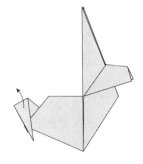

52) Crease this well and then unfold it.

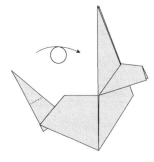

53) Turn the paper over.

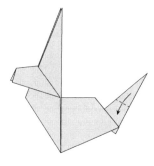

54) Fold the paper down along the dotted line.

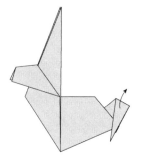

55) Crease this well and then unfold it.

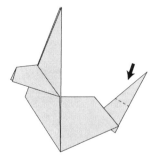

56) Make an Inside Reverse Fold along the existing creases.

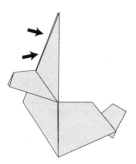

57) Open up both the ears giving them a round shape.

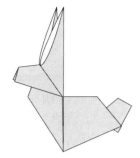

The completed rabbit.

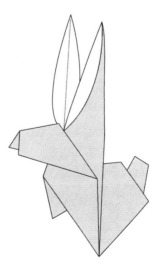

Rabbit Page **217**

Table

This model uses the Square Base in a more unique way than usual.

Techniques Used: Mountain and Valley Folds, Square Base, Squash Fold and Petal Fold.

Before You Start: Begin with a square sheet of paper with the white side facing up.

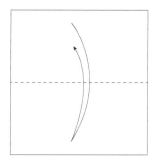

1) Fold the paper in half horizontally and then unfold it.

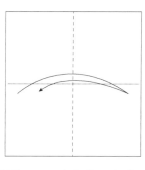

2) Fold the paper in half vertically and then unfold it.

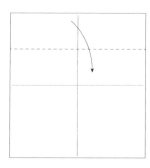

3) Fold the top part of the paper down towards the center along the dotted line.

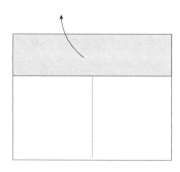

4) Crease this well and then unfold it.

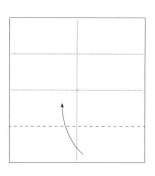

5) Fold the bottom part of the paper up towards the center along the dotted line.

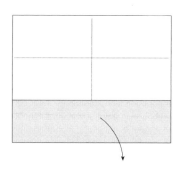

6) Crease this well and then unfold it.

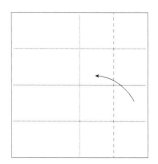

7) Fold the right side of the paper towards the center along the dotted line.

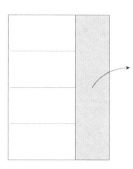

8) Crease this well and then unfold it.

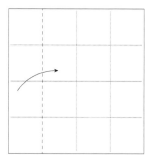

9) Fold the left side of the paper towards the center along the dotted line.

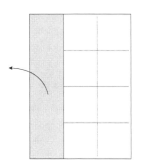

10) Crease this well and then unfold it.

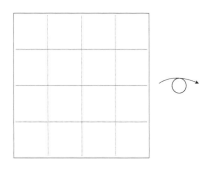

11) Turn the paper over.

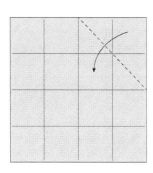

12) Fold the top right corner of paper to the center. Crease it well.

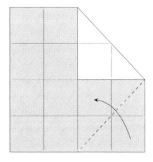

13) Fold the bottom right corner of paper to the center. Crease it well.

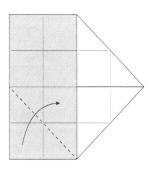

14) Fold the bottom left corner of paper to the center. Crease it well.

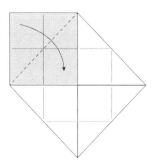

15) Fold the top left corner of paper to the center. Crease it well.

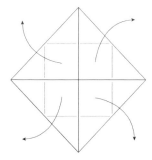

16) Unfold all 4 corners.

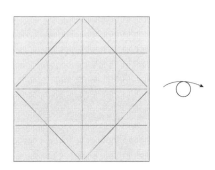

17) Turn the paper over.

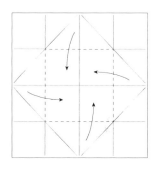

18) Fold each side of the paper towards the center along the dotted lines. Fold only the middle part of the existing creases.

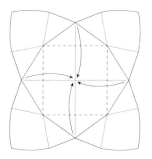

19) The paper will begin to take on a shape like what you see here. Fold each of those 4 points to the center.

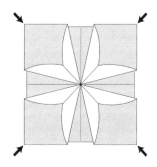

20) Squash Fold each of the 4 flaps of paper on the 4 corners.

21) Fold the top right square of paper in half along the dotted line and then unfold it.

Table

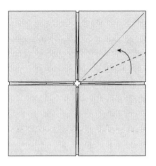

22) Fold the bottom part of this square to the center along the dotted line.

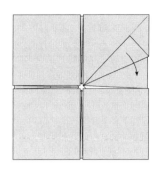

23) Crease this well and then unfold it.

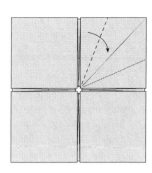

24) Fold the left side of tis square to the center along the dotted line.

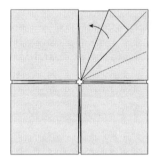

25) Crease this well and then unfold it.

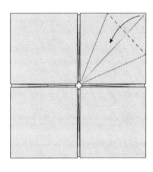

26) Fold the top of this square down along the dotted line.

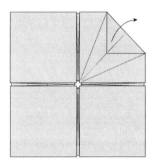

27) Crease this well and then unfold it.

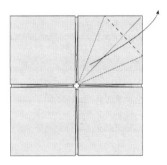

28) Lift up the top layer of paper along the dotted line.

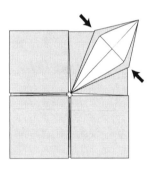

29) Fold in both sides making a Petal Fold.

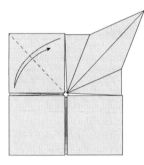

30) Fold the top left square of paper in half along the dotted line and then unfold it.

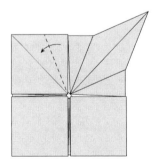

31) Fold the right side of this square to the center along the dotted line.

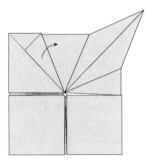

32) Crease this well and then unfold it.

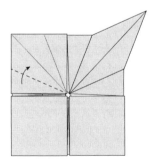

33) Fold the bottom part of this square to the center along the dotted line.

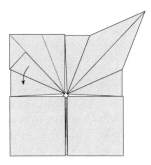

34) Crease this well and then unfold it.

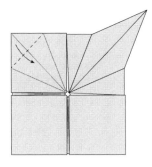

35) Fold the top of this square down along the dotted line.

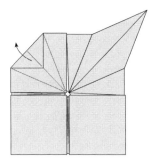

36) Crease this well and then unfold it.

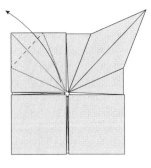

37) Lift up the top layer of paper along the dotted line.

38) Fold in both sides making a Petal Fold.

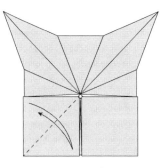

39) Fold the bottom left square of paper in half along the dotted line.

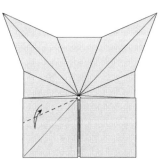

40) Fold the top part of this square to the center along the dotted line. Crease it well and then unfold it.

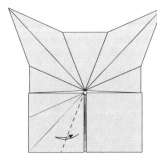

41) Fold the right side of this square to the center along the dotted line. Crease it well and then unfold it.

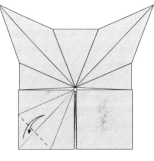

42) Fold the bottom corner of this square up along the dotted line. Crease it well and then unfold it.

43) Make a Petal Fold using the existing creases.

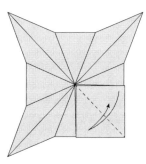

44) Fold the bottom right square in half along the dotted line and then unfold it.

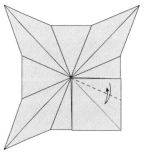

45) Fold the top part of this square to the center along the dotted line. Crease it well and then unfold it.

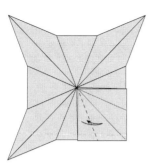

46) Fold the left side of this square to the center along the dotted line. Crease it well and then unfold it.

47) Fold the bottom corner of this square up along the dotted line. Crease it well and then unfold it.

48) Make a Petal Fold using the existing creases.

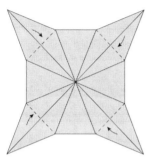

49) The four Petal Folds will form the legs of the table. Fold each of them up along the dotted line.

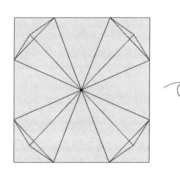

50) Turn the model over.

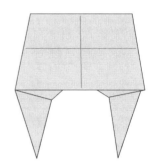

The completed Table.

Water Bomb

This is the traditional Water Bomb from which the Water Bomb Base gets its name.

Techniques Used: Mountain and Valley Folds and Water Bomb Base.

Before You Start: Begin with a square sheet of paper with the colored side facing up.

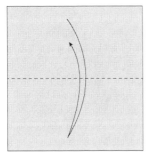

1) Fold the paper in half horizontally. Crease it well and then unfold it.

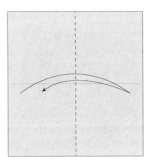

2) Fold the paper in half vertically. Crease it well and then unfold it.

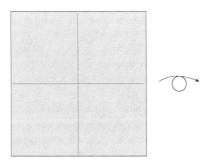

3) Turn the paper over.

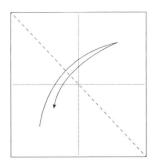

4) Fold the paper in half diagonally. Crease it well and then unfold it.

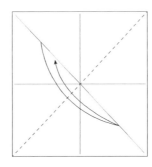

5) Fold the paper in half diagonally the other way. Crease it well and then unfold it.

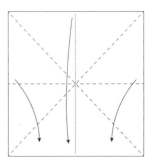

6) Fold the sides and top of the paper down to the bottom along the existing creases to form a Water Bomb Base.

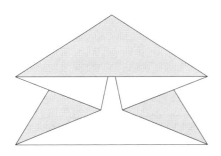

7) Push everything flat.

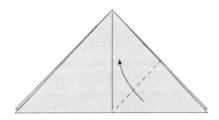

8) Fold the top right flap of paper up along the dotted line.

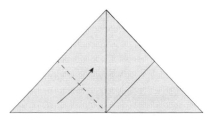

9) Fold the top left flap of paper up along the dotted line.

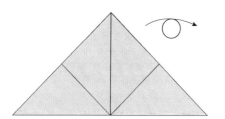

10) Turn the paper over.

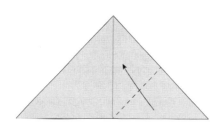

11) Fold the right flap of paper up along the dotted line.

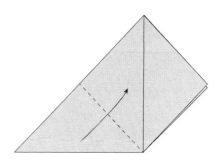

12) Fold the left flap of paper up along the dotted line.

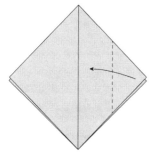

13) Fold the top right flap of paper towards the center along the dotted line.

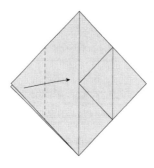

14) Fold the top left flap of paper towards the center along the dotted line.

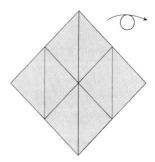

15) Turn the paper over.

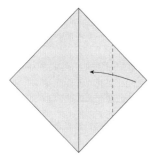

16) Fold the right flap of paper towards the center along the dotted line.

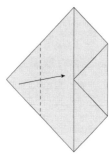

17) Fold the left flap of paper towards the center along the dotted line.

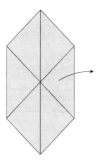

18) Unfold the right flap of paper.

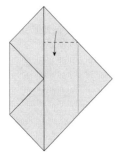

19) Fold the top of the top right flap of paper down along the dotted line.

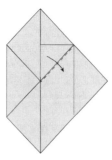

20) Fold this flap of paper down again along the dotted line.

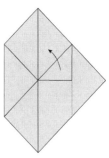

21) Crease this well and then unfold it.

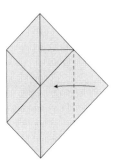

22) Fold the right side back to the center along the existing crease.

23) Fold the flap of paper into the pocket along the existing crease.

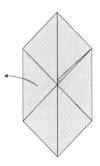

24) Unfold the left flap of paper.

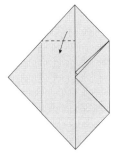

25) Fold the top of the top left flap of paper down along the dotted line.

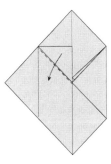

26) Fold this flap of paper down again along the dotted line.

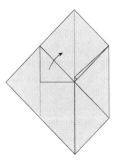

27) Crease this well and then unfold it.

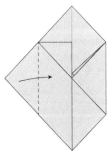

28) Fold the left side back to the center along the existing crease.

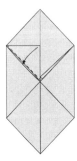

29) Fold the flap of paper into the pocket along the existing crease.

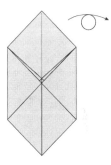

30) Turn the paper over.

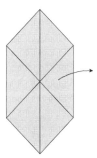

31) Unfold the right flap of paper.

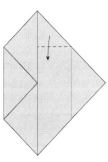

32) Fold the top of the top right flap of paper down along the dotted line.

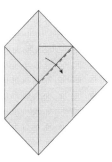

33) Fold this flap of paper down again along the dotted line.

Water Bomb

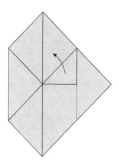

34) Crease this well and then unfold it.

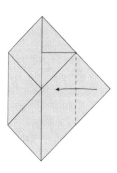

35) Fold the right side back to the center along the existing crease.

36) Fold the flap of paper into the pocket along the existing crease.

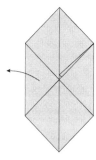

37) Unfold the left flap of paper.

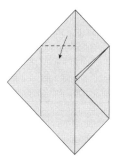

38) Fold the top of the top left flap of paper down along the dotted line.

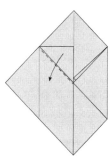

39) Fold this flap of paper down again along the dotted line.

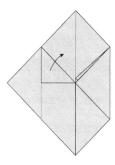

40) Crease this well and then unfold it.

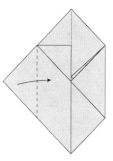

41) Fold the left side back to the center along the existing crease.

42) Fold the flap of paper into the pocket along the existing crease.

43) Blow air into the tiny hole at the bottom of the model to inflate it like a balloon.

The completed Water Bomb.

Tulip

This model begins from a Water Bomb Base. If you're already familiar with this base you can skip ahead to step 8.

Techniques Used: Mountain and Valley Folds and Water Bomb Base.

Before You Start: Begin with a square sheet of paper with the colored side facing up.

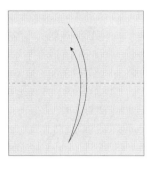

1) Fold the paper in half horizontally. Crease it well and then unfold it.

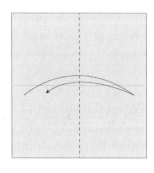

2) Fold the paper in half vertically. Crease it well and then unfold it.

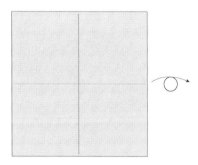

3) Turn the paper over.

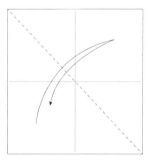

4) Fold the paper in half diagonally. Crease it well and then unfold it.

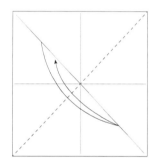

5) Fold the paper in half diagonally the other way. Crease it well and then unfold it.

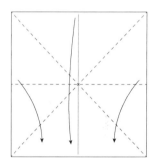

6) Fold the sides and top of the paper down to the bottom along the existing creases to form a Water Bomb Base.

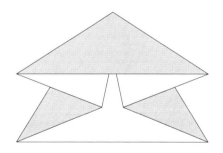

7) Push everything flat.

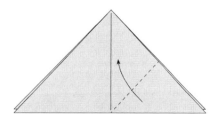

8) Fold the top right flap of paper up along the dotted line.

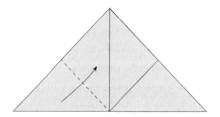

9) Fold the top left flap of paper up along the dotted line.

Tulip   Page **227**

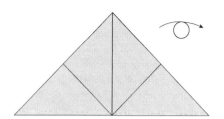

10) Turn the paper over.

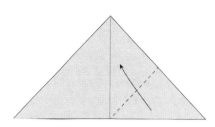

11) Fold the right flap of paper up along the dotted line.

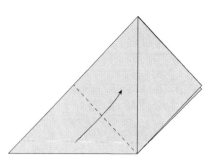

12) Fold the left flap of paper up along the dotted line.

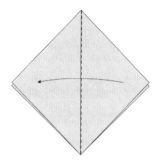

13) Fold the top right flap over to the left along the dotted line.

14) Turn the paper over.

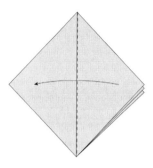

15) Fold the top right flap over to the left along the dotted line.

16) Fold the top left flap of paper over to the right along the dotted line.

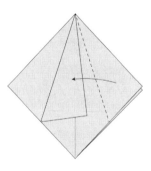

17) Fold the top right flap of paper over to the left along the dotted line.

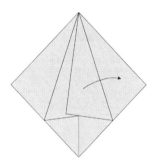

18) Crease this well and then unfold it.

19) Fold the top right flap of paper back over to the left using the existing crease and tuck it inside the flap on the left. This doesn't have to be perfect.

20) Turn the paper over.

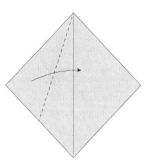

21) Fold the left flap of paper over to the right along the dotted line.

Tulip

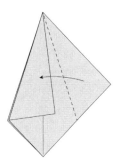

22) Fold the right flap of paper over to the left along the dotted line.

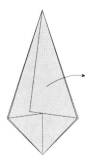

23) Crease this well and then unfold it.

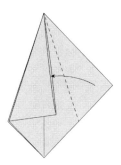

24) Fold the right flap of paper back over to the left using the existing crease and tuck it inside the flap on the left. This doesn't have to be perfect.

25) Blow air into the tiny hole at the bottom to inflate the model into a 3D shape.

26) Carefully peel down the four flaps of paper to form the tulip petals.

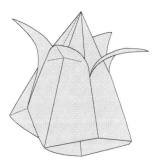

The completed Tulip.

Bunny Balloon

This model begins from a Water Bomb Base. If you're already familiar with this base you can skip ahead to step 8.

Techniques Used: Mountain and Valley Folds and Water Bomb Base.

Before You Start: Begin with a square sheet of paper with the colored side facing up.

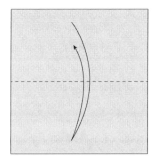

1) Fold the paper in half horizontally. Crease it well and then unfold it.

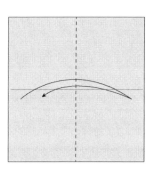

2) Fold the paper in half vertically. Crease it well and then unfold it.

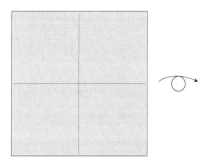

3) Turn the paper over.

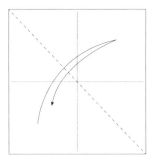

4) Fold the paper in half diagonally. Crease it well and then unfold it.

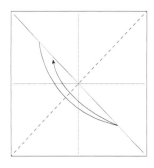

5) Fold the paper in half diagonally the other way. Crease it well and then unfold it.

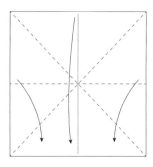

6) Fold the sides and top of the paper down to the bottom along the existing creases to form a Water Bomb Base.

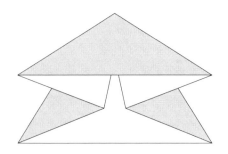

7) Push everything flat.

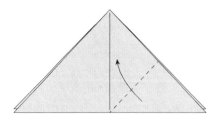

8) Fold the top right flap of paper up along the dotted line.

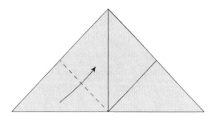

9) Fold the top left flap of paper up along the dotted line.

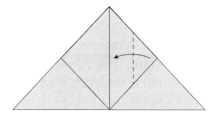

10) Fold the top right flap to the center along the dotted line.

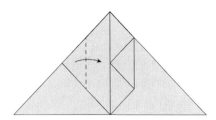

11) Fold the top left flap of paper to the center along the dotted line.

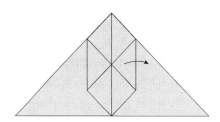

12) Unfold the flap of paper on the right.

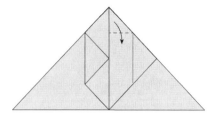

13) Fold the top of the right flap of paper down along the dotted line.

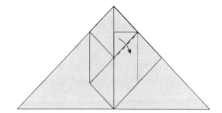

14) Fold this down again along the dotted line.

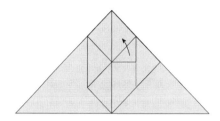

15) Crease this well and then unfold it.

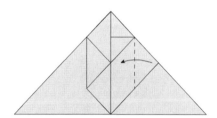

16) Fold the right side back to the center along the existing crease.

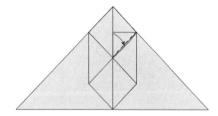

17) Fold the flap of paper into the pocket along the existing crease.

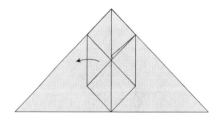

18) Unfold the flap of paper on the left.

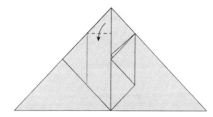

19) Fold the top of the left flap of paper down along the dotted line.

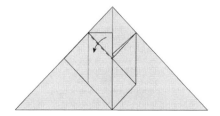

20) Fold this down again along the dotted line.

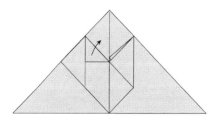

21) Crease this well and then unfold it.

Bunny Balloon

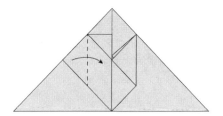

22) Fold the left side back to the center along the existing crease.

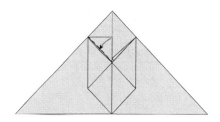

23) Fold the flap of paper into the pocket along the existing crease.

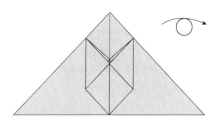

24) Turn the paper over.

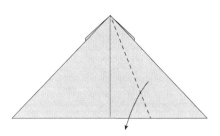

25) Fold the right flap of paper down along the dotted line.

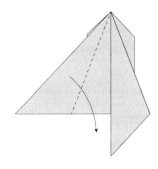

26) Fold the left flap of paper down along the dotted line.

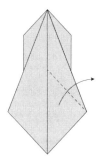

27) Fold the right flap of paper up along the dotted line.

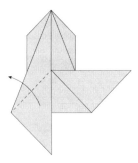

28) Fold the left flap of paper up along the dotted line.

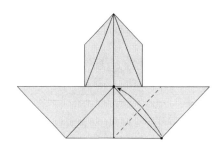

29) Fold the right section of paper along the dotted line bringing the two marked points together.

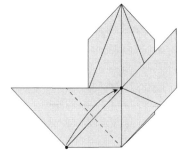

30) Fold the left section of paper along the dotted line bringing the two marked points together.

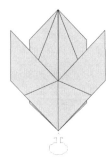

31) Blow air into the tiny hole at the bottom of the model to inflate it like a balloon.

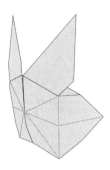

The completed Bunny Balloon.

Goldfish Balloon

This model begins from a Water Bomb Base. If you're already familiar with this base you can skip ahead to step 8.

Techniques Used: Mountain and Valley Folds and Water Bomb Base.

Before You Start: Begin with a square sheet of paper with the colored side facing up.

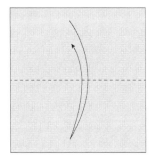

1) Fold the paper in half horizontally. Crease it well and then unfold it.

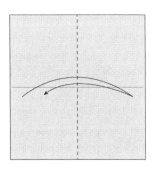

2) Fold the paper in half vertically. Crease it well and then unfold it.

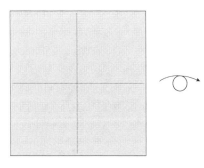

3) Turn the paper over.

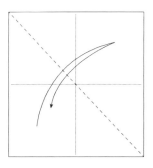

4) Fold the paper in half diagonally. Crease it well and then unfold it.

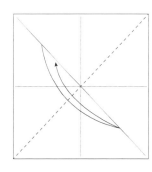

5) Fold the paper in half diagonally the other way. Crease it well and then unfold it.

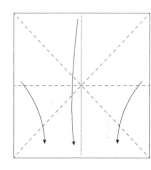

6) Fold the sides and top of the paper down to the bottom along the existing creases to form a Water Bomb Base.

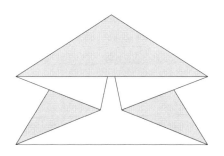

7) Push everything flat.

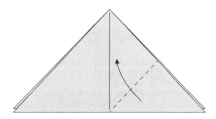

8) Fold the top right flap of paper up along the dotted line.

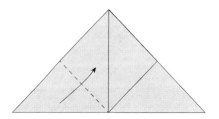

9) Fold the top left flap of paper up along the dotted line.

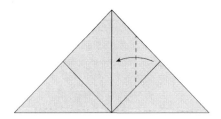

10) Fold the top right flap to the center along the dotted line.

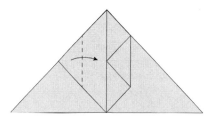

11) Fold the top left flap of paper to the center along the dotted line.

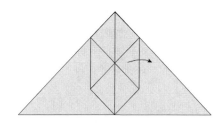

12) Unfold the flap of paper on the right.

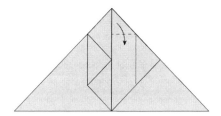

13) Fold the top of the right flap of paper down along the dotted line.

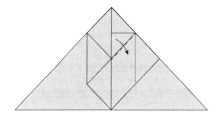

14) Fold this down again along the dotted line.

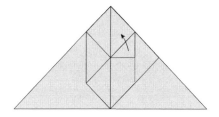

15) Crease this well and then unfold it.

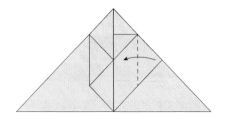

16) Fold the right side back to the center along the existing crease.

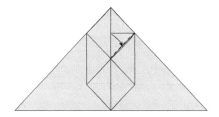

17) Fold the flap of paper into the pocket along the existing crease.

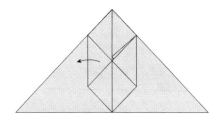

18) Unfold the flap of paper on the left.

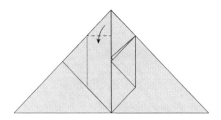

19) Fold the top of the left flap of paper down along the dotted line.

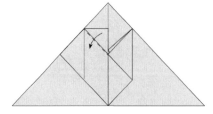

20) Fold this down again along the dotted line.

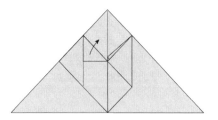

21) Crease this well and then unfold it.

Goldfish Balloon

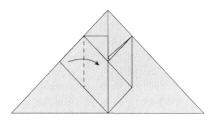

22) Fold the left side back to the center along the existing crease.

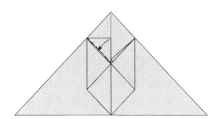

23) Fold the flap of paper into the pocket along the existing crease.

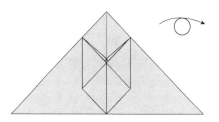

24) Turn the paper over.

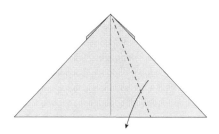

25) Fold the right flap of paper down along the dotted line.

26) Fold the left flap of paper down along the dotted line.

27) Fold the left flap of paper up along the dotted line.

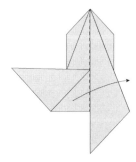

28) Fold the left flap of paper to the right along the dotted line in the middle.

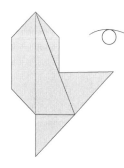

29) Turn the paper over.

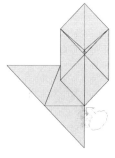

30) Blow air into the tiny hole at the bottom of the model to inflate it like a balloon.

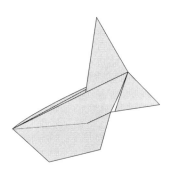

The completed Goldfish Balloon.

Jumping Frog

This is another really excellent action origami model. If you push down on this frog's back you can make it jump pretty far!

Techniques Used: Mountain and Valley Folds, Pleat and Water Bomb Base.

Before You Start: Begin with a square sheet of paper with the white side facing up.

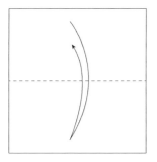

1) Fold the paper in half horizontally and then unfold it.

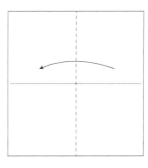

2) Fold the paper in half vertically.

3) Fold the paper in half vertically again and then unfold it.

4) Fold the paper down along the dotted line.

5) Crease this well and then unfold it.

6) Fold the paper down along the dotted line.

7) Crease this well and then unfold it.

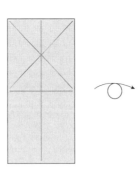

8) Turn the paper over.

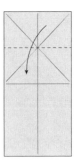

9) Fold the paper down along the horizontal dotted line.

Jumping Frog

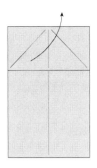

10) Crease this well and then unfold it.

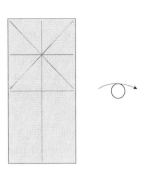

11) Turn the paper back over to the way it was before.

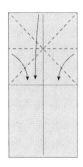

12) Fold the paper down along the existing creases just like a Water Bomb Base.

13) Push everything down flat.

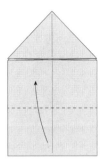

14) Fold the bottom part of the paper up along the dotted line.

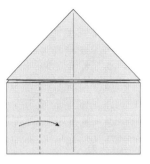

15) Fold the left side of the paper towards the center along the dotted line. Don't fold the top triangle. The paper will tuck in behind it.

16) Fold the right side of the paper towards the center along the dotted line. Again, don't fold the top triangle but tuck the paper in behind it.

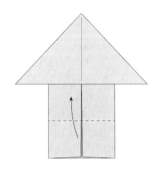

17) Fold the bottom part of the paper up along the dotted line.

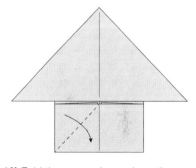

18) Fold the paper down along the dotted line.

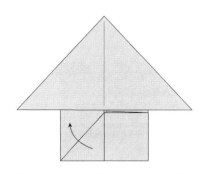

19) Crease this well and then unfold it.

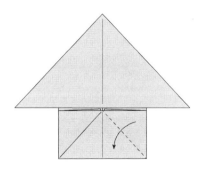

20) Fold the paper down along the dotted line.

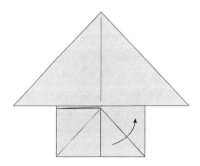

21) Crease this well and then unfold it.

Jumping Frog

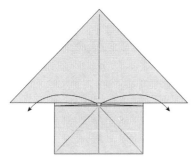

22) Pull the two flaps of paper on the inside of either side out.

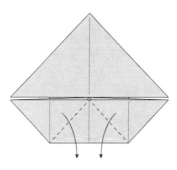

23) Fold the two flaps of paper on each side down along the dotted lines.

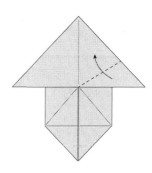

24) Fold the top right part of the paper up along the dotted line.

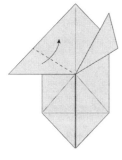

25) Fold the left part of the paper up along the dotted line.

26) Fold the bottom right part of the paper up along the dotted line.

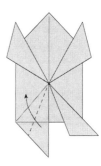

27) Fold the bottom left part of the paper up along the dotted line.

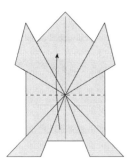

28) Fold the entire model up along the dotted line.

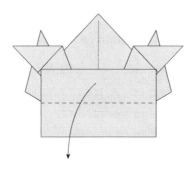

29) Fold the top part of the model down along the dotted line.

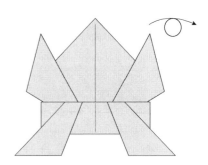

30) Turn the whole model over.

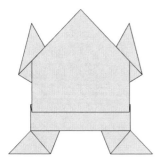

The completed jumping frog.

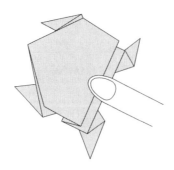

If you push down on the folds on it's back you can make it jump!

Butterfly

This butterfly begins from the same sequence of folds as the traditional pinwheel on page 112.

Techniques Used: Mountain and Valley Folds.

Before You Start: Begin with a square sheet of paper with the white side facing up.

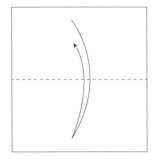

1) Fold the paper in half horizontally, crease it well and then unfold it.

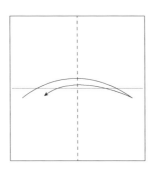

2) Fold the paper in half vertically, crease it well and then unfold it.

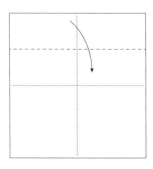

3) Fold the top quarter of the paper along the dotted line to the center line.

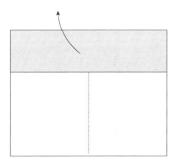

4) Crease this fold well and then unfold it.

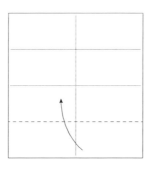

5) Fold the bottom quarter of the paper along the dotted line to the center line.

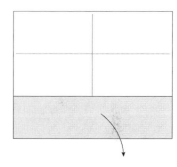

6) Crease this fold well and then unfold it.

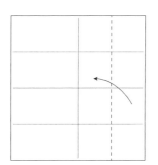

7) Fold the right quarter of the paper along the dotted line to the center line.

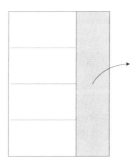

8) Crease this fold well and then unfold it.

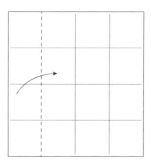

9) Fold the left quarter of the paper along the dotted line to the center line.

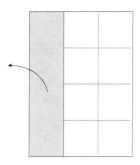

10) Crease this fold well and then unfold it.

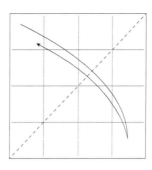

11) Fold the paper in half diagonally. Crease it well and then unfold it.

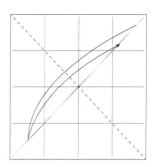

12) Fold the paper in half diagonally the other way. Crease it well and then unfold it.

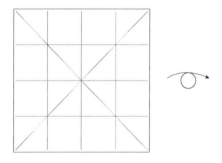

13) Turn the paper over so the colored side is facing up.

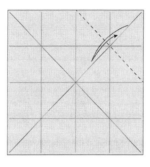

14) Fold the corner of the paper to the center along the dotted line. Crease this fold well and then unfold it.

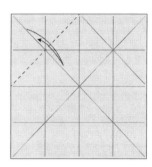

15) Fold the next corner of the paper to the center along the dotted line. Crease this fold well and then unfold it.

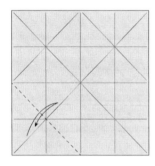

16) Fold the next corner of the paper to the center along the dotted line. Crease this fold well and then unfold it.

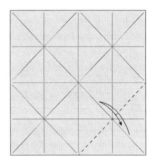

17) Fold the final corner of the paper to the center along the dotted line. Crease this fold well and then unfold it.

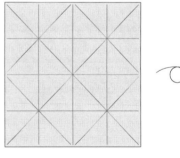

18) Turn the paper over so the white side is facing up again.

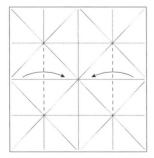

19) Fold both sides towards the center along the dotted lines. These are already existing creases. Only fold along the part with the dotted line.

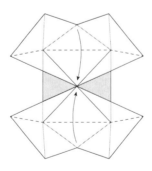

20) You should have a shape that resembles what you see here. Fold both the top and bottom of the model along the dotted lines to the center.

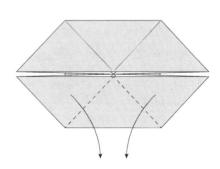

21) Fold the bottom two flaps of paper down along the dotted lines.

Butterfly

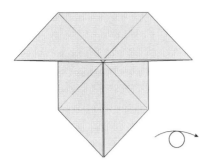

22) Turn the paper over.

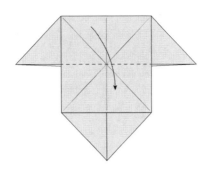

23) Fold the top part of the paper down along the dotted line.

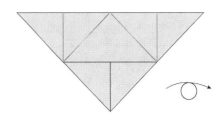

24) Turn the paper over.

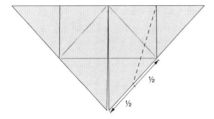

25) Fold the top flap of paper on the right along the dotted line towards the center. The fold goes from the top corner to halfway down the side edge.

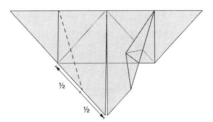

26) Fold the top flap of paper on the left along the dotted line towards the center. The fold goes from the top corner to halfway down the side edge.

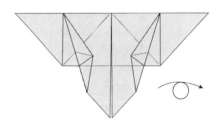

27) Flip the model over.

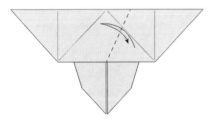

28) Valley Fold along the dotted line in the direction of the arrow in the diagram. Crease this fold well and then unfold it.

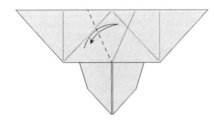

29) Valley Fold along the dotted line on the other side in the direction of the arrow in the diagram. Crease this fold well and then unfold it.

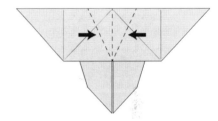

30) Pinch the middle of the model along the existing creases and form a Mountain Fold along the vertical line in the middle.

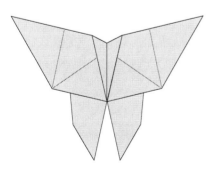

The completed butterfly.

Butterfly

Lotus Flower

Step 19 to 34 of these instructions are used to create guide creases for making the folds in steps 35 to 38. Once you get comfortable with this model you may be able to skip them and jump straight to the folds in steps 35-38.

Techniques Used: Mountain and Valley Folds, Blintz Base and Squash Fold.

Before You Start: Begin with a square sheet of paper rotated 45 degrees with the white side up.

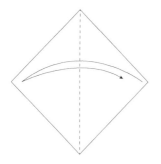

1) Fold the paper in half vertically and then unfold it.

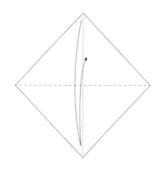

2) Fold the paper in half horizontally and then unfold it.

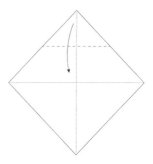

3) Fold the top corner of the paper down to the center.

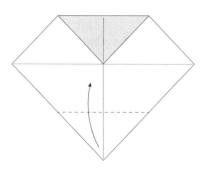

4) Fold the bottom corner of the paper up to the center.

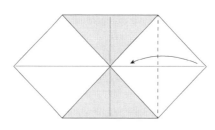

5) Fold the right corner of the paper to the center.

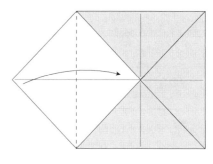

6) Fold the left corner of the paper to the center.

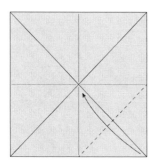

7) Fold the bottom right corner of the paper to the center.

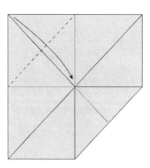

8) Fold the top left corner of the paper to the center.

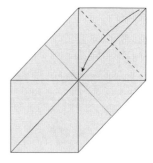

9) Fold the top right corner of the paper to the center.

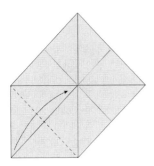

10) Fold the bottom left corner of the paper to the center.

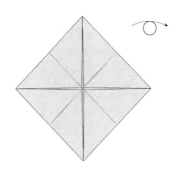

11) Turn the paper over.

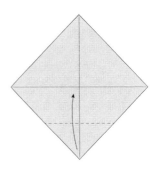

12) Fold the bottom corner up to the center.

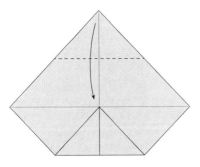

13) Fold the top corner down to the center.

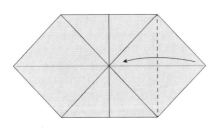

14) Fold the right corner to the center.

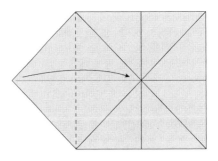

15) Fold the left corner to the center.

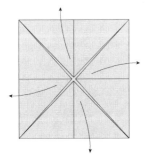

16) Crease all four of these folds well and then unfold them.

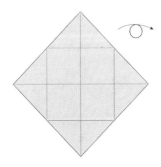

17) Turn the paper over.

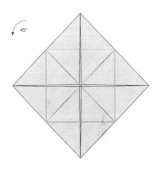

18) Rotate the paper to the left 45 degrees.

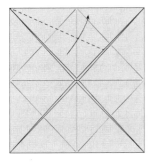

19) Fold the top flap of paper at the top up along the dotted line.

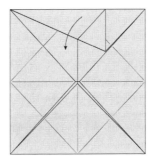

20) Crease this well and then unfold it.

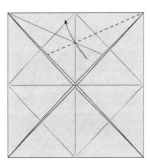

21) Fold the top flap of paper at the top up along the dotted line.

Lotus Flower

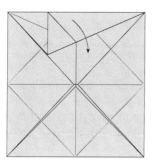

22) Crease this well and then unfold it.

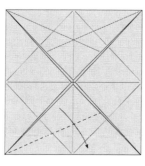

23) Fold the top flap of paper at the bottom down along the dotted line.

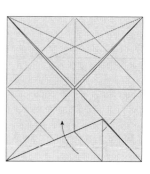

24) Crease this well and then unfold it.

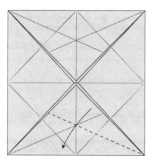

25) Fold the top flap of paper at the bottom down along the dotted line.

26) Crease this well and then unfold it.

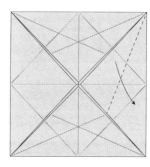

27) Fold the top flap of paper on the right down along the dotted line.

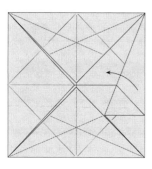

28) Crease this well and then unfold it.

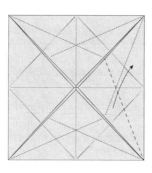

29) Fold the top flap of paper on the right up along the dotted line.

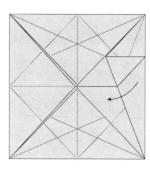

30) Crease this well and then unfold it.

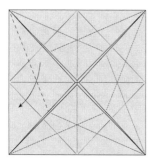

31) Fold the top flap of paper on the left down along the dotted line.

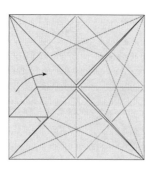

32) Crease this well and then unfold it.

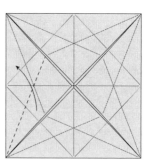

33) Fold the top flap of paper on the left up along the dotted line.

Lotus Flower

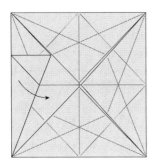

34) Crease this well and then unfold it.

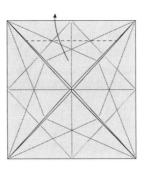

35) Fold the top flap of paper at the top up along the dotted line. Notice that this fold passes through where the existing creases meet in two places.

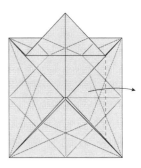

36) Fold the top flap of paper on the right along the dotted line. Notice that this fold passes through where the existing creases meet in two places.

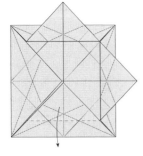

37) Fold the top flap of paper at the bottom along the dotted line. Notice that this fold passes through where the existing creases meet in two places.

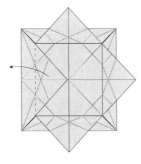

38) Fold the top flap of paper on the right along the dotted line. Notice that this fold passes through where the existing creases meet in two places.

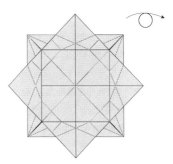

39) Turn the paper over.

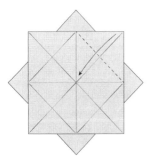

40) Fold the top right corner to the center. You won't be able to make this completely flat yet.

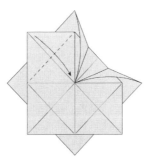

41) Fold the top left corner to the center. You won't be able to make this completely flat yet.

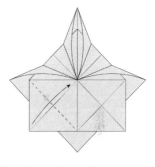

42) Fold the bottom left corner to the center. You won't be able to make this completely flat yet.

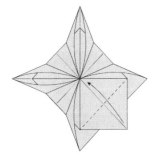

43) Fold the bottom right corner to the center. You won't be able to make this completely flat yet.

44) Squash Fold the flap of paper at the top down along the dotted line.

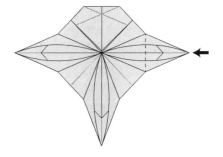

45) Squash fold the flap of paper on the right towards the center along the dotted line.

Lotus Flower

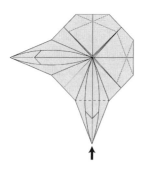

46) Squash fold the flap of paper at the bottom up along the dotted line.

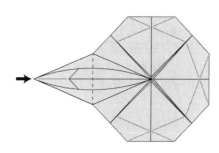

47) Squash fold the flap of paper on the left towards the center along the dotted line.

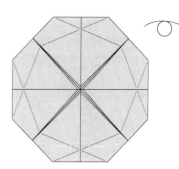

48) Turn the paper over.

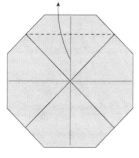

49) Fold the top layer of paper at the top up along the dotted line.

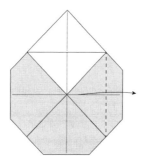

50) Fold the top layer of paper on the right along the dotted line.

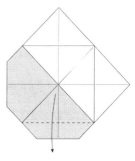

51) Fold the top layer of paper at the bottom down along the dotted line.

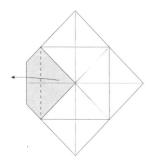

52) Fold the top layer of paper on the left along the dotted line.

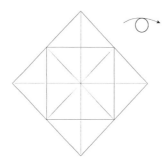

53) Turn the paper over.

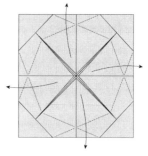

54) Open up each of the four Squash Folds and round them to give the Lotus Flower its shape.

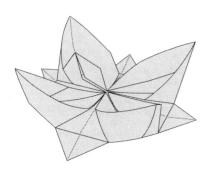

The completed Lotus Flower.

Masu Box

A Masu Box is a traditional wooden box used to measure portions of rice back in Feudal Japan.

Techniques Used: Mountain and Valley Folds and Blintz Base.

Before You Start: Begin with a square sheet of paper with the white side up.

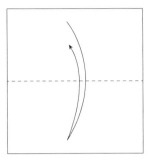

1) Fold the paper in half horizontally along the dotted line and then unfold it.

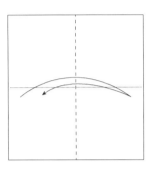

2) Fold the paper in half vertically along the dotted line and then unfold it.

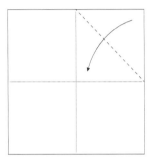

3) Fold the top right corner to the center along the dotted line.

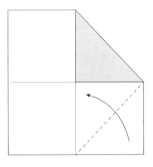

4) Fold the bottom right corner to the center along the dotted line.

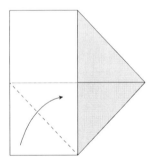

5) Fold the bottom left corner to the center along the dotted line.

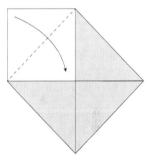

6) Fold the top left corner to the center along the dotted line.

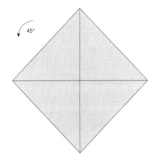

7) Rotate the paper 45 degrees.

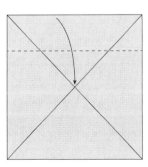

8) Fold the top of the paper to the center along the dotted line.

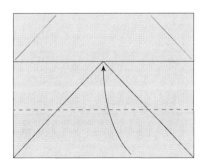

9) Fold the bottom of the paper to the center along the dotted line.

Masu Box

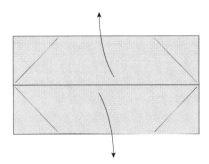

10) Crease both these folds well and then unfold them.

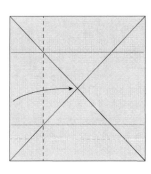

11) Fold the left side of the paper to the center along the dotted line.

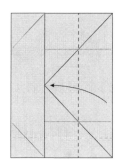

12) Fold the right side of the paper to the center along the dotted line.

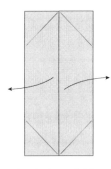

13) Crease both these folds well and then unfold them.

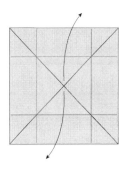

14) Unfold the top and bottom triangle shaped flaps of paper.

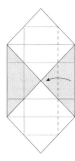

15) Fold the right side of the model towards the center along the dotted line.

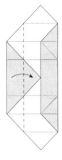

16) Fold the left side of the model towards the center along the dotted line.

17) Open up the paper along the dotted lines. These are already existing creases.

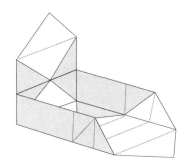

18) You should end up with a shape that looks like this.

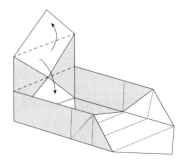

19) Fold the side down. Fold the top triangle of paper up and tuck it in place with the other triangle flaps of paper at the bottom of the inside of the box.

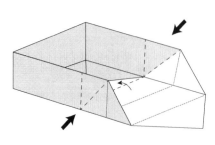

20) Fold the other side of the box along the dotted lines just like in step 17. These are also already existing creases.

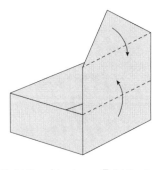

21) Fold the side down. Fold the top triangle of paper up and tuck it in place with the other triangle flaps of paper at the bottom of the inside of the box.

Masu Box

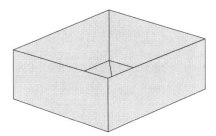

The completed Masu Box.

Masu Box Lid

The instructions for the Masu Box Lid are almost exactly the same as the Masu Box itself. A couple of the steps are a little bit different to give the lid a slightly larger size so it fits over the box.

Techniques Used: Mountain and Valley Folds and Blintz Base.

Before You Start: Begin with a square sheet of paper with the white side up.

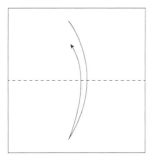

1) Fold the paper in half horizontally along the dotted line and then unfold it.

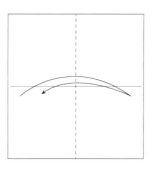

2) Fold the paper in half vertically along the dotted line and then unfold it.

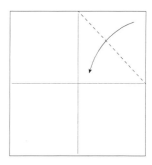

3) Fold the top right corner to the center along the dotted line.

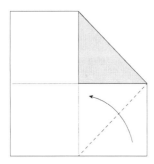

4) Fold the bottom right corner to the center along the dotted line.

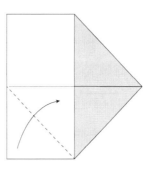

5) Fold the bottom left corner to the center along the dotted line.

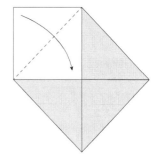

6) Fold the top left corner to the center along the dotted line.

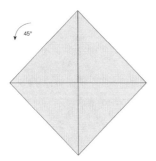

7) Rotate the paper 45 degrees.

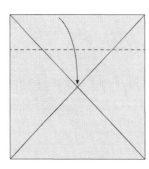

8) Fold the top of the paper to the center along the dotted line. Leave a tiny gap between the edge of the paper and the center of the model.

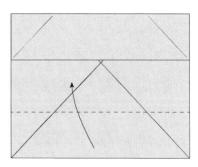

9) Fold the bottom of the paper to the center along the dotted line. Leave a tiny gap between the edge of the paper and the center of the model.

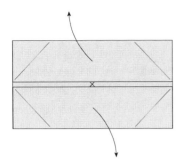

10) Crease both these folds well and then unfold them.

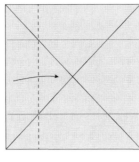

11) Fold the left side of the paper to the center along the dotted line. Leave a tiny gap between the edge of the paper and the center of the model.

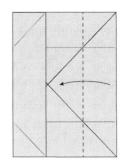

12) Fold the right side of the paper to the center along the dotted line. Leave a tiny gap between the edge of the paper and the center of the model.

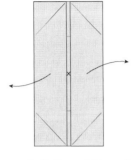

13) Crease both these folds well and then unfold them.

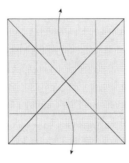

14) Unfold the top and bottom triangle shaped flaps of paper.

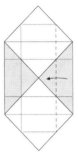

15) Fold the right side of the model towards the center along the dotted line.

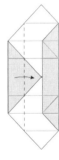

16) Fold the left side of the model towards the center along the dotted line.

17) Open up the paper along the dotted lines. These are already existing creases.

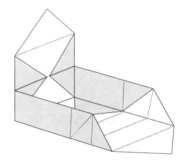

18) You should end up with a shape that looks like this.

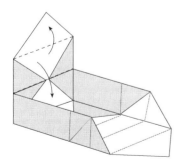

19) Fold the side down. Fold the top triangle of paper up and tuck it in place with the other triangle flaps of paper at the bottom of the inside of the box.

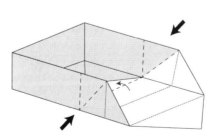

20) Fold the other side of the box along the dotted lines just like in step 17. These are also already existing creases.

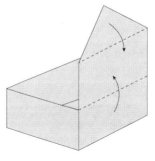

21) Fold the side down. Fold the top triangle of paper up and tuck it in place with the other triangle flaps of paper at the bottom of the inside of the box.

Masu Box Lid

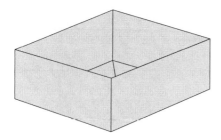

The completed Masu Box Lid.

Challenging

Masu Box Divider

Designed by: Paolo Bascetta

This model uses a series of almost random looking folds to create guides that are used for later creases.

Techniques Used: Mountain and Valley Folds and Water Bomb Base.

Before You Start: Begin with a square sheet of paper with the white side up.

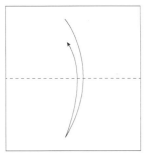

1) Fold the paper in half horizontally along the dotted line. Crease it well and then unfold it.

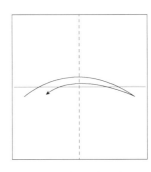

2) Fold the paper in half vertically along the dotted line. Crease it well and then unfold it.

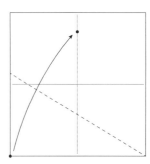

3) Fold the paper up along the dotted line bringing the corner of the paper to the crease you made in step 2.

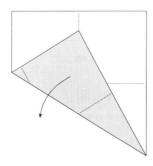

4) Crease only a little bit along the left of side of the fold and then unfold it. You will use this crease as a guide.

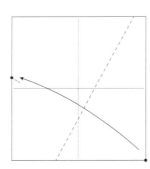

5) Fold the paper along the dotted line bringing the bottom right corner to the end of the crease you made in step 4.

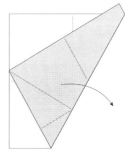

6) Crease only a little bit along the bottom of the fold and then unfold it. You will also use this crease as a guide.

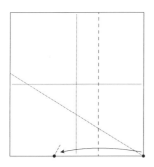

7) Fold the right side of the paper along the dotted line bringing the bottom right corner to the end of the crease you made in step 6.

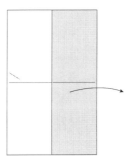

8) Crease this well and then unfold it.

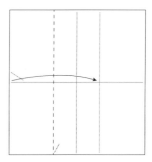

9) Fold the left side of the paper along the dotted line bringing the left edge of the paper to the crease you made in step 8.

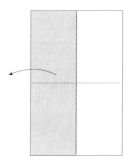

10) Crease this well and then unfold it.

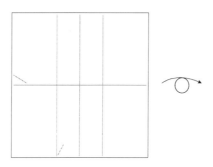

11) You now have two creases that are exactly 1/3 of the distance from the center of the paper to the edge of the paper. Turn the paper over.

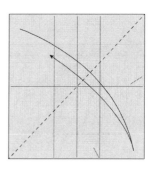

12) Fold the paper in half diagonally. Crease this well and then unfold it.

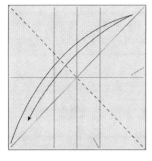

13) Fold the paper in half diagonally the other way. Crease this well and then unfold it.

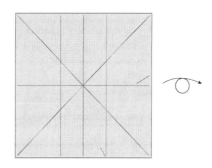

14) Turn the paper over.

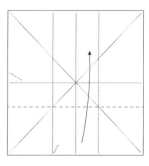

15) Fold the paper up along the dotted line. This fold goes through the points where the two vertical creases intersect the two diagonal creases.

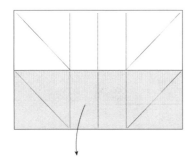

16) Crease this well and then unfold it.

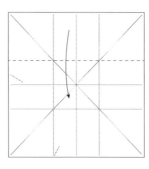

17) Fold the top of the paper down along the dotted line bringing the edge of the paper to the crease you just made.

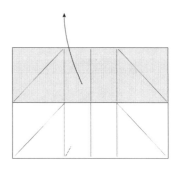

18) Crease this well and then unfold it.

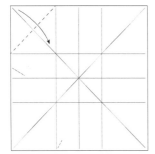

19) The paper should now be divided into 9 equally sized squares. Fold the top left corner of the paper towards the center along the dotted line.

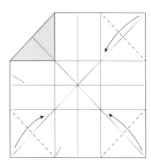

20) Fold the remaining corners of the paper towards the center along the dotted lines.

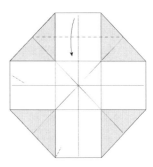

21) Fold the top part of the paper down towards the center along the dotted line bringing the edge of the paper to the horizontal crease.

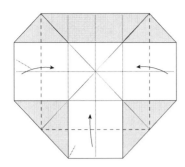

22) Fold the other three edges of the paper towards the center along the dotted lines.

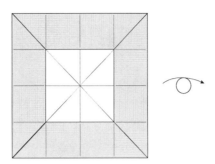

23) Turn the paper over.

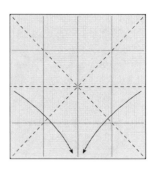

24) Fold a Water Bomb Base using the existing creases.

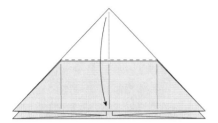

25) Fold the top triangle of paper down.

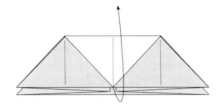

26) Open up the model bringing the top layer of paper up and out.

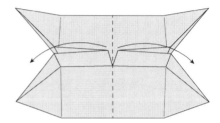

27) Make a mountain fold along the dotted line bringing the paper down towards both sides.

28) Push everything flat into a shape that looks like what you see here.

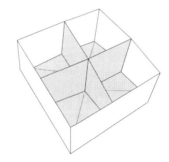

The completed Masu Box Divider.

Masu Box Divider

Sitting Crane

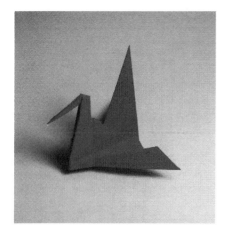

This is a somewhat fancier and more complex version of the traditional origami crane.

Techniques Used: Mountain and Valley Folds, Inside Reverse Fold, Square Base, Petal Fold and Bird Base.

Before You Start: Begin with a square sheet of paper with the white side facing up.

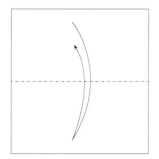

1) Fold the paper in half horizontally. Crease it well and then unfold.

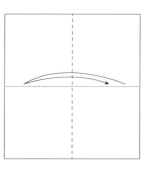

2) Fold the paper in half vertically. Crease it well and then unfold it.

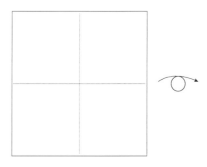

3) Turn the paper over.

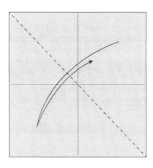

4) Fold the paper in half diagonally. Crease it well and then unfold it.

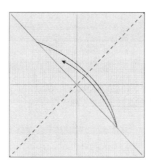

5) Fold the paper in half diagonally the other way. Crease it well and then unfold it.

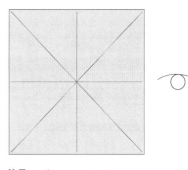

6) Turn the paper over.

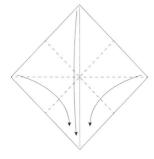

7) Fold the paper along the existing creases bringing the left, right and top corners to the bottom into a Square base.

8) Fold the flap of paper on the right to the center along the dotted line.

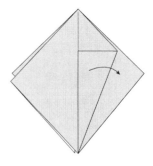

9) Crease this well and then unfold it.

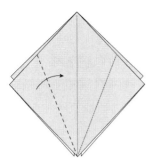

10) Fold the flap of paper on the left to the center along the dotted line.

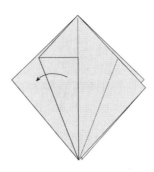

11) Crease this well and then unfold it.

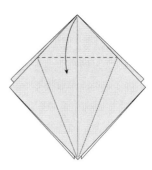

12) Fold the top of the model down along the dotted line. The ends of this dotted line will line up with the previous two creases you made.

13) Crease this well and then unfold it.

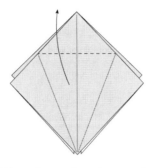

14) Lift up the top flap of paper along the horizontal crease you just made.

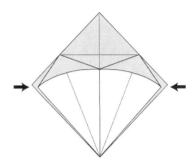

15) As you lift the paper up fold in both sides along the existing creases making a Petal Fold.

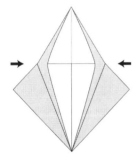

16) Push everything flat along the existing creases.

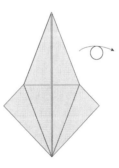

17) Turn the paper over.

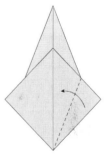

18) Fold the flap of paper on the right to the center along the dotted line.

19) Crease this well and then unfold it.

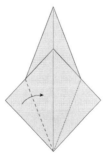

20) Fold the flap of paper on the left to the center along the dotted line.

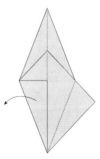

21) Crease this well and then unfold it.

Sitting Crane

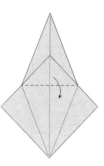

22) Fold the top of the model down along the dotted line. The ends of this dotted line will line up with the previous two creases you made.

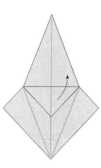

23) Crease this well and then unfold it.

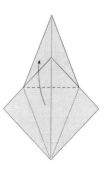

24) Lift up the top flap of paper along the horizontal crease you just made.

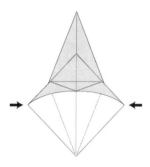

25) As you lift the paper up fold in both sides along the existing creases making a Petal Fold.

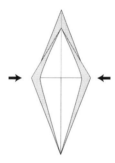

26) Push everything flat along the existing creases.

27) Fold the top right flap of paper over to the left along the dotted line.

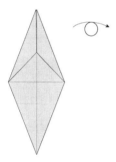

28) Turn the paper over.

29) Fold the top flap on the right over to the left along the dotted line.

30) Fold the top flap of paper up along the dotted line.

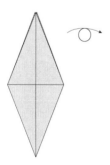

31) Turn the paper over.

32) Fold the top flap of paper up along the dotted line.

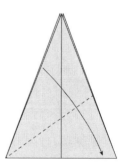

33) Fold the top flap of paper down along the dotted line bringing the left edge to the bottom edge.

Sitting Crane

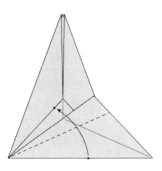

34) Fold the top flap of paper up along the dotted line bringing the marked edge to the other marked edge.

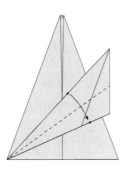

35) Fold the top flap of paper down along the dotted line bringing the marked edge to the other marked edge.

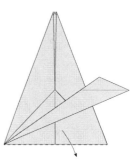

36) Fold the top flap of paper back down along the dotted line.

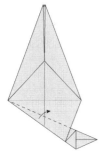

37) Fold the paper up along the dotted line.

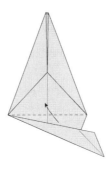

38) Fold the top flap of paper back up along the dotted line.

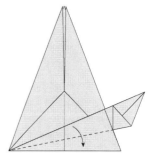

39) Fold the paper down along the dotted line bringing the top edge to the bottom edge.

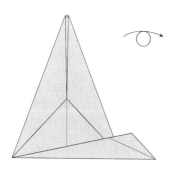

40) Turn the paper over.

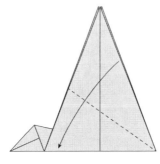

41) Fold the top flap of paper down along the dotted line bringing the right edge to the bottom edge.

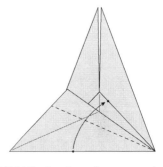

42) Fold the top flap of paper up along the dotted line bringing the marked edge to the other marked edge.

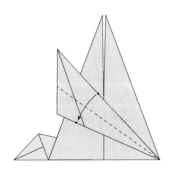

43) Fold the top flap of paper down along the dotted line bringing the marked edge to the other marked edge.

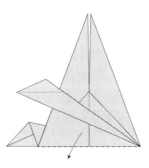

44) Fold the top flap of paper back down along the dotted line.

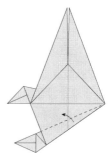

45) Fold the paper up along the dotted line.

Sitting Crane

46) Fold the top flap of paper back up along the dotted line.

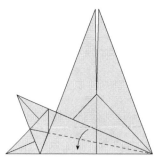

47) Fold the paper down along the dotted line bringing the top edge to the bottom edge.

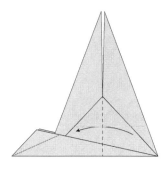

48) Fold the top flap of paper on the right over to the left along the dotted line.

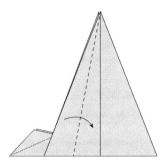

49) Fold this flap of paper along the dotted line bringing the left edge to the center.

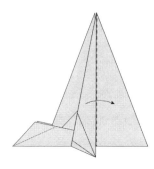

50) Fold this flap of paper back over to the right.

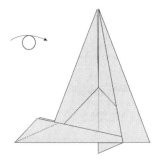

51) Turn the paper over.

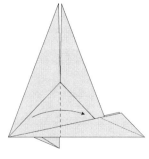

52) Fold the top flap of paper on the left over to the right along the dotted line.

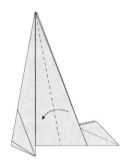

53) Fold this flap of paper along the dotted line bringing the right edge to the center.

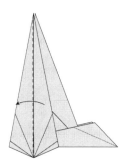

54) Fold this flap of paper back over to the left.

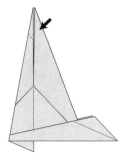

55) Make an Inside Reverse Fold along the dotted line to form the crane's head.

56) Pull the tail section of paper down and to the right. Push everything flat along the new creases.

57) Open up both wings on both sides.

Sitting Crane

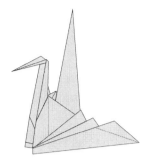

The completed Sitting Crane.

Star Box

If you use two sided paper the inside and outside parts of this box will be different colors.

Techniques Used: Mountain and Valley Folds, Square Base and Squash Fold.

Before You Start: Begin with a square sheet of paper with the colored side facing up.

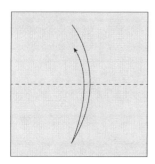

1) Fold the paper in half horizontally. Crease it well and then unfold.

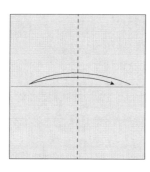

2) Fold the paper in half vertically. Crease it well and then unfold it.

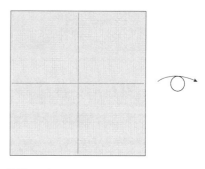

3) Turn the paper over.

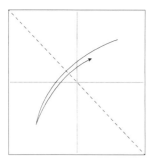

4) Fold the paper in half diagonally. Crease it well and then unfold it.

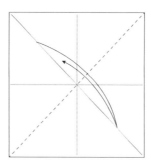

5) Fold the paper in half diagonally the other way. Crease it well and then unfold it.

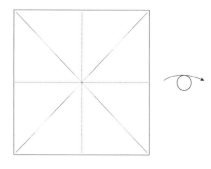

6) Turn the paper over.

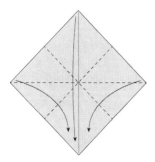

7) Fold the paper along the existing creases bringing the left, right and top corners to the bottom into a Square base.

8) Rotate the paper 180 degrees.

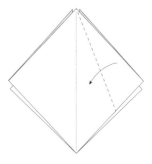

9) Fold the top right flap of paper to the center along the dotted line.

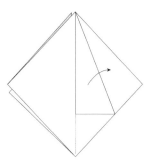

10) Crease this well and then unfold it.

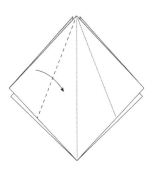

11) Fold the top left flap of paper to the center along the dotted line.

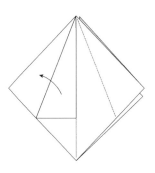

12) Crease this well and then unfold it.

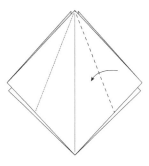

13) Bring the top right flap of paper up along the existing crease.

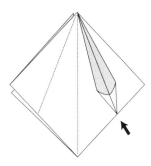

14) Squash Fold this flap of paper down.

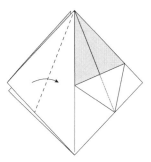

15) Bring the top left flap of paper up along the existing crease.

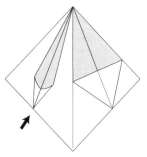

16) Squash Fold this flap of paper down.

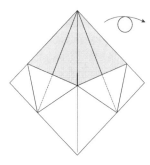

17) Turn the paper over.

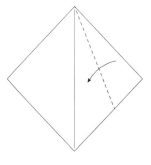

18) Fold the top right flap of paper to the center along the dotted line.

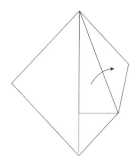

19) Crease this well and then unfold it.

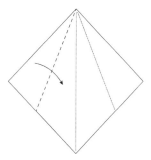

20) Fold the top left flap of paper to the center along the dotted line.

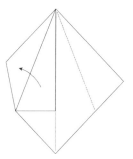

21) Crease this well and then unfold it.

Star Box

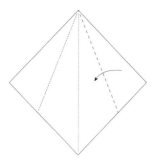

22) Bring the top right flap of paper up along the existing crease.

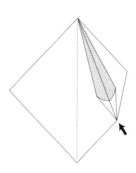

23) Squash Fold this flap of paper down.

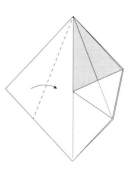

24) Bring the top left flap of paper up along the existing crease.

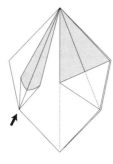

25) Squash Fold this flap of paper down.

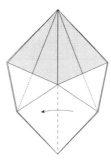

26) Fold the right flap of paper over to the left along the dotted line.

27) Fold the right side of the paper to the center along the dotted line.

28) Fold the top left flap of paper to the center along the dotted line.

29) Fold the top left flap of paper over to the right along the dotted line.

30) Fold the top left flap of paper over to the right along the dotted line.

31) Fold the top right flap of paper to the center along the dotted line.

32) Fold the left side of the paper to the center along the dotted line.

33) Fold the top right flap of paper over to the left along the dotted line.

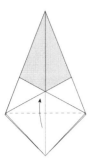

34) Fold the bottom triangle of paper up along the dotted line.

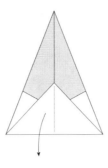

35) Crease this well and then unfold it.

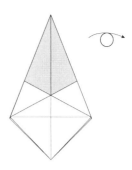

36) Turn the paper over.

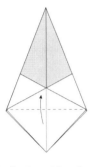

37) Fold the bottom triangle of paper up along the dotted line. This is the opposite direction of the previous fold made on the other side.

38) Crease this well and then unfold it.

39) Fold the top flap of paper down along the dotted line.

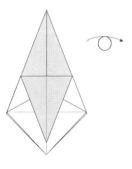

40) Turn the paper over.

41) Fold the top flap of paper down along the dotted line.

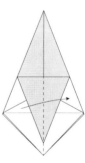

42) Fold the top left flap of paper over to the right along the dotted line.

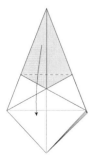

43) Fold the top flap of paper down along the dotted line.

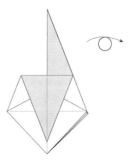

44) Turn the paper over.

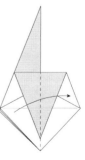

45) Fold the top left flap of paper over to the right along the dotted line.

Star Box

46) Fold the top flap of paper down along the dotted line.

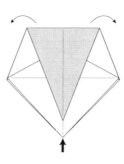

47) Open up the top of the model while pushing in the bottom.

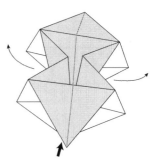

48) Continue opening the top of the model and pull out the two triangle shaped flaps of paper on each side. Continue pushing in the bottom until the base of the box forms along the existing creases.

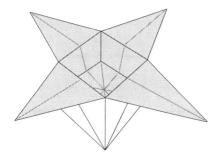

The completed Star Box.

Owl

There are two variations of this origami owl, one with the wings stretched out and one with them folded in.

Techniques Used: Mountain and Valley Folds, Pleat, Square Base, Petal Fold, Swivel Fold, Bird Base and Scissors.

Before You Start: Begin with a square sheet of paper with the white side facing up.

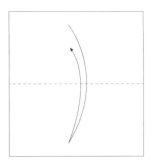

1) Fold the paper in half horizontally. Crease it well and then unfold.

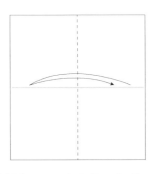

2) Fold the paper in half vertically. Crease it well and then unfold it.

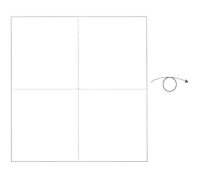

3) Turn the paper over.

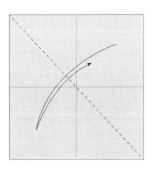

4) Fold the paper in half diagonally. Crease it well and then unfold it.

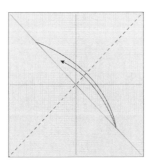

5) Fold the paper in half diagonally the other way. Crease it well and then unfold it.

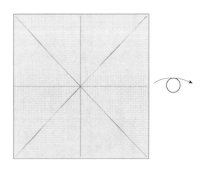

6) Turn the paper over.

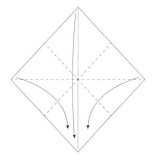

7) Fold the paper along the existing creases bringing the left, right and top corners to the bottom into a Square base.

8) Fold the flap of paper on the right to the center along the dotted line.

9) Crease this well and then unfold it.

Owl   Page 269

10) Fold the flap of paper on the left to the center along the dotted line.

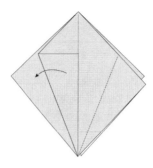

11) Crease this well and then unfold it.

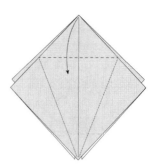

12) Fold the top of the model down along the dotted line. The ends of this dotted line will line up with the previous two creases you made.

13) Crease this well and then unfold it.

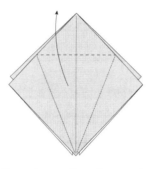

14) Lift up the top flap of paper along the horizontal crease you just made.

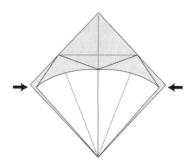

15) As you lift the paper up fold in both sides along the existing creases making a Petal Fold.

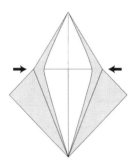

16) Push everything flat along the existing creases.

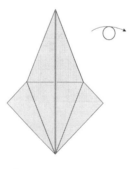

17) Turn the paper over.

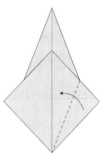

18) Fold the flap of paper on the right to the center along the dotted line.

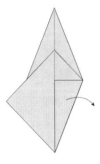

19) Crease this well and then unfold it.

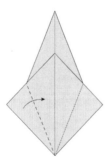

20) Fold the flap of paper on the left to the center along the dotted line.

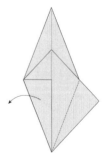

21) Crease this well and then unfold it.

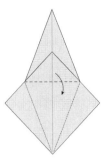 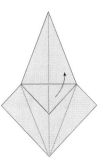 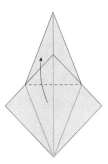

22) Fold the top of the model down along the dotted line. The ends of this dotted line will line up with the previous two creases you made.

23) Crease this well and then unfold it.

24) Lift up the top flap of paper along the horizontal crease you just made.

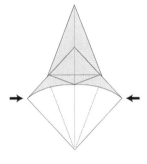 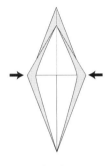 

25) As you lift the paper up fold in both sides along the existing creases making a Petal Fold.

26) Push everything flat along the existing creases.

27) Fold the top flap of paper down along the dotted line.

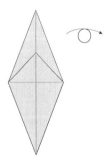  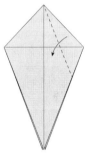

28) Turn the paper over.

29) Fold the top flap of paper down along the dotted line.

30) Fold the top flap of paper on the right to the center along the dotted line.

 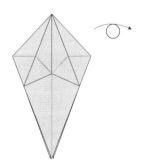 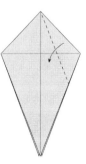

31) Fold the top flap of paper on the left to the center along the dotted line.

32) Turn the paper over.

33) Fold the top flap of paper on the right to the center along the dotted line.

34) Fold the top flap of paper on the left to the center along the dotted line.

35) Fold the top right flap of paper over to the left.

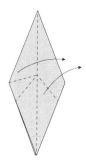

36) Lift the top flap of paper up and to the right making creases along the dotted lines.

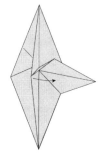

37) As you make this fold bring the top flap of paper on the left side back over to the right and push everything flat.

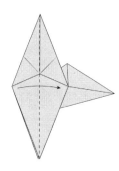

38) Fold the top left flap of paper over to the right.

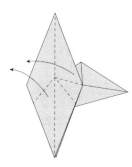

39) Lift the top flap of paper up and to the left making creases along the dotted lines.

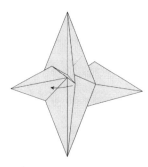

40) As you make this fold bring the top flap of paper on the right side back over to the left and push everything flat.

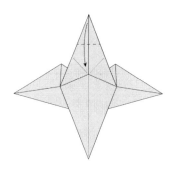

41) Fold the top part of the paper down along the dotted line.

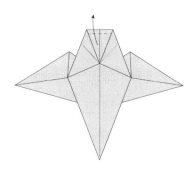

42) Fold it back up along the dotted line.

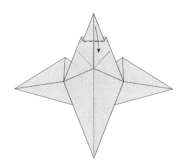

43) Fold the top part of the paper down along the dotted line.

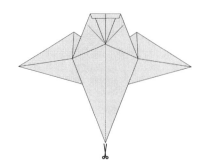

44) Carefully cut only the top flap of paper down the middle stopping a short distance from the bottom tip.

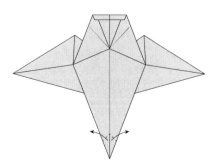

45) Fold both tips of paper at the bottom out to the sides along the dotted lines.

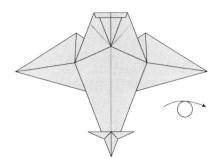

46) Turn the paper over.

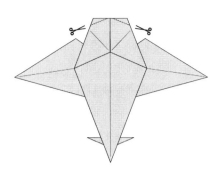

47) Carefully make two cuts through the top flap of paper along the dotted lines.

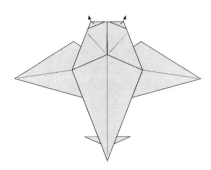

48) Fold both of these tips of paper up along the existing crease.

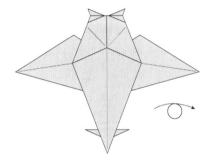

49) Turn the paper over.

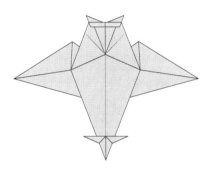

The completed Owl. If you'd like to make a variation with the wings tucked in see the next diagram.

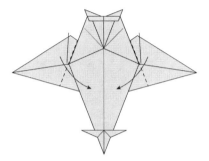

50) Fold both wings down and to the center along the dotted line.

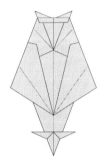

The completed Owl.

Owl

Page 273

Dragon

This dragon looks really great and is actually easier to fold than you might think.

Techniques Used: Mountain and Valley Folds, Outside Reverse Fold, Crimp, Square Base, Petal Fold and Bird Base.

Before You Start: Begin with a square sheet of paper with the white side facing up.

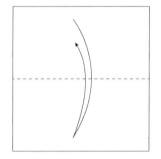

1) Fold the paper in half horizontally. Crease it well and then unfold.

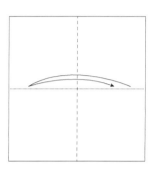

2) Fold the paper in half vertically. Crease it well and then unfold it.

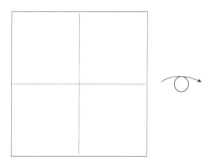

3) Turn the paper over.

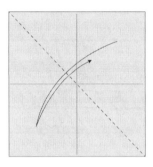

4) Fold the paper in half diagonally. Crease it well and then unfold it.

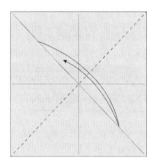

5) Fold the paper in half diagonally the other way. Crease it well and then unfold it.

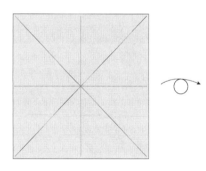

6) Turn the paper over.

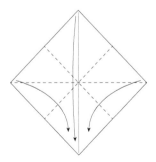

7) Fold the paper along the existing creases bringing the left, right and top corners to the bottom into a Square base.

8) Fold the flap of paper on the right to the center along the dotted line.

9) Crease this well and then unfold it.

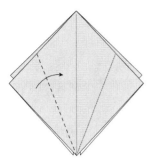

10) Fold the flap of paper on the left to the center along the dotted line.

11) Crease this well and then unfold it.

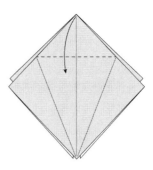

12) Fold the top of the model down along the dotted line. The ends of this dotted line will line up with the previous two creases you made.

13) Crease this well and then unfold it.

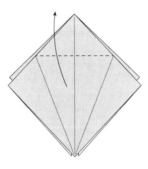

14) Lift up the top flap of paper along the horizontal crease you just made.

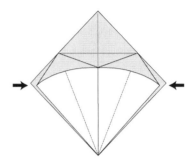

15) As you lift the paper up fold in both sides along the existing creases making a Petal Fold.

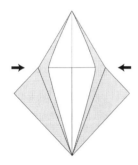

16) Push everything flat along the existing creases.

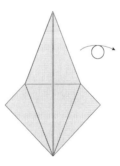

17) Turn the paper over.

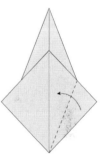

18) Fold the flap of paper on the right to the center along the dotted line.

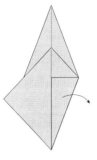

19) Crease this well and then unfold it.

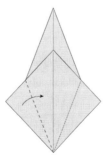

20) Fold the flap of paper on the left to the center along the dotted line.

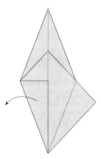

21) Crease this well and then unfold it.

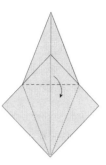

22) Fold the top of the model down along the dotted line. The ends of this dotted line will line up with the previous two creases you made.

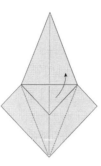

23) Crease this well and then unfold it.

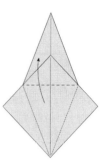

24) Lift up the top flap of paper along the horizontal crease you just made.

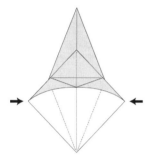

25) As you lift the paper up fold in both sides along the existing creases making a Petal Fold.

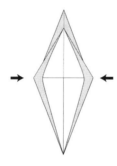

26) Push everything flat along the existing creases.

27) Fold the top right section of paper towards the center along the dotted line.

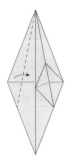

28) Fold the top left section of paper towards the center along the dotted line.

29) Fold the top right flap of paper over to the left along the dotted line in the center.

30) Turn the paper over.

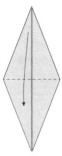

31) Fold the top flap of paper down along the dotted line.

32) Fold the right flap of paper to the left along the dotted line.

33) Fold the top flap of paper up along the dotted line.

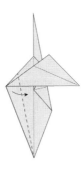

34) Fold the top flap of paper down along the dotted line.

35) Fold the left of the paper towards the center along the dotted line.

36) Fold the triangle shaped flap of paper up along the dotted line.

37) Fold this flap of paper down along the dotted line.

38) Turn the paper over.

39) Fold the top flap of paper up along the dotted line.

40) Fold this flap of paper down along the dotted line.

41) Fold the paper on the right side towards the center along the dotted line.

42) Fold the triangle shaped flap of paper up along the dotted line.

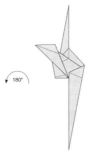

43) Fold this flap of paper down along the dotted line.

44) Rotate the model 180 degrees.

45) Fold the top section of paper down along the dotted line.

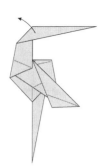

46) Crease this well and then unfold it.

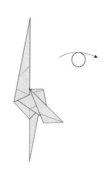

47) Turn the paper over.

48) Fold the top section of paper down along the dotted line. This is the opposite direction of the previous crease.

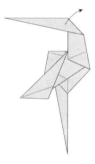

49) Crease this well and then unfold it.

50) Make an Outside Reverse Fold along the existing creases.

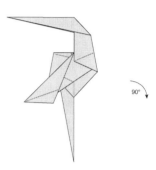

51) Rotate the model 90 degrees to the right.

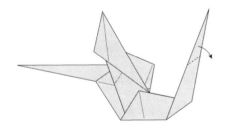

52) Fold the paper down along the dotted line.

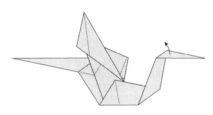

53) Crease this well and then unfold it.

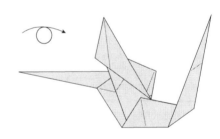

54) Turn the paper over.

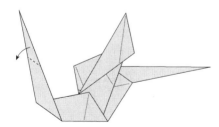

55) Fold the paper down along the dotted line. This is the opposite direction of the fold on the other side.

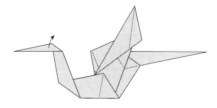

56) Crease this well and then unfold it.

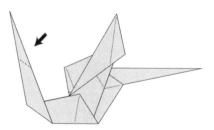

57) Make an Outside Reverse Fold along the existing creases.

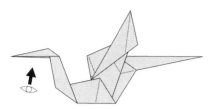 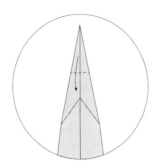 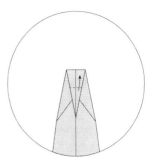

58) The next few steps take place underneath the head. Look underneath the model where the arrow indicates and open the paper up a little bit.

59) Fold the tip of the paper down along the dotted line.

60) Fold the tip of the paper up along the dotted line.

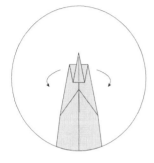 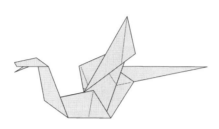

61) Close the head back up.

The completed dragon.

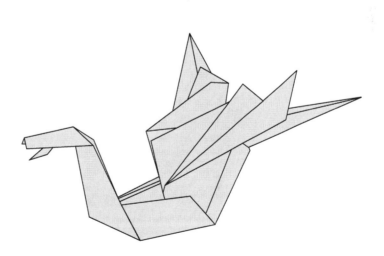

Dragon

Iris

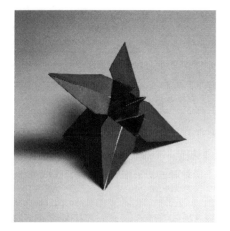

This Iris flower begins with a Frog Base. If you're already familiar with this base you can skip ahead to step 52.

Techniques Used: Mountain and Valley Folds, Square Base, Squash Fold, Petal Fold and Frog base.

Before You Start: Begin with a square sheet of paper with the white side facing up.

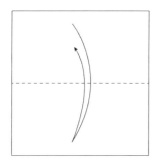

1) Fold the paper in half horizontally. Crease it well and then unfold.

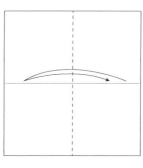

2) Fold the paper in half vertically. Crease it well and then unfold it.

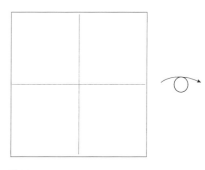

3) Turn the paper over.

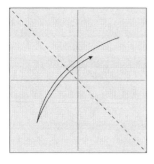

4) Fold the paper in half diagonally. Crease it well and then unfold it.

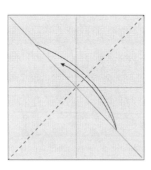

5) Fold the paper in half diagonally the other way. Crease it well and then unfold it.

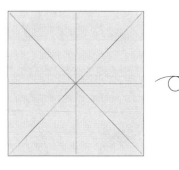

6) Turn the paper over.

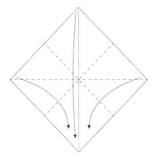

7) Fold the paper along the existing creases bringing the left, right and top corners to the bottom into a Square base.

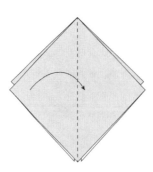

8) Bring the top left flap of paper up.

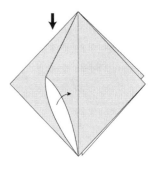

9) Make a Squash Fold on this flap.

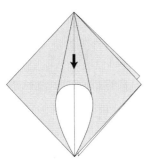

10) Complete the Squash Fold and push everything flat.

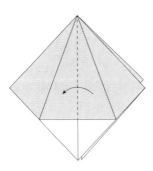

11) Fold the top right flap of paper over to the left.

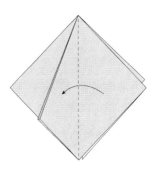

12) Bring the top right flap of paper up.

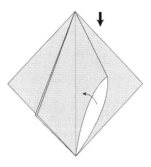

13) Make a Squash Fold on this flap.

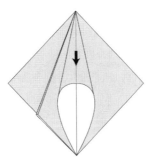

14) Complete the Squash Fold and push everything flat.

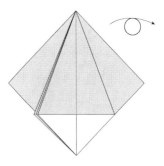

15) Turn the paper over.

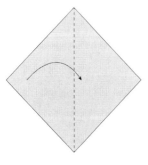

16) Bring the left flap of paper up.

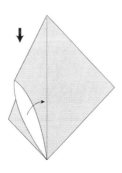

17) Make a Squash Fold on this flap.

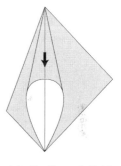

18) Complete the Squash Fold and push everything flat.

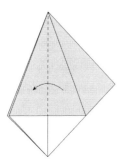

19) Fold the top right flap of paper over to the left.

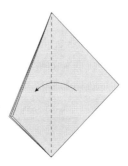

20) Bring the right flap of paper up.

21) Make a Squash Fold on this flap.

Iris

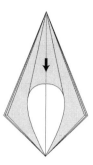

22) Complete the Squash Fold and push everything flat.

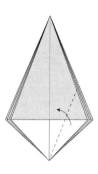

23) Fold the top right flap of paper to the center along the dotted line.

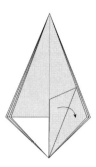

24) Crease this well and then unfold it.

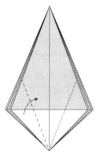

25) Fold the to left flap of paper to the center along the dotted line.

26) Crease this well and then unfold it.

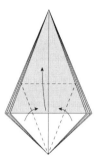

27) Make a Petal Fold using the existing creases.

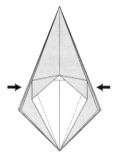

28) Complete the Petal Fold and push everything flat.

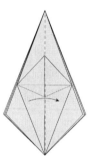

29) Fold the top left flap of paper over to the right.

30) Fold the top left flap of paper over to the right.

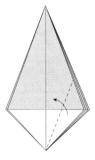

31) Fold the top right flap of paper to the center along the dotted line.

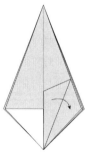

32) Crease this well and then unfold it.

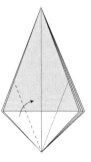

33) Fold the top left flap of paper to the center along the dotted line.

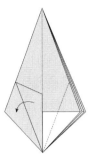

34) Crease this well and then unfold it.

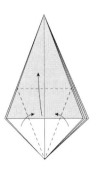

35) Make a Petal Fold using the existing creases.

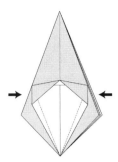

36) Complete the Petal Fold and push everything flat.

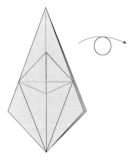

37) Turn the paper over.

38) Fold the top right flap of paper to the center along the dotted line.

39) Crease this well and then unfold it.

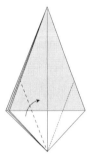

40) Fold the top left flap of paper to the center along the dotted line.

41) Crease this well and then unfold it.

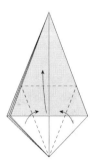

42) Make a Petal Fold using the existing creases.

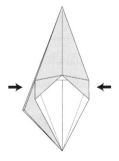

43) Complete the Petal Fold and push everything flat.

44) Fold the top left flap of paper to the right along the dotted line.

45) Fold the top left flap of paper to the right along the dotted line.

Iris

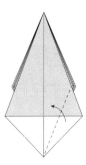

46) Fold the top right flap of paper to the center along the dotted line.

47) Crease this well and then unfold it.

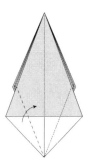

48) Fold the top left flap of paper to the center along the dotted line.

49) Crease this well and then unfold it.

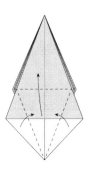

50) Make a Petal Fold using the existing creases.

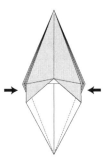

51) Complete the Petal Fold and push everything flat.

52) Fold the top triangle down along the dotted line.

53) Fold the top left flap of paper over to the right along the dotted line.

54) Fold the top left flap of paper over to the right along the dotted line.

55) Fold the top triangle down along the dotted line.

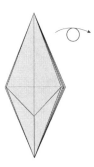

56) Turn the paper over.

57) Fold the top triangle down along the dotted line.

58) Fold the top left flap of paper over to the right along the dotted line.

59) Fold the top left flap of paper over to the right along the dotted line.

60) Fold the top triangle down along the dotted line.

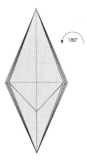

61) Rotate the paper 180 degrees.

62) Fold the top left flap of paper over to the right along the dotted line.

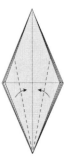

63) Fold the top right and left flaps of paper to the center along the dotted lines.

64) Fold the top left flap of paper over to the right along the dotted line.

65) Fold the top left flap of paper over to the right along the dotted line.

66) Fold the top right and left flaps of paper to the center along the dotted lines.

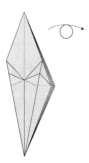

67) Turn the paper over.

68) Fold the top left flap of paper over to the right along the dotted line.

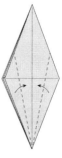

69) Fold the top right and left flaps of paper to the center along the dotted lines.

Iris

70) Fold the top left flap of paper over to the right along the dotted line.

71) Fold the top left flap of paper over to the right along the dotted line.

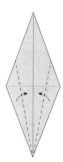

72) Fold the top right and left flaps of paper to the center along the dotted lines.

73) Fold the top flap of paper down along the dotted line.

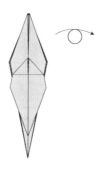

74) Turn the paper over.

75) Fold the top flap of paper down along the dotted line.

76) Fold the top left flap of paper over to the right along the dotted line.

77) Fold the top left flap of paper over to the right along the dotted line.

78) Fold the top flap of paper down along the dotted line.

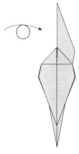

79) Turn the paper over.

80) Fold the top left flap of paper over to the right along the dotted line.

81) Fold the top left flap of paper over to the right along the dotted line.

 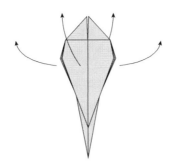 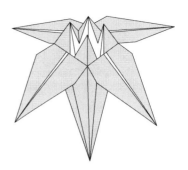

82) Fold the top flap of paper down along the dotted line.

83) Open up the model and pull the top flaps of paper from the front, back and two sides up.

The completed Iris.

Difficult

Dragonfly

This dragonfly has a couple of tricky folds on the wings. To help, try looking at the diagrams in the next steps to see how the paper needs to fold.

Techniques Used: Mountain and Valley Folds, Outside Reverse Fold, Square Base, Petal Fold, Swivel Fold, Bird Base and Scissors.

Before You Start: Begin with a square sheet of paper with the white side facing up.

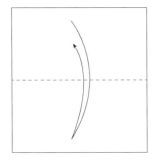

1) Fold the paper in half horizontally. Crease it well and then unfold.

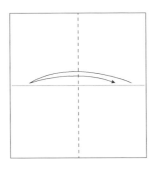

2) Fold the paper in half vertically. Crease it well and then unfold it.

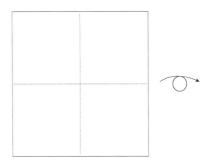

3) Turn the paper over.

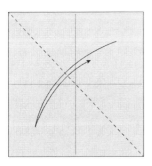

4) Fold the paper in half diagonally. Crease it well and then unfold it.

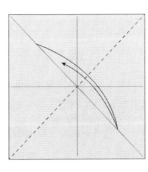

5) Fold the paper in half diagonally the other way. Crease it well and then unfold it.

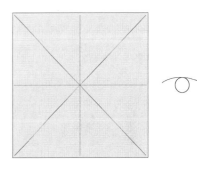

6) Turn the paper over.

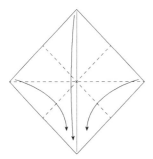

7) Fold the paper along the existing creases bringing the left, right and top corners to the bottom into a Square base.

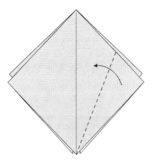

8) Fold the flap of paper on the right to the center along the dotted line.

9) Crease this well and then unfold it.

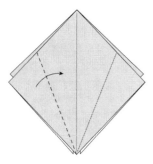

10) Fold the flap of paper on the left to the center along the dotted line.

11) Crease this well and then unfold it.

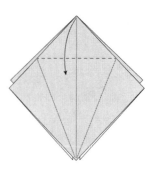

12) Fold the top of the model down along the dotted line. The ends of this dotted line will line up with the previous two creases you made.

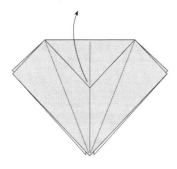

13) Crease this well and then unfold it.

14) Lift up the top flap of paper along the horizontal crease you just made.

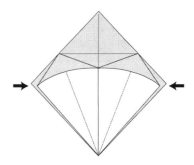

15) As you lift the paper up fold in both sides along the existing creases making a Petal Fold.

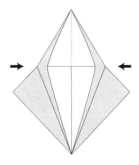

16) Push everything flat along the existing creases.

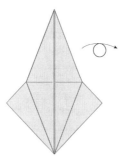

17) Turn the paper over.

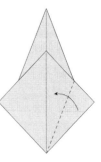

18) Fold the flap of paper on the right to the center along the dotted line.

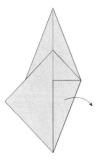

19) Crease this well and then unfold it.

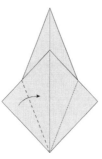

20) Fold the flap of paper on the left to the center along the dotted line.

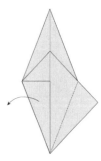

21) Crease this well and then unfold it.

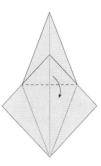
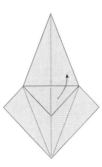
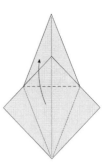

22) Fold the top of the model down along the dotted line. The ends of this dotted line will line up with the previous two creases you made.

23) Crease this well and then unfold it.

24) Lift up the top flap of paper along the horizontal crease you just made.

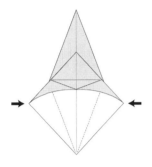
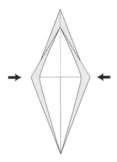
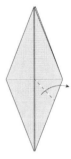

25) As you lift the paper up fold in both sides along the existing creases making a Petal Fold.

26) Push everything flat along the existing creases.

27) Fold the flap of paper on the right along the dotted line.

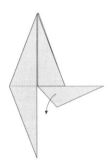
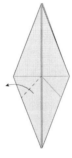
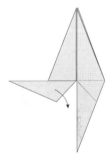

28) Crease this well and then unfold it.

29) Fold the flap of paper on the left along the dotted line.

30) Crease this well and then unfold it.

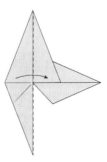

31) Fold the top flap of paper on the right over to the left along the dotted line.

32) Fold the top flap of paper up and to the right. Part of this fold is using an existing crease.

33) Fold the top flap of paper on the left over to the right along the dotted line.

Dragonfly

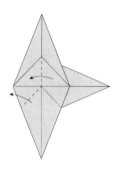

34) Fold the top flap of paper up and to the right. Part of this fold is using an existing crease.

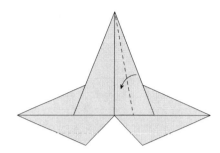

35) Fold the top right flap of paper towards the center along the dotted line. As you do, prepare to make a Swivel Fold with the paper underneath.

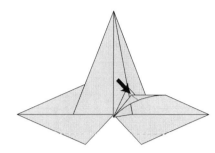

36) Complete the Swivel Fold and push everything flat.

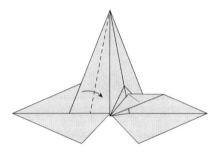

37) Fold the top left flap of paper towards the center along the dotted line. As you do, prepare to make a Swivel Fold with the paper underneath.

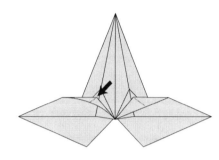

38) Complete the Swivel Fold and push everything flat.

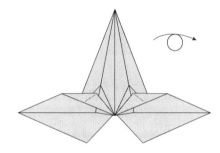

39) Turn the paper over.

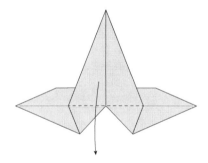

40) Fold the top flap of paper down along the dotted line.

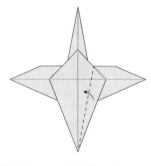

41) Fold the top right flap of paper towards the center along the dotted line. As you do, prepare to make a Swivel Fold with the paper underneath.

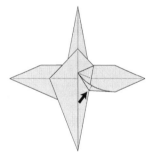

42) Compete the Swivel Fold and push everything flat.

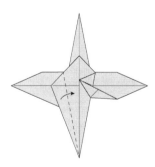

43) Fold the top left flap of paper towards the center along the dotted line. As you do, prepare to make a Swivel Fold with the paper underneath.

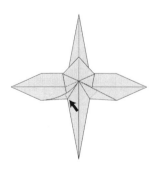

44) Complete the Swivel Fold and push everything flat.

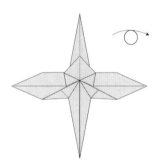

45) Turn the paper over.

Dragonfly

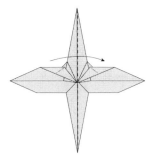

46) Fold the paper in half vertically along the dotted line.

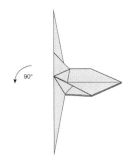

47) Rotate the model 90 degrees to the left.

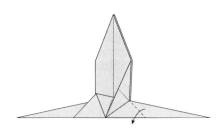

48) Fold the right long section of paper down along the dotted line.

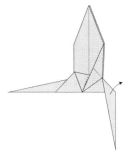

49) Crease this well and then unfold it.

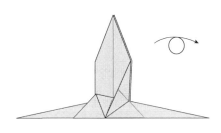

50) Turn the paper over.

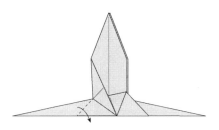

51) Fold the left long section of paper down along the dotted line. This is the opposite direction of the previous fold.

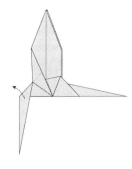

52) Crease this well and then unfold it.

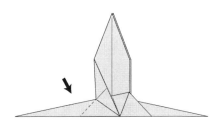

53) Make an Outside Reverse Fold using the existing creases.

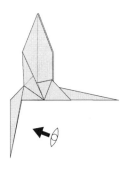

54) The next several steps take place on the underside of this flap of paper. Open it up a little bit and look at it from the direction of the arrow.

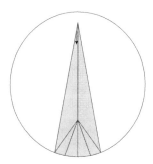

55) Fold the top part of the paper down along the dotted line.

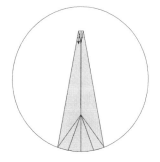

56) Fold the top part of the paper down along the dotted line.

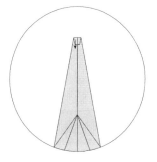

57) Fold the top layers of paper down along the dotted line.

Dragonfly

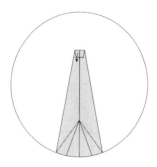

58) Fold the top layers of paper down along the dotted line.

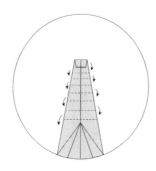

59) Continue folding the top layers of paper down until you reach the end where the rest of the creases begin.

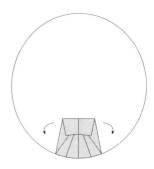

60) Close this flap of paper back up. There should be a very thick bulge of paper on both sides that will form the head of the dragonfly.

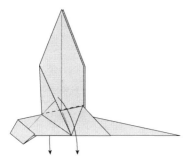

61) Fold the wings down on both sides of the model.

62) Cut through the center of each wing to divide the two wings into four wings.

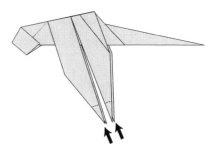

63) Make a small Inside Reverse Fold on the tip of each wing to give them their shape.

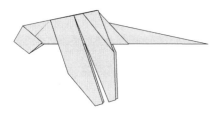

The completed dragonfly.

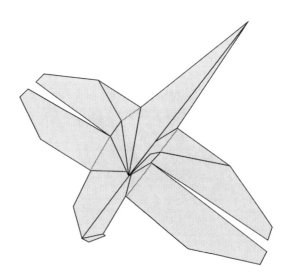

Dragonfly

Phoenix

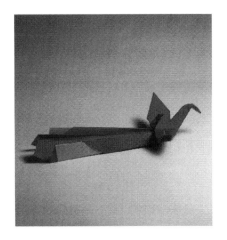

The instructions for this Phoenix look complex but they're actually very similar to the traditional origami crane.

Techniques Used: Mountain and Valley Folds, Inside Reverse Fold and Petal Fold.

Before You Start: Begin with a square sheet of paper with the colored side facing up.

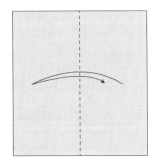

1) Fold the paper in half vertically and then unfold it.

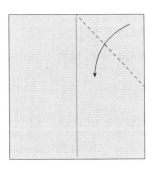

2) Fold the top right corner of paper down.

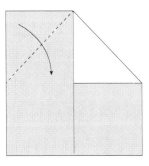

3) Fold the top left corner of the paper down.

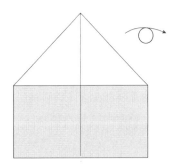

4) Turn the paper over.

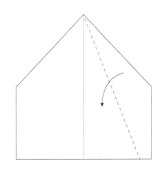

5) Fold the right side of the paper towards the center along the dotted line.. Let the white triangle of paper from behind out.

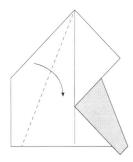

6) Fold the left side of the paper towards the center along the dotted line. Let the white triangle of paper from behind out.

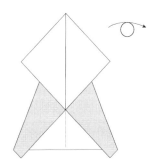

7) Turn the paper over.

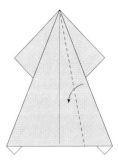

8) Fold the top right flap of paper towards the center along the dotted line.

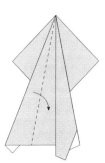

9) Fold the to left flap of paper towards the center along the dotted line.

Phoenix

10) Fold the top right flap of paper towards the center along the dotted line.

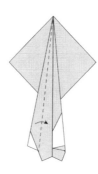

11) Fold the top left flap of paper towards the center along the dotted line.

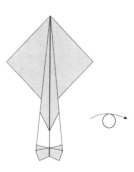

12) Turn the paper over.

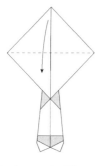

13) Fold the top part of the paper, including all the layers behind it down along the dotted line.

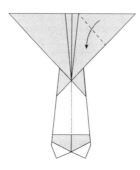

14) Fold the right side of the paper down along the dotted line.

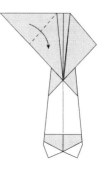

15) Fold the left side of the paper down along the dotted line.

16) Unfold both of the previous two folds.

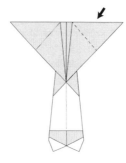

17) Make an Inside Reverse Fold along the existing crease on the right.

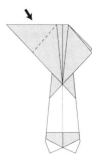

18) Make an Inside Reverse Fold along the existing crease on the left.

19) Fold the top left flap of paper over to the right along the dotted line opening this section up.

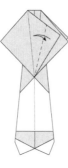

20) Fold the right side of this square to the center along the dotted line. Crease it well and then unfold it.

21) Fold the left side of this square to the center along the dotted line. Crease it well and then unfold it.

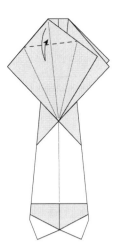

22) Fold the top part of this square down along the dotted line. Crease it well and then unfold it.

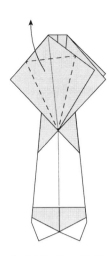

23) Make a Petal Fold using the existing creases.

24) Fold the right side of the Petal Fold to the center along the dotted line.

25) Fold the left side of the Petal Fold to the center along the dotted line.

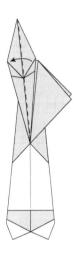

26) Fold the Petal Fold in half along the dotted line.

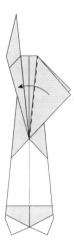

27) Fold the top right flap of paper over to the left along the dotted line opening this section up.

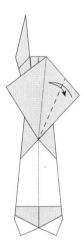

28) Fold the right side of this square to the center along the dotted line. Crease it well and then unfold it.

29) Fold the left side of this square to the center along the dotted line. Crease it well and then unfold it.

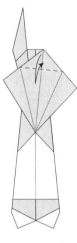

30) Fold the top part of this square down along the dotted line. Crease it well and then unfold it.

Phoenix

31) Make a Petal Fold using the existing creases.

32) Fold the right side of the Petal Fold to the center along the dotted line.

33) Fold the left side of the Petal Fold to the center along the dotted line.

34) Fold the Petal Fold in half along the dotted line.

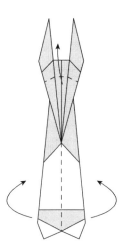

35) Fold the top part of the paper up along the dotted line while folding the bottom part back. The model will close up and the top part of the paper will form an Inside Reverse Fold.

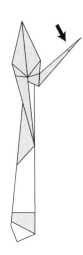

36) Make an Inside Reverse Fold to form the head.

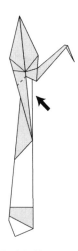

37) Make an Inside Reverse Fold to form the tail.

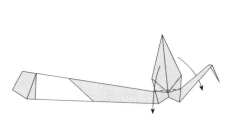

38) Fold both of the wings down.

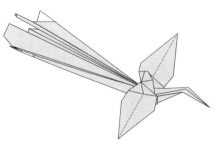

The completed Phoenix.

Frog

This is the most difficult model in this book and will test many of the techniques you have been practicing up until now. Good luck!

Techniques Used: Mountain and Valley Folds, Inside Reverse Fold, Square Base, Squash Fold, Petal Fold, Frog Base and Open Sink.

Before You Start: Begin with a square sheet of paper with the white side facing up.

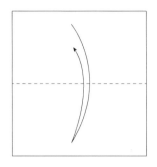

1) Fold the paper in half horizontally. Crease it well and then unfold.

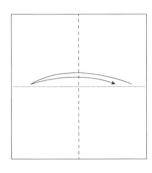

2) Fold the paper in half vertically. Crease it well and then unfold it.

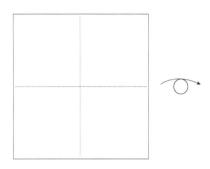

3) Turn the paper over.

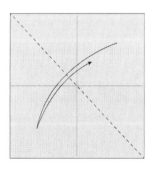

4) Fold the paper in half diagonally. Crease it well and then unfold it.

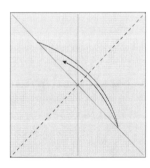

5) Fold the paper in half diagonally the other way. Crease it well and then unfold it.

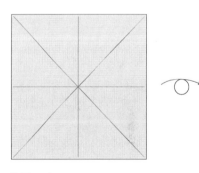

6) Turn the paper over.

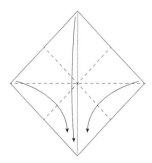

7) Fold the paper along the existing creases bringing the left, right and top corners to the bottom into a Square base.

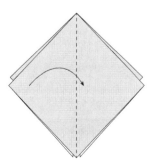

8) Bring the top left flap of paper up.

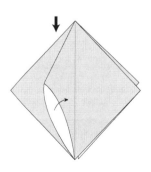

9) Make a Squash Fold on this flap.

Frog Page **301**

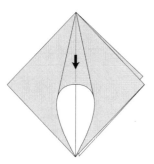

10) Complete the Squash Fold and push everything flat.

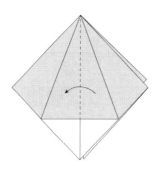

11) Fold the top right flap of paper over to the left.

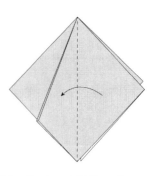

12) Bring the top right flap of paper up.

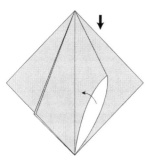

13) Make a Squash Fold on this flap.

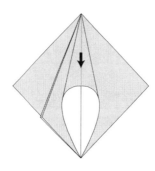

14) Complete the Squash Fold and push everything flat.

15) Turn the paper over.

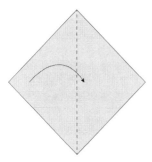

16) Bring the left flap of paper up.

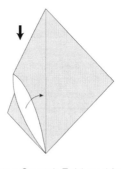

17) Make a Squash Fold on this flap.

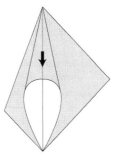

18) Complete the Squash Fold and push everything flat.

19) Fold the top right flap of paper over to the left.

20) Bring the right flap of paper up.

21) Make a Squash Fold on this flap.

Frog

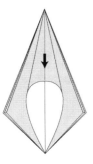

22) Complete the Squash Fold and push everything flat.

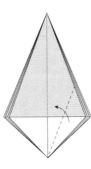

23) Fold the top right flap of paper to the center along the dotted line.

24) Crease this well and then unfold it.

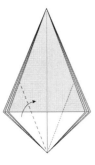

25) Fold the to left flap of paper to the center along the dotted line.

26) Crease this well and then unfold it.

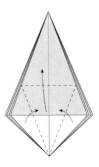

27) Make a Petal Fold using the existing creases.

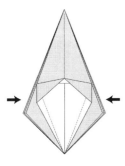

28) Complete the Petal Fold and push everything flat.

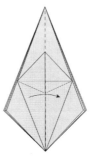

29) Fold the top left flap of paper over to the right.

30) Fold the top left flap of paper over to the right.

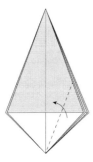

31) Fold the top right flap of paper to the center along the dotted line.

32) Crease this well and then unfold it.

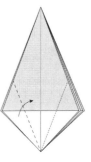

33) Fold the top left flap of paper to the center along the dotted line.

34) Crease this well and then unfold it.

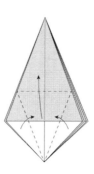

35) Make a Petal Fold using the existing creases.

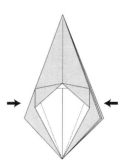

36) Complete the Petal Fold and push everything flat.

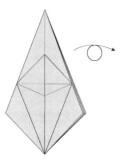

37) Turn the paper over.

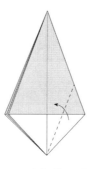

38) Fold the top right flap of paper to the center along the dotted line.

39) Crease this well and then unfold it.

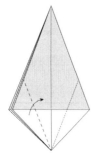

40) Fold the top left flap of paper to the center along the dotted line.

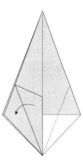

41) Crease this well and then unfold it.

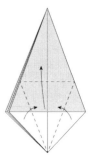

42) Make a Petal Fold using the existing creases.

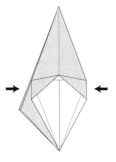

43) Complete the Petal Fold and push everything flat.

44) Fold the top left flap of paper to the right along the dotted line.

45) Fold the top left flap of paper to the right along the dotted line.

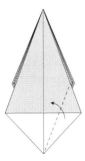  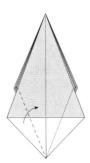

46) Fold the top right flap of paper to the center along the dotted line.

47) Crease this well and then unfold it.

48) Fold the top left flap of paper to the center along the dotted line.

 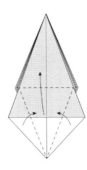 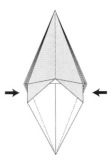

49) Crease this well and then unfold it.

50) Make a Petal Fold using the existing creases.

51) Complete the Petal Fold and push everything flat.

52) Fold the top left flap of paper over to the right along the dotted line.

53) Fold the top right and left flaps of paper to the center along the dotted lines.

54) Fold the top left flap of paper over to the right along the dotted line.

55) Fold the top left flap of paper over to the right along the dotted line.

56) Fold the top right and left flaps of paper to the center along the dotted lines.

57) Turn the paper over.

Frog

58) Fold the top left flap of paper over to the right along the dotted line.

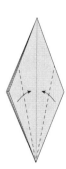

59) Fold the top right and left flaps of paper to the center along the dotted lines.

60) Fold the top left flap of paper over to the right along the dotted line.

61) Fold the top left flap of paper over to the right along the dotted line.

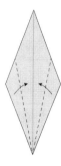

62) Fold the top right and left flaps of paper to the center along the dotted lines.

63) Fold the top flap of paper up to the top along the dotted line.

64) Fold the top left flap of paper over to the right along the dotted line.

65) Fold the top left flap of paper over to the right along the dotted line.

66) Fold the top flap of paper up to the top along the dotted line.

67) Fold the top right flap of paper over to the left along the dotted line.

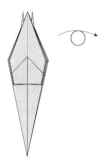

68) Turn the paper over.

69) Fold the top left flap of paper over to the right along the dotted line.

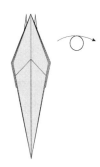

70) Turn the paper over.

71) Pull the two flaps of paper out to the sides and push them flat in their new position. These will form the front legs.

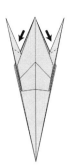

72) Make an Inside Reverse Fold on both of the front legs.

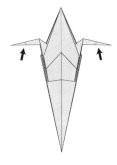

73) Make another Inside Reverse Fold on both of the front legs.

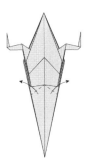

74) Make two Inside Reverse Folds on the two flaps of paper at the bottom. These will form the back legs.

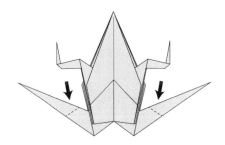

75) Make another Inside Reverse Fold on both of the back legs.

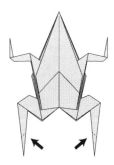

76) Make another Inside Reverse Fold on both of the back legs.

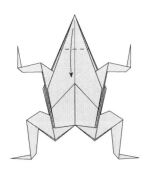

77) Fold the top of the model down along the dotted line.

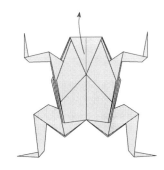

78) Crease this well and then unfold it.

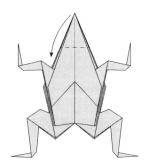

79) Fold the top of the model down along the dotted line in the other direction.

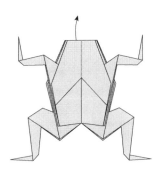

80) Crease this well and then unfold it.

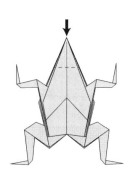

81) Make an Open Sink along the existing creases.

Frog

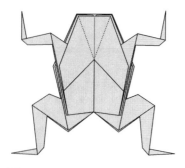

82) The dotted line shows the path of the paper inside the model after the Open Sink.

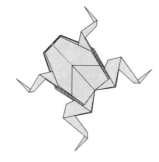

The completed Frog.

Additional Resources

Congratulations on working your way through this book! Here are some additional resources to help you on your origami journey.

If you'd like more origami to fold check out the diagram database at **www.origami.me/diagrams**. Here you'll find a massive collection of free origami diagrams from all over the Internet.

There's also a database of video tutorials at **www.origami.me/video-tutorials**. Videos are great because you can see all the intermediate steps between each fold.

If you were able to successfully fold all or most of the models in this book you should have no trouble folding anything there at a Beginner or Easy difficulty level. You can probably even try folding some Intermediate level models as well.

Instructions for the best origami models can only be found in books through. You can find a list of some of the best origami books out there at **www.origami.me/books**.

Finally, if you'd like to learn more about the different kinds of origami paper check out **www.origami.me/paper** for detailed information about the different varieties and how to use them.

Made in United States
Troutdale, OR
12/07/2023